1411

Volume II

Exploring World Literature

THE AGE OF REASON THROUGH MODERNISM

Custom Publishing

New York   Boston   San Francisco
London   Toronto   Sydney   Tokyo   Singapore   Madrid
Mexico City   Munich   Paris   Cape Town   Hong Kong   Montreal

Printed in the United States of America

10 9 8 7 6 5 4 3 2 1

2009240028

BW/LP

**Pearson
Custom Publishing**
is a division of

www.pearsonhighered.com

ISBN 10: 0-558-19833-3
ISBN 13: 978-0-558-19833-6

CONTENTS

Tartuffe or the Hypocrite 1

By Jean Baptiste Poqueline Moliere
Translated by Curtis Hidden Page

INTRODUCTORY NOTE 1

TARTUFFE (A COMEDY) 2

Phaedra   53

By Jean Baptiste Racine
Translated by Robert Bruce Boswell

Poetry   93

Hedda Gabler   121

By Henrik Isben
Translated by Edmund Gosse and William Archer
Introduction by William Archer

INTRODUCTION   121

TRANSCRIBER'S NOTE   126

HEDDA GABLER (PLAY IN FOUR ACTS)   127

The Cherry Orchard   185

By Anton Chekhov

THE CHERRY ORCHARD (A COMEDY IN FOUR ACTS)   185

Poetry   221

WILLIAM BUTLER YEATS   221

T. S. ELIOT   223

The Guest   243

By Albert Camus
Translated by Justin O'Brien

Jean Baptiste Poquelin Moliere
Tartuffe or the Hypocrite

Translated by Curtis Hidden Page

INTRODUCTORY NOTE

Jean Baptiste Poquelin, better known by his stage name of Moliere, stands without a rival at the head of French comedy. Born at Paris in January, 1622, where his father held a position in the royal household, he was educated at the Jesuit College de Clermont, and for some time studied law, which he soon abandoned for the stage. His life was spent in Paris and in the provinces, acting, directing performances, managing theaters, and writing plays. He had his share of applause from the king and from the public; but the satire in his comedies made him many enemies, and he was the object of the most venomous attacks and the most impossible slanders. Nor did he find much solace at home; for he married unfortunately, and the unhappiness that followed increased the bitterness that public hostility had brought into his life. On February 17, 1673, while acting in "La Malade Imaginaire," the last of his masterpieces, he was seized with illness and died a few hours later.

The first of the greater works of Moliere was "Les Precieuses Ridicules," produced in 1659. In this brilliant piece Moliere lifted French comedy to a new level and gave it a new purpose—the satirizing of contemporary manners and affectations by frank portrayal and criticism. In the great plays that followed, "The School for Husbands" and "The School for Wives," "The Misanthrope" and "The Hypocrite" (Tartuffe), "The Miser" and "The Hypochondriac," "The Learned Ladies," "The Doctor in Spite of Himself," "The Citizen Turned Gentleman," and many others, he exposed mercilessly one after another the vices and foibles of the day.

His characteristic qualities are nowhere better exhibited than in "Tartuffe." Compared with such characterization as Shakespeare's, Moliere's method of portraying life may seem to be lacking in complexity; but it is precisely the simplicity with which creations like Tartuffe embody the weakness or vice they represent that has given them their place as universally recognized types of human nature.

1

TARTUFFE

A COMEDY

Characters

MADAME PERNELLE, *mother of Orgon*
ORGON, *husband of Elmire*
ELMIRE, *wife of Orgon*
DAMIS, *son of Orgon*
MARIANE, *daughter of Orgon, in love with Valere*
CLEANTE, *brother-in-law of Orgon*
TARTUFFE, *a hypocrite*
DORING, *Mariane's maid*
M. LOYAL, *a bailiff*
A POLICE OFFICER
FLIPOTTE, *Madame Pernelle's servant*

The Scene is at Paris

Act I

Scene I

Madame Pernelle and Flipotte, her servant; Elmire, Mariane, Cleante, Damis, Dorine

MADAME PERNELLE: Come, come, Flipotte, and let me get away.
ELMIRE: You hurry so, I hardly can attend you.
MADAME PERNELLE: Then don't, my daughter-in law. Stay where you are.
        I can dispense with your polite attentions.
ELMIRE: We're only paying what is due you, mother.
        Why must you go away in such a hurry?
MADAME PERNELLE: Because I can't endure your carryings-on,
        And no one takes the slightest pains to please me.
        I leave your house, I tell you, quite disgusted;
10   You do the opposite of my instructions;
        You've no respect for anything; each one
        Must have his say; it's perfect pandemonium.
DORINE: If . . .
MADAME PERNELLE: You're a servant wench, my girl, and much
15   Too full of gab, and too impertinent
        And free with your advice on all occasions.
DAMIS: But . . .
MADAME PERNELLE: You're a fool, my boy—f, o, o, l
        Just spells your name. Let grandma tell you that
20   I've said a hundred times to my poor son,
        Your father, that you'd never come to good
        Or give him anything but plague and torment.
MARIANE: I think . . .
MADAME PERNELLE: O dearie me, his little sister!
25   You're all demureness, butter wouldn't melt

In your mouth, one would think to look at you.
Still waters, though, they say . . . you know the proverb;
And I don't like your doings on the sly.

ELMIRE: But, mother . . .

MADAME PERNELLE: Daughter, by your leave, your conduct
In everything is altogether wrong;
You ought to set a good example for 'em;
Their dear departed mother did much better.
You are extravagant; and it offends me,
35   To see you always decked out like a princess.
A woman who would please her husband's eyes
Alone, wants no such wealth of fineries.

CLEANTE: But, madam, after all . . .

MADAME PERNELLE: Sir, as for you,
40   The lady's brother, I esteem you highly,
Love and respect you. But, sir, all the same,
If I were in my son's, her husband's, place,
I'd urgently entreat you not to come
Within our doors. You preach a way of living
45   That decent people cannot tolerate.
I'm rather frank with you; but that's my way —
I don't mince matters, when I mean a thing.

DAMIS: Mr. Tartuffe, your friend, is mighty lucky . . .

MADAME PERNELLE: He is a holy man, and must be heeded;
50   I can't endure, with any show of patience,
To hear a scatterbrains like you attack him.

DAMIS: What! Shall I let a bigot criticaster
Come and usurp a tyrant's power here?
And shall we never dare amuse ourselves
55   Till this fine gentleman deigns to consent?

DORINE: If we must hark to him, and heed his maxims,
There's not a thing we do but what's a crime;
He censures everything, this zealous carper.

MADAME PERNELLE: And all he censures is well censured, too.
60   He wants to guide you on the way to heaven;
My son should train you all to love him well.

DAMIS: No, madam, look you, nothing — not my father
Nor anything — can make me tolerate him.
I should belie my feelings not to say so.
65   His actions rouse my wrath at every turn;
And I foresee that there must come of it
An open rupture with this sneaking scoundrel.

DORINE: Besides, 'tis downright scandalous to see
This unknown upstart master of the house —
70   This vagabond, who hadn't, when he came,
Shoes to his feet, or clothing worth six farthings,
And who so far forgets his place, as now
To censure everything, and rule the roost!

MADAME PERNELLE: Eh! Mercy sakes alive! Things would go better
75   If all were governed by his pious orders.
DORINE: He passes for a saint in your opinion.
        In fact, he's nothing but a hypocrite.
MADAME PERNELLE: Just listen to her tongue!
DORINE: I wouldn't trust him,
80   Nor yet his Lawrence, without bonds and surety.
MADAME PERNELLE: I don't know what the servant's character
        May be; but I can guarantee the master
        A holy man. You hate him and reject him
        Because he tells home truths to all of you.
85   'Tis sin alone that moves his heart to anger,
        And heaven's interest is his only motive.
DORINE: Of course. But why, especially of late,
        Can he let nobody come near the house?
        Is heaven offended at a civil call
90   That he should make so great a fuss about it?
        I'll tell you, if you like, just what I think;
        (Pointing to Elmire)
        Upon my word, he's jealous of our mistress.
MADAME PERNELLE: You hold your tongue, and think what you are saying.
95   He's not alone in censuring these visits;
        The turmoil that attends your sort of people,
        Their carriages forever at the door,
        And all their noisy footmen, flocked together,
        Annoy the neighbourhood, and raise a scandal.
100   I'd gladly think there's nothing really wrong;
        But it makes talk; and that's not as it should be.
CLEANTE: Eh! madam, can you hope to keep folk's tongues
        From wagging? It would be a grievous thing
        If, for the fear of idle talk about us,
105   We had to sacrifice our friends. No, no;
        Even if we could bring ourselves to do it,
        Think you that everyone would then be silenced?
        Against backbiting there is no defence
        So let us try to live in innocence,
110   To silly tattle pay no heed at all,
        And leave the gossips free to vent their gall.
DORINE: Our neighbour Daphne, and her little husband,
        Must be the ones who slander us, I'm thinking.
        Those whose own conduct's most ridiculous,
115   Are always quickest to speak ill of others;
        They never fail to seize at once upon
        The slightest hint of any love affair,
        And spread the news of it with glee, and give it
        The character they'd have the world believe in.
120   By others' actions, painted in their colours,
        They hope to justify their own; they think,
        In the false hope of some resemblance, either

To make their own intrigues seem innocent,
Or else to make their neighbours share the blame
125   Which they are loaded with by everybody.
MADAME PERNELLE: These arguments are nothing to the purpose.
Orante, we all know, lives a perfect life;
Her thoughts are all of heaven; and I have heard
That she condemns the company you keep.
DORINE: O admirable pattern! Virtuous dame!
She lives the model of austerity;
But age has brought this piety upon her,
And she's a prude, now she can't help herself.
As long as she could capture men's attentions
135   She made the most of her advantages;
But, now she sees her beauty vanishing,
She wants to leave the world, that's leaving her,
And in the specious veil of haughty virtue
She'd hide the weakness of her worn-out charms.
140   That is the way with all your old coquettes;
They find it hard to see their lovers leave 'em;
And thus abandoned, their forlorn estate
Can find no occupation but a prude's.
These pious dames, in their austerity,
145   Must carp at everything, and pardon nothing.
They loudly blame their neighbours' way of living,
Not for religion's sake, but out of envy,
Because they can't endure to see another
Enjoy the pleasures age has weaned them from.
MADAME PERNELLE: (To Elmire)
There! That's the kind of rigmarole to please you,
Daughter-in-law. One never has a chance
To get a word in edgewise, at your house,
Because this lady holds the floor all day;
155   But none the less, I mean to have my say, too.
I tell you that my son did nothing wiser
In all his life, than take this godly man
Into his household; heaven sent him here,
In your great need, to make you all repent;
160   For your salvation, you must hearken to him;
He censures nothing but deserves his censure.
These visits, these assemblies, and these balls,
Are all inventions of the evil spirit.
You never hear a word of godliness
165   At them—but idle cackle, nonsense, flimflam.
Our neighbour often comes in for a share,
The talk flies fast, and scandal fills the air;
It makes a sober person's head go round,
At these assemblies, just to hear the sound
170   Of so much gab, with not a word to say;
And as a learned man remarked one day

Most aptly, 'tis the Tower of Babylon,
Where all, beyond all limit, babble on.
And just to tell you how this point came in . . .

175   (To Cleante)
So! Now the gentlemen must snicker, must he?
Go find fools like yourself to make you laugh
And don't . . .
(To Elmire)

180   Daughter, good-bye; not one word more.
As for this house, I leave the half unsaid;
But I shan't soon set foot in it again,
(Cuffing Flipotte)
Come, you! What makes you dream and stand agape,

185   Hussy! I'll warm your ears in proper shape!
March, trollop, march!

SCENE II

Cleante, Dorine

CLEANTE: I won't escort her down,
For fear she might fall foul of me again;
The good old lady . . .

DORINE: Bless us! What a pity

5   She shouldn't hear the way you speak of her!
She'd surely tell you you're too "good" by half,
And that she's not so "old" as all that, neither!

CLEANTE: How she got angry with us all for nothing!
And how she seems possessed with her Tartuffe!

DORINE: Her case is nothing, though, beside her son's!
To see him, you would say he's ten times worse!
His conduct in our late unpleasantness [1]
Had won him much esteem, and proved his courage
In service of his king; but now he's like

15   A man besotted, since he's been so taken
With this Tartuffe. He calls him brother, loves him
A hundred times as much as mother, son,
Daughter, and wife. He tells him all his secrets
And lets him guide his acts, and rule his conscience.

20   He fondles and embraces him; a sweetheart
Could not, I think, be loved more tenderly;
At table he must have the seat of honour,
While with delight our master sees him eat
As much as six men could; we must give up

25   The choicest tidbits to him; if he belches,
('tis a servant speaking) [2]

[2] Moliere's note, inserted in the text of all the old editions. It is a curious illustration of the desire for uniformity and dignity of style in dramatic verse of the seventeenth century, that Moliere feels called on to apologize for a touch of realism like this. Indeed, these lines were even omitted when the play was given.

[1] Referring to the rebellion called La Fronde, during the minority of Louis XIV.

Master exclaims: "God bless you!"—Oh, he dotes
Upon him! he's his universe, his hero;
He's lost in constant admiration, quotes him
30 On all occasions, takes his trifling acts
For wonders, and his words for oracles.
The fellow knows his dupe, and makes the most on't,
He fools him with a hundred masks of virtue,
Gets money from him all the time by canting,
35 And takes upon himself to carp at us.
Even his silly coxcomb of a lackey
Makes it his business to instruct us too;
He comes with rolling eyes to preach at us,
And throws away our ribbons, rouge, and patches.
40 The wretch, the other day, tore up a kerchief
That he had found, pressed in the "Golden Legend",
Calling it a horrid crime for us to mingle
The devil's finery with holy things.

Scene III

Elmire, Mariane, Damis, Cleante, Dorine

ELMIRE: (To Cleante)
You're very lucky to have missed the speech
She gave us at the door. I see my husband
Is home again. He hasn't seen me yet,
5   So I'll go up and wait till he comes in.
CLEANTE: And I, to save time, will await him here;
I'll merely say good-morning, and be gone.

Scene IV

Cleante, Damis, Dorine

DAMIS: I wish you'd say a word to him about
My sister's marriage; I suspect Tartuffe
Opposes it, and puts my father up
To all these wretched shifts. You know, besides,
5   How nearly I'm concerned in it myself;
If love unites my sister and Valere,
I love his sister too; and if this marriage
Were to . . .
DORINE: He's coming.

Scene V

Orgon, Cleante, Dorine

ORGON: Ah! Good morning, brother.
CLEANTE: I was just going, but am glad to greet you.
Things are not far advanced yet, in the country?
ORGON: Dorine . . .
5   (To Cleante)
Just wait a bit, please, brother-in-law.

Let me allay my first anxiety
By asking news about the family.
(To Dorine)

10   Has everything gone well these last two days?
What's happening? And how is everybody?

DORINE: Madam had fever, and a splitting headache
Day before yesterday, all day and evening.

ORGON: And how about Tartuffe?

DORINE: Tartuffe? He's well;
He's mighty well; stout, fat, fair, rosy-lipped.

ORGON: Poor man!

DORINE: At evening she had nausea
And couldn't touch a single thing for supper,

20   Her headache still was so severe.

ORGON: And how
About Tartuffe?

DORINE: He supped alone, before her,
And unctuously ate up two partridges,

25   As well as half a leg o' mutton, deviled.

ORGON: Poor man!

DORINE: All night she couldn't get a wink
Of sleep, the fever racked her so; and we
Had to sit up with her till daylight.

ORGON: How
About Tartuffe?

DORINE: Gently inclined to slumber,
He left the table, went into his room,
Got himself straight into a good warm bed,

35   And slept quite undisturbed until next morning.

ORGON: Poor man!

DORINE: At last she let us all persuade her,
And got up courage to be bled; and then
She was relieved at once.

ORGON: And how about
Tartuffe?

DORINE: He plucked up courage properly,
Bravely entrenched his soul against all evils,
And to replace the blood that she had lost,

45   He drank at breakfast four huge draughts of wine.

ORGON: Poor man!

DORINE: So now they both are doing well;
And I'll go straightway and inform my mistress
How pleased you are at her recovery.

S CENE V I

Orgon, Cleante

CLEANTE: Brother, she ridicules you to your face;
And I, though I don't want to make you angry,
Must tell you candidly that she's quite right.

Was such infatuation ever heard of?
5   And can a man to-day have charms to make you
Forget all else, relieve his poverty,
Give him a home, and then . . .?

ORGON: Stop there, good brother,
You do not know the man you're speaking of.

CLEANTE: Since you will have it so, I do not know him;
But after all, to tell what sort of man
He is . . .

ORGON: Dear brother, you'd be charmed to know him;
Your raptures over him would have no end.
15   He is a man . . . who . . . ah!. . . in fact . . . a man
Whoever does his will, knows perfect peace,
And counts the whole world else, as so much dung.
His converse has transformed me quite; he weans
My heart from every friendship, teaches me
20   To have no love for anything on earth;
And I could see my brother, children, mother,
And wife, all die, and never care—a snap.

CLEANTE: Your feelings are humane, I must say, brother!

ORGON: Ah! If you'd seen him, as I saw him first,
25   You would have loved him just as much as I.
He came to church each day, with contrite mien,
Kneeled, on both knees, right opposite my place,
And drew the eyes of all the congregation,
To watch the fervour of his prayers to heaven;
30   With deep-drawn sighs and great ejaculations,
He humbly kissed the earth at every moment;
And when I left the church, he ran before me
To give me holy water at the door.
I learned his poverty, and who he was,
35   By questioning his servant, who is like him,
And gave him gifts; but in his modesty
He always wanted to return a part.
"It is too much," he'd say, "too much by half;
I am not worthy of your pity." Then,
40   When I refused to take it back, he'd go,
Before my eyes, and give it to the poor.
At length heaven bade me take him to my home,
And since that day, all seems to prosper here.
He censures everything, and for my sake
45   He even takes great interest in my wife;
He lets me know who ogles her, and seems
Six times as jealous as I am myself.
You'd not believe how far his zeal can go:
He calls himself a sinner just for trifles;
50   The merest nothing is enough to shock him;
So much so, that the other day I heard him
Accuse himself for having, while at prayer,
In too much anger caught and killed a flea.

CLEANTE: Zounds, brother, you are mad, I think! Or else
55   You're making sport of me, with such a speech.
         What are you driving at with all this nonsense . . . ?
ORGON: Brother, your language smacks of atheism;
         And I suspect your soul's a little tainted
         Therewith. I've preached to you a score of times
60   That you'll draw down some judgment on your head.
CLEANTE: That is the usual strain of all your kind;
         They must have every one as blind as they.
         They call you atheist if you have good eyes;
         And if you don't adore their vain grimaces,
65   You've neither faith nor care for sacred things.
         No, no; such talk can't frighten me; I know
         What I am saying; heaven sees my heart.
         We're not the dupes of all your canting mummers;
         There are false heroes—and false devotees;
70   And as true heroes never are the ones
         Who make much noise about their deeds of honour,
         Just so true devotees, whom we should follow,
         Are not the ones who make so much vain show.
         What! Will you find no difference between
75   Hypocrisy and genuine devoutness?
         And will you treat them both alike, and pay
         The self-same honour both to masks and faces
         Set artifice beside sincerity,
         Confuse the semblance with reality,
80   Esteem a phantom like a living person,
         And counterfeit as good as honest coin?
         Men, for the most part, are strange creatures, truly!
         You never find them keep the golden mean;
         The limits of good sense, too narrow for them,
85   Must always be passed by, in each direction;
         They often spoil the noblest things, because
         They go too far, and push them to extremes.
         I merely say this by the way, good brother.
ORGON: You are the sole expounder of the doctrine;
90   Wisdom shall die with you, no doubt, good brother,
         You are the only wise, the sole enlightened,
         The oracle, the Cato, of our age.
         All men, compared to you, are downright fools.
CLEANTE: I'm not the sole expounder of the doctrine,
95   And wisdom shall not die with me, good brother.
         But this I know, though it be all my knowledge,
         That there's a difference 'twixt false and true.
         And as I find no kind of hero more
         To be admired than men of true religion,
100   Nothing more noble or more beautiful
         Than is the holy zeal of true devoutness;
         Just so I think there's naught more odious

Than whited sepulchres of outward unction,
Those barefaced charlatans, those hireling zealots,
105   Whose sacrilegious, treacherous pretence
Deceives at will, and with impunity
Makes mockery of all that men hold sacred;
Men who, enslaved to selfish interests,
Make trade and merchandise of godliness,
110   And try to purchase influence and office
With false eye-rollings and affected raptures;
Those men, I say, who with uncommon zeal
Seek their own fortunes on the road to heaven;
Who, skilled in prayer, have always much to ask,
115   And live at court to preach retirement;
Who reconcile religion with their vices,
Are quick to anger, vengeful, faithless, tricky,
And, to destroy a man, will have the boldness
To call their private grudge the cause of heaven;
120   All the more dangerous, since in their anger
They use against us weapons men revere,
And since they make the world applaud their passion,
And seek to stab us with a sacred sword.
There are too many of this canting kind.
125   Still, the sincere are easy to distinguish;
And many splendid patterns may be found,
In our own time, before our very eyes
Look at Ariston, Periandre, Oronte,
Alcidamas, Clitandre, and Polydore;
130   No one denies their claim to true religion;
Yet they're no braggadocios of virtue,
They do not make insufferable display,
And their religion's human, tractable;
They are not always judging all our actions,
135   They'd think such judgment savoured of presumption;
And, leaving pride of words to other men,
'Tis by their deeds alone they censure ours.
Evil appearances find little credit
With them; they even incline to think the best
140   Of others. No caballers, no intriguers,
They mind the business of their own right living.
They don't attack a sinner tooth and nail,
For sin's the only object of their hatred;
Nor are they over-zealous to attempt
145   Far more in heaven's behalf than heaven would have 'em.
That is my kind of man, that is true living,
That is the pattern we should set ourselves.
Your fellow was not fashioned on this model;
You're quite sincere in boasting of his zeal;
150   But you're deceived, I think, by false pretences.
ORGON: My dear good brother-in-law, have you quite done?

CLEANTE: Yes.

ORGON: I'm your humble servant.
          (Starts to go.)

CLEANTE: Just a word.
          We'll drop that other subject. But you know
          Valere has had the promise of your daughter.

ORGON: Yes.

CLEANTE: You had named the happy day.

ORGON: 'Tis true.

CLEANTE: Then why put off the celebration of it?

ORGON: I can't say.

CLEANTE: Can you have some other plan
          In mind?

ORGON: Perhaps.

CLEANTE: You mean to break your word?

ORGON: I don't say that.

CLEANTE: I hope no obstacle
          Can keep you from performing what you've promised.

ORGON: Well, that depends.

CLEANTE: Why must you beat about?
          Valere has sent me here to settle matters.

ORGON: Heaven be praised!

CLEANTE: What answer shall I take him?

ORGON: Why, anything you please.

CLEANTE: But we must know
          Your plans. What are they?

ORGON: I shall do the will
          Of Heaven.

CLEANTE: Come, be serious. You've given
          Your promise to Valere. Now will you keep it?

ORGON: Good-bye.

CLEANTE: (alone)
          His love, methinks, has much to fear;
185   I must go let him know what's happening here.

A c t   I I

S c e n e   I

Orgon, Mariane

ORGON: Now, Mariane.

MARIANE: Yes, father?

ORGON: Come; I'll tell you
          A secret.

MARIANE: Yes . . . What are you looking for?

ORGON: (looking into a small closet-room)
          To see there's no one there to spy upon us;
          That little closet's mighty fit to hide in.
          There! We're all right now. Mariane, in you
10   I've always found a daughter dutiful

And gentle. So I've always love you dearly.
MARIANE: I'm grateful for your fatherly affection.
ORGON: Well spoken, daughter. Now, prove you deserve it
        By doing as I wish in all respects.
MARIANE: To do so is the height of my ambition.
ORGON: Excellent well. What say you of—Tartuffe?
MARIANE: Who? I?
ORGON: Yes, you. Look to it how you answer.
MARIANE: Why! I'll say of him—anything you please.

Scene II

Orgon, Mariane, Dorine (coming in quietly and standing behind Orgon,
so that he does not see her)

ORGON: Well spoken. A good girl. Say then, my daughter,
        That all his person shines with noble merit,
        That he has won your heart, and you would like
        To have him, by my choice, become your husband.
5   Eh?
MARIANE: Eh?
ORGON: What say you?
MARIANE: Please, what did you say?
ORGON: What?
MARIANE: Surely I mistook you, sir?
ORGON: How now?
MARIANE: Who is it, father, you would have me say
        Has won my heart, and I would like to have
        Become my husband, by your choice?
ORGON: Tartuffe.
MARIANE: But, father, I protest it isn't true!
        Why should you make me tell this dreadful lie?
ORGON: Because I mean to have it be the truth.
        Let this suffice for you: I've settled it.
MARIANE: What, father, you would . . . ?
ORGON: Yes, child, I'm resolved
        To graft Tartuffe into my family.
        So he must be your husband. That I've settled.
        And since your duty . .
25   (Seeing Dorine)
        What are you doing there?
        Your curiosity is keen, my girl,
        To make you come eavesdropping on us so.
DORINE: Upon my word, I don't know how the rumour
30   Got started—if 'twas guess-work or mere chance
        But I had heard already of this match,
        And treated it as utter stuff and nonsense.
ORGON: What! Is the thing incredible?
DORINE: So much so
35   I don't believe it even from yourself, sir.

ORGON: I know a way to make you credit it.
DORINE: No, no, you're telling us a fairly tale!
ORGON: I'm telling you just what will happen shortly.
DORINE: Stuff!
ORGON: Daughter, what I say is in good earnest.
DORINE: There, there, don't take your father seriously;
      He's fooling.
ORGON: But I tell you . . .
DORINE: No. No use.
45   They won't believe you.
ORGON: If I let my anger . . .
DORINE: Well, then, we do believe you; and the worse
      For you it is. What! Can a grown-up man
      With that expanse of beard across his face
50   Be mad enough to want . . . ?
ORGON: You hark me:
      You've taken on yourself here in this house
      A sort of free familiarity
      That I don't like, I tell you frankly, girl.
DORINE: There, there, let's not get angry, sir, I beg you.
      But are you making game of everybody?
      Your daughter's not cut out for bigot's meat;
      And he has more important things to think of.
      Besides, what can you gain by such a match?
60   How can a man of wealth, like you, go choose
      A wretched vagabond for son-in-law?
ORGON: You hold your tongue. And know, the less he has,
      The better cause have we to honour him.
      His poverty is honest poverty;
65   It should exalt him more than worldly grandeur,
      For he has let himself be robbed of all,
      Through careless disregard of temporal things
      And fixed attachment to the things eternal.
      My help may set him on his feet again,
70   Win back his property—a fair estate
      He has at home, so I'm informed—and prove him
      For what he is, a true-born gentleman.
DORINE: Yes, so he says himself. Such vanity
      But ill accords with pious living, sir.
75   The man who cares for holiness alone
      Should not so loudly boast his name and birth;
      The humble ways of genuine devoutness
      Brook not so much display of earthly pride.
      Why should he be so vain? . . . But I offend you:
80   Let's leave his rank, then,—take the man himself:
      Can you without compunction give a man
      Like him possession of a girl like her?
      Think what a scandal's sure to come of it!
      Virtue is at the mercy of the fates,

85   When a girl's married to a man she hates;
The best intent to live an honest woman
Depends upon the husband's being human,
And men whose brows are pointed at afar
May thank themselves their wives are what they are.
90   For to be true is more than woman can,
With husbands built upon a certain plan;
And he who weds his child against her will
Owes heaven account for it, if she do ill.
Think then what perils wait on your design.

ORGON: (to Mariane)
So! I must learn what's what from her, you see!

DORINE: You might do worse than follow my advice.

ORGON: Daughter, we can't waste time upon this nonsense;
I know what's good for you, and I'm your father.
100   True, I had promised you to young Valere;
But, first, they tell me he's inclined to gamble,
And then, I fear his faith is not quite sound.
I haven't noticed that he's regular
At church.

DORINE: You'd have him run there just when you do.
Like those who go on purpose to be seen?

ORGON: I don't ask your opinion on the matter.
In short, the other is in Heaven's best graces,
And that is riches quite beyond compare.
110   This match will bring you every joy you long for;
'Twill be all steeped in sweetness and delight.
You'll live together, in your faithful loves,
Like two sweet children, like two turtle-doves;
You'll never fail to quarrel, scold, or tease,
115   And you may do with him whate'er you please.

DORINE: With him? Do naught but give him horns, I'll warrant.

ORGON: Out on thee, wench!

DORINE: I tell you he's cut out for't;
However great your daughter's virtue, sir,
120   His destiny is sure to prove the stronger.

ORGON: Have done with interrupting. Hold your tongue.
Don't poke your nose in other people's business.

DORINE: (She keeps interrupting him, just as he turns and starts
to speak to his daughter).
125   If I make bold, sir, 'tis for your own good.

ORGON: You're too officious; pray you, hold your tongue.

DORINE: 'Tis love of you . . .

ORGON: I want none of your love.

DORINE: Then I will love you in your own despite.

ORGON: You will, eh?

DORINE: Yes, your honour's dear to me;
I can't endure to see you made the butt
Of all men's ridicule.

ORGON: Won't you be still?

DORINE: 'Twould be a sin to let you make this match.

ORGON: Won't you be still, I say, you impudent viper!

DORINE: What! you are pious, and you lose your temper?

ORGON: I'm all wrought up, with your confounded nonsense;
        Now, once for all, I tell you hold your tongue.

DORINE: Then mum's the word; I'll take it out in thinking.

ORGON: Think all you please; but not a syllable
        To me about it, or . . . you understand!
        (Turning to his daughter.)
        As a wise father, I've considered all
145   With due deliberation.

DORINE: I'll go mad
        If I can't speak.
        (She stops the instant he turns his head.)

ORGON: Though he's no lady's man,
150   Tartuffe is well enough . . .

DORINE: A pretty phiz!

ORGON: So that, although you may not care at all
        For his best qualities . . .

DORINE: A handsome dowry!

155   (Orgon turns and stands in front of her, with arms folded, eyeing her.)
        Were I in her place, any man should rue it
        Who married me by force, that's mighty certain;
        I'd let him know, and that within a week,
        A woman's vengeance isn't far to seek.

ORGON: (to Dorine)
        So—nothing that I say has any weight?

DORINE: Eh? What's wrong now? I didn't speak to you.

ORGON: What were you doing?

DORINE: Talking to myself.

ORGON: Oh! Very well. (Aside.) Her monstrous impudence
        Must be chastised with one good slap in the face.
        (He stands ready to strike her, and, each time he speaks to his daughter, he
        glances toward her; but she stands still and says not a word.) [3]

ORGON: Daughter, you must approve of my design. . . .
170   Think of this husband . . . I have chosen for you. . .
        (To Dorine)
        Why don't you talk to yourself?

DORINE: Nothing to say.

[3] As given at the Comedie francaise, the action is as follows: While Orgon says, "You must approve of my design,"
Dorine is making signs to Mariane to resist his orders; Orgon turns around suddenly; but Dorine quickly changes her gesture
and with the hand which she had lifted calmly arranges her hair and her cap. Orgon goes on, "Think of the husband . . ."
and stops before the middle of his sentence to turn and catch the beginning of Dorine's gesture; but he is too quick this
time, and Dorine stands looking at his furious countenance with a sweet and gentle expression. He turns and goes on, and
the obstinate Dorine again lifts her hand behind his shoulder to urge Mariane to resistance: this time he catches her; but
just as he swings his shoulder to give her the promised blow, she stops him by changing the intent of her gesture, and carefully picking from the top of his sleeve a bit of fluff which she holds carefully between her fingers, then blows into the air,
and watches intently as it floats away. Orgon is paralysed by her innocence of expression, and compelled to hide his
rage.—Regnier, "Le Tartuffe des Comediens".]

ORGON: One little word more.

DORINE: Oh, no, thanks. Not now.

ORGON: Sure, I'd have caught you.

DORINE: Faith, I'm no such fool.

ORGON: So, daughter, now obedience is the word;
    You must accept my choice with reverence.

DORINE: (running away)
    You'd never catch me marrying such a creature.

ORGON: (swinging his hand at her and missing her)
    Daughter, you've such a pestilent hussy there
    I can't live with her longer, without sin.

185 I can't discuss things in the state I'm in.
    My mind's so flustered by her insolent talk,
    To calm myself, I must go take a walk.

SCENE III

Mariane, Dorine

DORINE: Say, have you lost the tongue from out your head?
    And must I speak your role from A to Zed?
    You let them broach a project that's absurd,
    And don't oppose it with a single word!

MARIANE: What can I do? My father is the master.

DORINE: Do? Everything, to ward off such disaster.

MARIANE: But what?

DORINE: Tell him one doesn't love by proxy;
    Tell him you'll marry for yourself, not him;

10 Since you're the one for whom the thing is done,
    You are the one, not he, the man must please;
    If his Tartuffe has charmed him so, why let him
    Just marry him himself—no one will hinder.

MARIANE: A father's rights are such, it seems to me,

15 That I could never dare to say a word.

DORINE: Came, talk it out. Valere has asked your hand:
    Now do you love him, pray, or do you not?

MARIANE: Dorine! How can you wrong my love so much,
    And ask me such a question? Have I not

20 A hundred times laid bare my heart to you?
    Do you know how ardently I love him?

DORINE: How do I know if heart and words agree,
    And if in honest truth you really love him?

MARIANE: Dorine, you wrong me greatly if you doubt it;

25 I've shown my inmost feelings, all too plainly.

DORINF: So then, you love him?

MARIANE: Yes, devotedly.

DORINE: And he returns your love, apparently?

MARIANE: I think so.

DORINE: And you both alike are eager
    To be well married to each other?

MARIANE: Surely.

DORINE: Then what's your plan about this other match?

MARIANE: To kill myself, if it is forced upon me.

DORINE: Good! That's a remedy I hadn't thought of.
Just die, and everything will be all right.
This medicine is marvellous, indeed!
It drives me mad to hear folk talk such nonsense.

MARIANE: Oh dear, Dorine you get in such a temper!
40   You have no sympathy for people's troubles.

DORINE: I have no sympathy when folk talk nonsense,
And flatten out as you do, at a pinch.

MARIANE: But what can you expect?—if one is timid?—

DORINE: But what is love worth, if it has no courage?

MARIANE: Am I not constant in my love for him?
Is't not his place to win me from my father?

DORINE: But if your father is a crazy fool,
And quite bewitched with his Tartuffe? And breaks
His bounden word? Is that your lover's fault?

MARIANE: But shall I publicly refuse and scorn
This match, and make it plain that I'm in love?
Shall I cast off for him, whate'er he be,
Womanly modesty and filial duty?
You ask me to display my love in public . . .?

DORINE: No, no, I ask you nothing. You shall be
Mister Tartuffe's; why, now I think of it,
I should be wrong to turn you from this marriage.
What cause can I have to oppose your wishes?
So fine a match! An excellent good match!
60   Mister Tartuffe! Oh ho! No mean proposal!
Mister Tartuffe, sure, take it all in all,
Is not a man to sneeze at—oh, by no means!
'Tis no small luck to be his happy spouse.
The whole world joins to sing his praise already;
65   He's noble—in his parish; handsome too;
Red ears and high complexion—oh, my lud!
You'll be too happy, sure, with him for husband.

MARIANE: Oh dear! . . .

DORINE: What joy and pride will fill your heart
70   To be the bride of such a handsome fellow!

MARIANE: Oh, stop, I beg you; try to find some way
To help break off the match. I quite give in,
I'm ready to do anything you say.

DORINE: No, no, a daughter must obey her father,
75   Though he should want to make her wed a monkey.
Besides, your fate is fine. What could be better!
You'll take the stage-coach to his little village,
And find it full of uncles and of cousins,
Whose conversation will delight you. Then
80   You'll be presented in their best society.

You'll even go to call, by way of welcome,
On Mrs. Bailiff, Mrs. Tax-Collector,
Who'll patronise you with a folding-stool.
There, once a year, at carnival, you'll have
85   Perhaps—a ball; with orchestra—two bag-pipes;
And sometimes a trained ape, and Punch and Judy;
Though if your husband . . .

MARIANE: Oh, you'll kill me. Please
Contrive to help me out with your advice.

DORINE: I thank you kindly.

MARIANE: Oh! Dorine, I beg you . . .

DORINE: To serve you right, this marriage must go through.

MARIANE: Dear girl!

DORINE: No.

MARIANE: If I say I love Valere . . .

DORINE: No, no. Tartuffe's your man, and you shall taste him.

MARIANE: You know I've always trusted you; now help me . . .

DORINE: No, you shall be, my faith! Tartuffified.

MARIANE: Well, then, since you've no pity for my fate
100   Let me take counsel only of despair;
It will advise and help and give me courage;
There's one sure cure, I know, for all my troubles.
(She starts to go.)

DORINE: There, there! Come back. I can't be angry long.
105   I must take pity on you, after all.

MARIANE: Oh, don't you see, Dorine, if I must bear
This martyrdom, I certainly shall die.

DORINE: Now don't you fret. We'll surely find some way.
To hinder this . . . But here's Valere, your lover.

SCENE IV

Valere, Mariane, Dorine

VALERE: Madam, a piece of news—quite new to me—
Has just come out, and very fine it is.

MARIANE: What piece of news?

VALERE: Your marriage with Tartuffe.

MARIANE: 'Tis true my father has this plan in mind.

VALERE: Your father, madam . . .

MARIANE: Yes, he's changed his plans,
And did but now propose it to me.

VALERE: What!
10   Seriously?

MARIANE: Yes, he was serious,
And openly insisted on the match.

VALERE: And what's your resolution in the matter,
Madam?

MARIANE: I don't know.

VALERE: That's a pretty answer.
You don't know?

MARIANE: No.

VALERE: No?

MARIANE: What do you advise?

VALERE: I? My advice is, marry him, by all means.

MARIANE: That's your advice?

VALERE: Yes.

MARIANE: Do you mean it?

VALERE: Surely.

       A splendid choice, and worthy of your acceptance.

MARIANE: Oh, very well, sir! I shall take your counsel.

VALERE: You'll find no trouble taking it, I warrant.

MARIANE: No more than you did giving it, be sure.

VALERE: I gave it, truly, to oblige you, madam.

MARIANE: And I shall take it to oblige you, sir.

DORINE: (withdrawing to the back of the stage)

       Let's see what this affair will come to.

VALERE: So,

35   That is your love? And it was all deceit

       When you . . .

MARIANE: I beg you, say no more of that.

       You told me, squarely, sir, I should accept

       The husband that is offered me; and I

40   Will tell you squarely that I mean to do so,

       Since you have given me this good advice.

VALERE: Don't shield yourself with talk of my advice.

       You had your mind made up, that's evident;

       And now you're snatching at a trifling pretext

45   To justify the breaking of your word.

MARIANE: Exactly so.

VALERE: Of course it is; your heart

       Has never known true love for me.

MARIANE: Alas!

50   You're free to think so, if you please.

VALERE: Yes, yes,

       I'm free to think so; and my outraged love

       May yet forestall you in your perfidy,

       And offer elsewhere both my heart and hand.

MARIANE: No doubt of it; the love your high deserts

       May win . . .

VALERE: Good Lord, have done with my deserts!

       I know I have but few, and you have proved it.

       But I may find more kindness in another;

60   I know of someone, who'll not be ashamed

       To take your leavings, and make up my loss.

MARIANE: The loss is not so great; you'll easily

       Console yourself completely for this change.

VALERE: I'll try my best, that you may well believe.

65   When we're forgotten by a woman's heart,

       Our pride is challenged; we, too, must forget;

Or if we cannot, must at least pretend to.
No other way can man such baseness prove,
As be a lover scorned, and still in love.

MARIANE: In faith, a high and noble sentiment.

VALERE: Yes; and it's one that all men must approve.
What! Would you have me keep my love alive,
And see you fly into another's arms
Before my very eyes; and never offer
75   To someone else the heart that you had scorned?

MARIANE: Oh, no, indeed! For my part, I could wish
That it were done already.

VALERE: What! You wish it?

MARIANE: Yes.

VALERE: This is insult heaped on injury;
I'll go at once and do as you desire
(He takes a step or two as if to go away.)

MARIANE: Oh, very well then.

VALERE: (turning back)
85   But remember this.
'Twas you that drove me to this desperate pass.

MARIANE: Of course.

VALERE: (turning back again)
And in the plan that I have formed
90   I only follow your example.

MARIANE: Yes.

VALERE: (at the door)
Enough; you shall be punctually obeyed.

MARIANE: So much the better.

VALERE: (coming back again)
This is once for all.

MARIANE: So be it, then.

VALERE: (He goes toward the door, but just as he reaches it, turns around)
Eh?

MARIANE: What?

VALERE: You didn't call me?

MARIANE: I? You are dreaming.

VALERE: Very well, I'm gone. Madam, farewell.
(He walks slowly away.)

MARIANE: Farewell, sir.

DORINE: I must say
You've lost your senses and both gone clean daft!
I've let you fight it out to the end o' the chapter
To see how far the thing could go. Oho, there,
110   Mister Valere!
(She goes and seizes him by the arm, to stop him. He makes a great show of
resistance.)

VALERE: What do you want, Dorine?

DORINE: Come here.

VALERE: No, no, I'm quite beside myself.

Don't hinder me from doing as she wishes.

DORINE: Stop!

VALERE: No. You see, I'm fixed, resolved, determined.

DORINE: So!

MARIANE: (aside)

Since my presence pains him, makes him go,
I'd better go myself, and leave him free.

DORINE: (leaving Valere, and running after Mariane)

Now t'other! Where are you going?

MARIANE: Let me be.

DORINE: Come back.

MARIANE: No, no, it isn't any use.

VALERE: (aside)

'Tis clear the sight of me is torture to her;
130   No doubt, t'were better I should free her from it.

DORINE: (leaving Mariane and running after Valere)

Same thing again! Deuce take you both, I say.
Now stop your fooling; come here, you; and you.
(She pulls first one, then the other, toward the middle of the stage.)

VALERE: (to Dorine)

What's your idea?

MARIANE: (to Dorine)

What can you mean to do?

DORINE: Set you to rights, and pull you out o' the scrape.
140   (To Valere)

Are you quite mad, to quarrel with her now?

VALERE: Didn't you hear the things she said to me?

DORINE: (to Mariane)

Are you quite mad, to get in such a passion?

MARIANE: Didn't you see the way he treated me?

DORINE: Fools, both of you.

(To Valere)

· She thinks of nothing else
But to keep faith with you, I vouch for it.
150   (To Mariane)

And he loves none but you, and longs for nothing
But just to marry you, I stake my life on't.

MARIANE: (to Valere)

Why did you give me such advice then, pray?

VALERE: (to Mariane)

Why ask for my advice on such a matter?

DORINE: You both are daft, I tell you. Here, your hands.

(To Valere)

Come, yours.

VALERE: (giving Dorine his hand)

What for?

DORINE: (to Mariane)

Now, yours.

MARIANE: (giving Dorine her hand)

165   But what's the use?

DORINE: Oh, quick now, come along. There, both of you—
        You love each other better than you think
        (Valere and Mariane hold each other's hands some time without looking
        at each other.)

VALERE: (at last turning toward Mariane)
        Come, don't be so ungracious now about it;
        Look at a man as if you didn't hate him.
        (Mariane looks sideways toward Valere, with just a bit of a smile.)

DORINE: My faith and troth, what fools these lovers be!

VALERE: (to Mariane)
        But come now, have I not a just complaint?
        And truly, are you not a wicked creature
        To take delight in saying what would pain me?

MARIANE: And are you not yourself the most ungrateful . . . ?

DORINE: Leave this discussion till another time;
        Now, think how you'll stave off this plaguy marriage.

MARIANE: Then tell us how to go about it.

DORINE: Well,
        We'll try all sorts of ways.

185   (To Mariane)
        Your father's daft;
        (To Valere)
        This plan is nonsense.
        (To Mariane)

190   You had better humour
        His notions by a semblance of consent,
        So that in case of danger, you can still
        Find means to block the marriage by delay.
        If you gain time, the rest is easy, trust me.

195   One day you'll fool them with a sudden illness,
        Causing delay; another day, ill omens:
        You've met a funeral, or broke a mirror,
        Or dreamed of muddy water. Best of all,
        They cannot marry you to anyone

200   Without your saying yes. But now, methinks,
        They mustn't find you chattering together.
        (To Valere)
        You, go at once and set your friends at work
        To make him keep his word to you; while we

205   Will bring the brother's influence to bear,
        And get the step-mother on our side, too.
        Good-bye.

VALERE: (to Mariane)
        Whatever efforts we may make,

210   My greatest hope, be sure, must rest on you.

MARIANE: (to Valere)
        I cannot answer for my father's whims;
        But no one save Valere shall ever have me.

VALERE: You thrill me through with joy! Whatever comes . . .
DORINE: Oho! These lovers! Never done with prattling!
      Now go.
VALERE: (starting to go, and coming back again)
      One last word . . .
DORINE: What a gabble and pother!
220   Be off! By this door, you. And you, by t'other.
      (She pushes them off, by the shoulders, in opposite directions.)

ACT III

SCENE I

Damis, Dorine

DAMIS: May lightning strike me dead this very instant,
      May I be everywhere proclaimed a scoundrel,
      If any reverence or power shall stop me,
      And if I don't do straightway something desperate!
DORINE: I beg you, moderate this towering passion;
      Your father did but merely mention it.
      Not all things that are talked of turn to facts;
      The road is long, sometimes, from plans to acts.
DAMIS: No, I must end this paltry fellow's plots,
10   And he shall hear from me a truth or two.
DORINE: So ho! Go slow now. Just you leave the fellow—
      Your father too—in your step-mother's hands.
      She has some influence with this Tartuffe,
      He makes a point of heeding all she says,
15   And I suspect that he is fond of her.
      Would God 'twere true!—'Twould be the height of humour
      Now, she has sent for him, in your behalf,
      To sound him on this marriage, to find out
      What his ideas are, and to show him plainly
20   What troubles he may cause, if he persists
      In giving countenance to this design.
      His man says, he's at prayers, I mustn't see him,
      But likewise says, he'll presently be down.
      So off with you, and let me wait for him.
DAMIS: I may be present at this interview.
DORINE: No, no! They must be left alone.
DAMIS: I won't
      So much as speak to him.
DORINE: Go on! We know you
30   And your high tantrums. Just the way to spoil things!
      Be off.
DAMIS: No, I must see—I'll keep my temper.
DORINE: Out on you, what a plague! He's coming. Hide!
      (Damis goes and hides in the closet at the back of the stage.)

SCENE II

Tartuffe, Dorine

TARTUFFE: (speaking to his valet, off the stage, as soon as he sees
      Dorine is there)
      Lawrence, put up my hair-cloth shirt and scourge,
      And pray that Heaven may shed its light upon you.
5   If any come to see me, say I'm gone
      To share my alms among the prisoners.

DORINE: (aside)
      What affectation and what showing off!

TARTUFFE: What do you want with me?

DORINE: To tell you . . .

TARTUFFE: (taking a handkerchief from his pocket)
      Ah!
      Before you speak, pray take this handkerchief.

DORINE: What?

TARTUFFE: Cover up that bosom, which I can't
      Endure to look on. Things like that offend
      Our souls, and fill our minds with sinful thoughts.

DORINE: Are you so tender to temptation, then,
      And has the flesh such power upon your senses?
20   I don't know how you get in such a heat;
      For my part, I am not so prone to lust,
      And I could see you stripped from head to foot,
      And all your hide not tempt me in the least

TARTUFFE: Show in your speech some little modesty,
25   Or I must instantly take leave of you.

DORINE: No, no, I'll leave you to yourself; I've only
      One thing to say: Madam will soon be down,
      And begs the favour of a word with you.

TARTUFFE: Ah! Willingly.

DORINE: (aside)
      How gentle all at once!
      My faith, I still believe I've hit upon it.

TARTUFFE: Will she come soon?

DORINE: I think I hear her now.
35   Yes, here she is herself; I'll leave you with her.

SCENE III

Elmire, Tartuffe

TARTUFFE: May Heaven's overflowing kindness ever
      Give you good health of body and of soul,
      And bless your days according to the wishes
      And prayers of its most humble votary!

ELMIRE: I'm very grateful for your pious wishes.
      But let's sit down, so we may talk at ease.

TARTUFFE: (after sitting down)
      And how are you recovered from your illness?

ELMIRE: (sitting down also)
10   Quite well; the fever soon let go its hold.
TARTUFFE: My prayers, I fear, have not sufficient merit
           To have drawn down this favour from on high;
           But each entreaty that I made to Heaven
           Had for its object your recovery.
ELMIRE: You're too solicitous on my behalf.
TARTUFFE: We could not cherish your dear health too much;
           I would have given mine, to help restore it.
ELMIRE: That's pushing Christian charity too far;
         I owe you many thanks for so much kindness.
TARTUFFE: I do far less for you than you deserve.
ELMIRE: There is a matter that I wished to speak of
         In private; I am glad there's no one here
         To listen.
TARTUFFE: Madam, I am overjoyed.
25   'Tis sweet to find myself alone with you.
           This is an opportunity I've asked
           Of Heaven, many a time; till now, in vain.
ELMIRE: All that I wish, is just a word from you,
         Quite frank and open, hiding nothing from me.
30   (DAMIS, without their seeing him, opens the closet door halfway.)
TARTUFFE: I too could wish, as Heaven's especial favour,
           To lay my soul quite open to your eyes,
           And swear to you, the trouble that I made
           About those visits which your charms attract,
35   Does not result from any hatred toward you,
           But rather from a passionate devotion,
           And purest motives . . .
ELMIRE: That is how I take it,
         I think 'tis my salvation that concerns you.
TARTUFFE: (pressing her finger tips)
           Madam, 'tis so; and such is my devotion . . .
ELMIRE: Ouch! but you squeeze too hard.
TARTUFFE: Excess of zeal.
           In no way could I ever mean to hurt you,
45   And I'd as soon . . .
           (He puts his hand on her knee.)
ELMIRE: What's your hand doing there?
TARTUFFE: Feeling your gown; the stuff is very soft.
ELMIRE: Let be, I beg you; I am very ticklish.
50   (She moves her chair away, and Tartuffe brings his nearer.)
TARTUFFE: (handling the lace yoke of Elmire's dress)
           Dear me how wonderful in workmanship
           This lace is! They do marvels, nowadays;
           Things of all kinds were never better made.
ELMIRE: Yes, very true. But let us come to business.
         They say my husband means to break his word.
         And marry Mariane to you. Is't so?

TARTUFFE: He did hint some such thing; but truly, madam,
         That's not the happiness I'm yearning after;
60   I see elsewhere the sweet compelling charms
         Of such a joy as fills my every wish.
ELMIRE: You mean you cannot love terrestrial things.
TARTUFFE: The heart within my bosom is not stone.
ELMIRE: I well believe your sighs all tend to Heaven,
65   And nothing here below can stay your thoughts.
TARTUFFE: Love for the beauty of eternal things
         Cannot destroy our love for earthly beauty;
         Our mortal senses well may be entranced
         By perfect works that Heaven has fashioned here.
70   Its charms reflected shine in such as you,
         And in yourself, its rarest miracles;
         It has displayed such marvels in your face,
         That eyes are dazed, and hearts are rapt away;
         I could not look on you, the perfect creature,
75   Without admiring Nature's great Creator,
         And feeling all my heart inflamed with love
         For you, His fairest image of Himself.
         At first I trembled lest this secret love
         Might be the Evil Spirit's artful snare;
80   I even schooled my heart to flee your beauty,
         Thinking it was a bar to my salvation.
         But soon, enlightened, O all lovely one,
         I saw how this my passion may be blameless,
         How I may make it fit with modesty,
85   And thus completely yield my heart to it.
         'Tis I must own, a great presumption in me
         To dare make you the offer of my heart;
         My love hopes all things from your perfect goodness,
         And nothing from my own poor weak endeavour.
90   You are my hope, my stay, my peace of heart;
         On you depends my torment or my bliss;
         And by your doom of judgment, I shall be
         Blest, if you will; or damned, by your decree.
ELMIRE: Your declaration's turned most gallantly;
95   But truly, it is just a bit surprising.
         You should have better armed your heart, methinks,
         And taken thought somewhat on such a matter.
         A pious man like you, known everywhere . . .
TARTUFFE: Though pious, I am none the less a man;
100   And when a man beholds your heavenly charms,
         The heart surrenders, and can think no more.
         I know such words seem strange, coming from me;
         But, madam, I'm no angel, after all;
         If you condemn my frankly made avowal
105   You only have your charming self to blame.
         Soon as I saw your more than human beauty,

You were thenceforth the sovereign of my soul;
Sweetness ineffable was in your eyes,
That took by storm my still resisting heart,
110   And conquered everything, fasts, prayers, and tears,
And turned my worship wholly to yourself.
My looks, my sighs, have spoke a thousand times;
Now, to express it all, my voice must speak.
If but you will look down with gracious favour
115   Upon the sorrows of your worthless slave,
If in your goodness you will give me comfort
And condescend unto my nothingness,
I'll ever pay you, O sweet miracle,
An unexampled worship and devotion.
120   Then too, with me your honour runs no risk;
With me you need not fear a public scandal.
These court gallants, that women are so fond of,
Are boastful of their acts, and vain in speech;
They always brag in public of their progress;
125   Soon as a favour's granted, they'll divulge it;
Their tattling tongues, if you but trust to them,
Will foul the altar where their hearts have worshipped.
But men like me are so discreet in love,
That you may trust their lasting secrecy.
130   The care we take to guard our own good name
May fully guarantee the one we love;
So you may find, with hearts like ours sincere,
Love without scandal, pleasure without fear.
ELMIRE: I've heard you through—your speech is clear, at least.
135   But don't you fear that I may take a fancy
To tell my husband of your gallant passion,
And that a prompt report of this affair
May somewhat change the friendship which he bears you?
TARTUFFE: I know that you're too good and generous,
140   That you will pardon my temerity,
Excuse, upon the score of human frailty,
The violence of passion that offends you,
And not forget, when you consult your mirror,
That I'm not blind, and man is made of flesh.
ELMIRE: Some women might do otherwise, perhaps,
But I am willing to employ discretion,
And not repeat the matter to my husband;
But in return, I'll ask one thing of you:
That you urge forward, frankly and sincerely,
150   The marriage of Valere to Mariane;
That you give up the unjust influence
By which you hope to win another's rights;
And . . .

S CENE I V

Elmire, Damis, Tartuffe

DAMIS: (coming out of the closet-room where he had been hiding)
No, I say! This thing must be made public.
I was just there, and overheard it all;
And Heaven's goodness must have brought me there
5   On purpose to confound this scoundrel's pride
And grant me means to take a signal vengeance
On his hypocrisy and arrogance,
And undeceive my father, showing up
The rascal caught at making love to you.

ELMIRE: No, no; it is enough if he reforms,
Endeavouring to deserve the favour shown him.
And since I've promised, do not you belie me.
'Tis not my way to make a public scandal;
An honest wife will scorn to heed such follies,
15   And never fret her husband's ears with them.

DAMIS: You've reasons of your own for acting thus;
And I have mine for doing otherwise.
To spare him now would be a mockery;
His bigot's pride has triumphed all too long
20   Over my righteous anger, and has caused
Far too much trouble in our family.
The rascal all too long has ruled my father,
And crossed my sister's love, and mine as well.
The traitor now must be unmasked before him:
25   And Providence has given me means to do it.
To Heaven I owe the opportunity,
And if I did not use it now I have it,
I should deserve to lose it once for all.

ELMIRE: Damis . . .

DAMIS: No, by your leave; I'll not be counselled.
I'm overjoyed. You needn't try to tell me
I must give up the pleasure of revenge.
I'll make an end of this affair at once;
And, to content me, here's my father now.

S CENE V

Orgon, Elmire, Damis, Tartuffe

DAMIS: Father, we've news to welcome your arrival,
That's altogether novel, and surprising.
You are well paid for your caressing care,
And this fine gentleman rewards your love
5   Most handsomely, with zeal that seeks no less
Than your dishonour, as has now been proven.
I've just surprised him making to your wife
The shameful offer of a guilty love.
She, somewhat over gentle and discreet,

10   Insisted that the thing should be concealed;
        But I will not condone such shamelessness,
        Nor so far wrong you as to keep it secret.
ELMIRE: Yes, I believe a wife should never trouble
        Her husband's peace of mind with such vain gossip;
15   A woman's honour does not hang on telling;
        It is enough if she defend herself;
        Or so I think; Damis, you'd not have spoken,
        If you would but have heeded my advice.

SCENE VI

Orgon, Damis, Tartuffe

ORGON: Just Heaven! Can what I hear be credited?
TARTUFFE: Yes, brother, I am wicked, I am guilty,
        A miserable sinner, steeped in evil,
        The greatest criminal that ever lived.
5   Each moment of my life is stained with soilures;
        And all is but a mass of crime and filth;
        Heaven, for my punishment, I see it plainly,
        Would mortify me now. Whatever wrong
        They find to charge me with, I'll not deny it
10   But guard against the pride of self-defence.
        Believe their stories, arm your wrath against me,
        And drive me like a villain from your house;
        I cannot have so great a share of shame
        But what I have deserved a greater still.
ORGON: (to his son)
        You miscreant, can you dare, with such a falsehood,
        To try to stain the whiteness of his virtue?
DAMIS: What! The feigned meekness of this hypocrite
          Makes you discredit . . .
ORGON: Silence, cursed plague!
TARTUFFE: Ah! Let him speak; you chide him wrongfully;
        You'd do far better to believe his tales.
        Why favour me so much in such a matter?
        How can you know of what I'm capable?
25   And should you trust my outward semblance, brother,
        Or judge therefrom that I'm the better man?
        No, no; you let appearances deceive you;
        I'm anything but what I'm thought to be,
        Alas! and though all men believe me godly,
30   The simple truth is, I'm a worthless creature.
        (To Damis)
        Yes, my dear son, say on, and call me traitor,
        Abandoned scoundrel, thief, and murderer;
        Heap on me names yet more detestable,
35   And I shall not gainsay you; I've deserved them;
        I'll bear this ignominy on my knees,
        To expiate in shame the crimes I've done.

ORGON: (to Tartuffe)

    Ah, brother, 'tis too much!

40   (To his son)

    You'll not relent,

    You blackguard?

DAMIS: What! His talk can so deceive you . . .

ORGON: Silence, you scoundrel!

45   (To Tartuffe)

    Brother, rise, I beg you.

    (To his son)

    Infamous villain!

DAMIS: Can he . . .

ORGON: Silence!

DAMIS: What . . .

ORGON: Another word, I'll break your every bone.

TARTUFFE: Brother, in God's name, don't be angry with him!

    I'd rather bear myself the bitterest torture

55   Than have him get a scratch on my account.

ORGON: (to his son)

    Ungrateful monster!

TARTUFFE: Stop. Upon my knees

    I beg you pardon him . . .

ORGON: (throwing himself on his knees too, and embracing Tartuffe)

    Alas! How can you?

    (To his son)

    Villain! Behold his goodness!

DAMIS: So . . .

ORGON: Be still.

DAMIS: What! I . . .

ORGON: Be still, I say. I know your motives

    For this attack. You hate him, all of you;

    Wife, children, servants, all let loose upon him,

70   You have recourse to every shameful trick

    To drive this godly man out of my house;

    The more you strive to rid yourselves of him,

    The more I'll strive to make him stay with me;

    I'll have him straightway married to my daughter,

75   Just to confound the pride of all of you.

DAMIS: What! Will you force her to accept his hand?

ORGON: Yes, and this very evening, to enrage you,

    Young rascal! Ah! I'll brave you all, and show you

    That I'm the master, and must be obeyed.

80   Now, down upon your knees this instant, rogue,

    And take back what you said, and ask his pardon.

DAMIS: Who? I? Ask pardon of that cheating scoundrel . . . ?

ORGON: Do you resist, you beggar, and insult him?

    A cudgel, here! a cudgel!

85   (To Tartuffe)

    Don't restrain me

(To his son)

Off with you! Leave my house this instant, sirrah,

And never dare set foot in it again.

DAMIS: Yes, I will leave your house, but . . .

ORGON: Leave it quickly.

You reprobate, I disinherit you,

And give you, too, my curse into the bargain.

SCENE VII

Orgon, Tartuffe

ORGON: What! So insult a saintly man of God!

TARTUFFE: Heaven, forgive him all the pain he gives me! [4]

(To Orgon)

Could you but know with what distress I see

5   Them try to vilify me to my brother!

ORGON: Ah!

TARTUFFE: The mere thought of such ingratitude

Makes my soul suffer torture, bitterly . . .

My horror at it . . . Ah! my heart's so full

10   I cannot speak . . . I think I'll die of it.

ORGON: (in tears, running to the door through which he drove away his son)

Scoundrel! I wish I'd never let you go,

But slain you on the spot with my own hand.

(To Tartuffe)

15   Brother, compose yourself, and don't be angry.

TARTUFFE: Nay, brother, let us end these painful quarrels.

I see what troublous times I bring upon you,

And think 'tis needful that I leave this house.

ORGON: What! You can't mean it?

TARTUFFE: Yes, they hate me here,

And try, I find, to make you doubt my faith.

ORGON: What of it? Do you find I listen to them?

TARTUFFE: No doubt they won't stop there. These same reports

You now reject, may some day win a hearing.

ORGON: No, brother, never.

TARTUFFE: Ah! my friend, a woman

May easily mislead her husband's mind.

ORGON: No, no.

TARTUFFE: So let me quickly go away

30   And thus remove all cause for such attacks.

ORGON: No, you shall stay; my life depends upon it.

TARTUFFE: Then I must mortify myself. And yet,

If you should wish . . .

ORGON: No, never!

---

[4] Some modern editions have adopted the reading, preserved by tradition as that of the earliest stage version: Heaven, forgive him even as I forgive him! Voltaire gives still another reading: Heaven, forgive me even as I forgive him! Whichever was the original version, it appears in none of the early editions, and Moliere probably felt forced to change it on account of its too close resemblance to the Biblical phrase.

TARTUFFE: Very well, then;
      No more of that. But I shall rule my conduct
      To fit the case. Honour is delicate,
      And friendship binds me to forestall suspicion,
      Prevent all scandal, and avoid your wife.
ORGON: No, you shall haunt her, just to spite them all.
      'Tis my delight to set them in a rage;
      You shall be seen together at all hours
      And what is more, the better to defy them,
      I'll have no other heir but you; and straightway
45   I'll go and make a deed of gift to you,
      Drawn in due form, of all my property.
      A good true friend, my son-in-law to be,
      Is more to me than son, and wife, and kindred.
      You will accept my offer, will you not?
TARTUFFE: Heaven's will be done in everything!
ORGON: Poor man!
      We'll go make haste to draw the deed aright,
      And then let envy burst itself with spite!

ACT IV

SCENE I

Cleante, Tartuffe

CLEANTE: Yes, it's become the talk of all the town,
      And make a stir that's scarcely to your credit;
      And I have met you, sir, most opportunely,
      To tell you in a word my frank opinion.
5   Not to sift out this scandal to the bottom,
      Suppose the worst for us—suppose Damis
      Acted the traitor, and accused you falsely;
      Should not a Christian pardon this offence,
      And stifle in his heart all wish for vengeance?
10   Should you permit that, for your petty quarrel,
      A son be driven from his father's house?
      I tell you yet again, and tell you frankly,
      Everyone, high or low, is scandalised;
      If you'll take my advice, you'll make it up,
15   And not push matters to extremities.
      Make sacrifice to God of your resentment;
      Restore the son to favour with his father.
TARTUFFE: Alas! So far as I'm concerned, how gladly
      Would I do so! I bear him no ill will;
20   I pardon all, lay nothing to his charge,
      And wish with all my heart that I might serve him;
      But Heaven's interests cannot allow it;
      If he returns, then I must leave the house.
      After his conduct, quite unparalleled,
25   All intercourse between us would bring scandal;

God knows what everyone's first thought would be!
They would attribute it to merest scheming
On my part—say that conscious of my guilt
I feigned a Christian love for my accuser,
30   But feared him in my heart, and hoped to win him
And underhandedly secure his silence.
CLEANTE: You try to put us off with specious phrases;
        But all your arguments are too far-fetched.
        Why take upon yourself the cause of Heaven?
35   Does Heaven need our help to punish sinners?
        Leave to itself the care of its own vengeance,
        And keep in mind the pardon it commands us;
        Besides, think somewhat less of men's opinions,
        When you are following the will of Heaven.
40   Shall petty fear of what the world may think
        Prevent the doing of a noble deed?
        No!—let us always do as Heaven commands,
        And not perplex our brains with further questions.
TARTUFFE: Already I have told you I forgive him;
45   And that is doing, sir, as Heaven commands.
        But after this day's scandal and affront
        Heaven does not order me to live with him.
CLEANTE: And does it order you to lend your ear
        To what mere whim suggested to his father,
50   And to accept gift of his estates,
        On which, in justice, you can make no claim?
TARTUFFE: No one who knows me, sir, can have the thought
        That I am acting from a selfish motive.
        The goods of this world have no charms for me;
55   I am not dazzled by their treacherous glamour;
        And if I bring myself to take the gift
        Which he insists on giving me, I do so,
        To tell the truth, only because I fear
        This whole estate may fall into bad hands,
60   And those to whom it comes may use it ill
        And not employ it, as is my design,
        For Heaven's glory and my neighbours' good.
CLEANTE: Eh, sir, give up these conscientious scruples
        That well may cause a rightful heir's complaints.
65   Don't take so much upon yourself, but let him
        Possess what's his, at his own risk and peril;
        Consider, it were better he misused it,
        Than you should be accused of robbing him.
        I am astounded that unblushingly
70   You could allow such offers to be made!
        Tell me—has true religion any maxim
        That teaches us to rob the lawful heir?
        If Heaven has made it quite impossible
        Damis and you should live together here,

75   Were it not better you should quietly
And honourably withdraw, than let the son
Be driven out for your sake, dead against
All reason? 'Twould be giving, sir, believe me,
Such an example of your probity . . .

TARTUFFE: Sir, it is half-past three; certain devotions
Recall me to my closet; you'll forgive me
For leaving you so soon.

CLEANTE: (alone)
Ah!

S C E N E   I I

Elmire, Mariane, Cleante, Dorine

DORINE: (to Cleante)
Sir, we beg you
To help us all you can in her behalf;
She's suffering almost more than heart can bear;
5   This match her father means to make to-night
Drives her each moment to despair. He's coming.
Let us unite our efforts now, we beg you,
And try by strength or skill to change his purpose.

S C E N E   I I I

Orgon, Elmire, Mariane, Cleante, Dorine

ORGON: So ho! I'm glad to find you all together.
(To Mariane)
Here is the contract that shall make you happy,
My dear. You know already what it means.

MARIANE: (on her knees before Orgon)
Father, I beg you, in the name of Heaven
That knows my grief, and by whate'er can move you,
Relax a little your paternal rights,
And free my love from this obedience!
10   Oh, do not make me, by your harsh command,
Complain to Heaven you ever were my father;
Do not make wretched this poor life you gave me.
If, crossing that fond hope which I had formed,
You'll not permit me to belong to one
15   Whom I have dared to love, at least, I beg you
Upon my knees, oh, save me from the torment
Of being possessed by one whom I abhor!
And do not drive me to some desperate act
By exercising all your rights upon me.

ORGON: (a little touched)
Come, come, my heart, be firm! no human weakness!

MARIANE: I am not jealous of your love for him;
Display it freely; give him your estate,
And if that's not enough, add all of mine;

25   I willingly agree, and give it up,
        If only you'll not give him me, your daughter;
        Oh, rather let a convent's rigid rule
        Wear out the wretched days that Heaven allots me.

ORGON: These girls are ninnies!—always turning nuns
30   When fathers thwart their silly love-affairs.
        Get on your feet! The more you hate to have him,
        The more 'twill help you earn your soul's salvation.
        So, mortify your senses by this marriage,
        And don't vex me about it any more.

DORINE: But what . . . ?

ORGON: You hold your tongue, before your betters.
        Don't dare to say a single word, I tell you.

CLEANTE: If you will let me answer, and advise . . .

ORGON: Brother, I value your advice most highly;
40   'Tis well thought out; no better can be had;
        But you'll allow me—not to follow it.

ELMIRE: (to her husband)
        I can't find words to cope with such a case;
        Your blindness makes me quite astounded at you.
45   You are bewitched with him, to disbelieve
        The things we tell you happened here to-day.

ORGON: I am your humble servant, and can see
        Things, when they're plain as noses on folks' faces,
        I know you're partial to my rascal son,
50   And didn't dare to disavow the trick
        He tried to play on this poor man; besides,
        You were too calm, to be believed; if that
        Had happened, you'd have been far more disturbed.

ELMIRE: And must our honour always rush to arms
55   At the mere mention of illicit love?
        Or can we answer no attack upon it
        Except with blazing eyes and lips of scorn?
        For my part, I just laugh away such nonsense;
        I've no desire to make a loud to-do.
60   Our virtue should, I think, be gentle-natured;
        Nor can I quite approve those savage prudes
        Whose honour arms itself with teeth and claws
        To tear men's eyes out at the slightest word.
        Heaven preserve me from that kind of honour!
65   I like my virtue not to be a vixen,
        And I believe a quiet cold rebuff
        No less effective to repulse a lover.

ORGON: I know . . . and you can't throw me off the scent.

ELMIRE: Once more, I am astounded at your weakness;
70   I wonder what your unbelief would answer,
        If I should let you see we've told the truth?

ORGON: See it?

ELMIRE: Yes.

ORGON: Nonsense.

ELMIRE: Come! If I should find
A way to make you see it clear as day?

ORGON: All rubbish.

ELMIRE: What a man! But answer me.
I'm not proposing now that you believe us;
80   But let's suppose that here, from proper hiding,
You should be made to see and hear all plainly;
What would you say then, to your man of virtue?

ORGON: Why, then, I'd say . . . say nothing. It can't be.

ELMIRE: Your error has endured too long already,
85   And quite too long you've branded me a liar.
I must at once, for my own satisfaction,
Make you a witness of the things we've told you.

ORGON: Amen! I take you at your word. We'll see
What tricks you have, and how you'll keep your promise.

ELMIRE: (to Dorine)
Send him to me.

DORINE: (to Elmire)
The man's a crafty codger,
Perhaps you'll find it difficult to catch him.

ELMIRE: (to Dorine)
Oh no! A lover's never hard to cheat,
And self-conceit leads straight to self-deceit.
Bid him come down to me.
(To Cleante and Mariane)
100   And you, withdraw.

SCENE IV

Elmire, Orgon

ELMIRE: Bring up this table, and get under it.

ORGON: What?

ELMIRE: One essential is to hide you well.

ORGON: Why under there?

ELMIRE: Oh, dear! Do as I say;
I know what I'm about, as you shall see.
Get under, now, I tell you; and once there
Be careful no one either sees or hears you.

ORGON: I'm going a long way to humour you,
10   I must say; but I'll see you through your scheme.

ELMIRE: And then you'll have, I think, no more to say.
(To her husband, who is now under the table.)
But mind, I'm going to meddle with strange matters;
Prepare yourself to be in no wise shocked.
15   Whatever I may say must pass, because
'Tis only to convince you, as I promised.
By wheedling speeches, since I'm forced to do it,
I'll make this hypocrite put off his mask,
Flatter the longings of his shameless passion,

20   And give free play to all his impudence.
       But, since 'tis for your sake, to prove to you
       His guilt, that I shall feign to share his love,
       I can leave off as soon as you're convinced,
       And things shall go no farther than you choose.
25   So, when you think they've gone quite far enough,
       It is for you to stop his mad pursuit,
       To spare your wife, and not expose me farther
       Than you shall need, yourself, to undeceive you.
       It is your own affair, and you must end it
30   When . . . Here he comes. Keep still, don't show yourself.

SCENE V

Tartuffe, Elmire; Orgon (under the table)

TARTUFFE: They told me that you wished to see me here.
ELMIRE: Yes. I have secrets for your ear alone.
       But shut the door first, and look everywhere
       For fear of spies.
5   (Tartuffe goes and closes the door, and comes back.)
       We surely can't afford
       Another scene like that we had just now;
       Was ever anyone so caught before!
       Damis did frighten me most terribly
10   On your account; you saw I did my best
       To baffle his design, and calm his anger.
       But I was so confused, I never thought
       To contradict his story; still, thank Heaven,
       Things turned out all the better, as it happened,
15   And now we're on an even safer footing.
       The high esteem you're held in, laid the storm;
       My husband can have no suspicion of you,
       And even insists, to spite the scandal-mongers,
       That we shall be together constantly;
20   So that is how, without the risk of blame,
       I can be here locked up with you alone,
       And can reveal to you my heart, perhaps
       Only too ready to allow your passion.
TARTUFFE: Your words are somewhat hard to understand,
25   Madam; just now you used a different style.
ELMIRE: If that refusal has offended you,
       How little do you know a woman's heart!
       How ill you guess what it would have you know,
       When it presents so feeble a defence!
30   Always, at first, our modesty resists
       The tender feelings you inspire us with.
       Whatever cause we find to justify
       The love that masters us, we still must feel
       Some little shame in owning it; and strive
35   To make as though we would not, when we would.

But from the very way we go about it
We let a lover know our heart surrenders,
The while our lips, for honour's sake, oppose
Our heart's desire, and in refusing promise.
40   I'm telling you my secret all too freely
And with too little heed to modesty.
But—now that I've made bold to speak—pray tell me.
Should I have tried to keep Damis from speaking,
Should I have heard the offer of your heart
45   So quietly, and suffered all your pleading,
And taken it just as I did—remember—
If such a declaration had not pleased me,
And, when I tried my utmost to persuade you
Not to accept the marriage that was talked of,
50   What should my earnestness have hinted to you
If not the interest that you've inspired,
And my chagrin, should such a match compel me
To share a heart I want all to myself?
TARTUFFE: 'Tis, past a doubt, the height of happiness,
55   To hear such words from lips we dote upon;
Their honeyed sweetness pours through all my senses
Long draughts of suavity ineffable.
My heart employs its utmost zeal to please you,
And counts your love its one beatitude;
60   And yet that heart must beg that you allow it
To doubt a little its felicity.
I well might think these words an honest trick
To make me break off this approaching marriage;
And if I may express myself quite plainly,
65   I cannot trust these too enchanting words
Until the granting of some little favour
I sigh for, shall assure me of their truth
And build within my soul, on firm foundations,
A lasting faith in your sweet charity.
ELMIRE: (coughing to draw her husband's attention)
What! Must you go so fast?—and all at once
Exhaust the whole love of a woman's heart?
She does herself the violence to make
This dear confession of her love, and you
75   Are not yet satisfied, and will not be
Without the granting of her utmost favours?
TARTUFFE: The less a blessing is deserved, the less
We dare to hope for it; and words alone
Can ill assuage our love's desires. A fate
80   Too full of happiness, seems doubtful still;
We must enjoy it ere we can believe it.
And I, who know how little I deserve
Your goodness, doubt the fortunes of my daring;
So I shall trust to nothing, madam, till

85   You have convinced my love by something real.
ELMIRE: Ah! How your love enacts the tyrant's role,
          And throws my mind into a strange confusion!
          With what fierce sway it rules a conquered heart,
          And violently will have its wishes granted!
90   What! Is there no escape from your pursuit?
          No respite even?—not a breathing space?
          Nay, is it decent to be so exacting,
          And so abuse by urgency the weakness
          You may discover in a woman's heart?
TARTUFFE: But if my worship wins your gracious favour,
          Then why refuse me some sure proof thereof?
ELMIRE: But how can I consent to what you wish,
          Without offending Heaven you talk so much of?
TARTUFFE: If Heaven is all that stands now in my way,
100   I'll easily remove that little hindrance;
          Your heart need not hold back for such a trifle.
ELMIRE: But they affright us so with Heaven's commands!
TARTUFFE: I can dispel these foolish fears, dear madam;
          I know the art of pacifying scruples
105   Heaven forbids, 'tis true, some satisfactions;
          But we find means to make things right with Heaven.
          ('Tis a scoundrel speaking.) [5]
          There is a science, madam, that instructs us
          How to enlarge the limits of our conscience
110   According to our various occasions,
          And rectify the evil of the deed
          According to our purity of motive.
          I'll duly teach you all these secrets, madam;
          You only need to let yourself be guided.
115   Content my wishes, have no fear at all;
          I answer for't, and take the sin upon me.
          (Elmire coughs still louder.)
          Your cough is very bad.
ELMIRE: Yes, I'm in torture.
TARTUFFE: Would you accept this bit of licorice?
ELMIRE: The case is obstinate, I find; and all
          The licorice in the world will do no good.
TARTUFFE: 'Tis very trying.
ELMIRE: More than words can say.
TARTUFFE: In any case, your scruple's easily
          Removed. With me you're sure of secrecy,
          And there's no harm unless a thing is known.
          The public scandal is what brings offence,
          And secret sinning is not sin at all.

[5] Moliere's note, in the original edition.

ELMIRE: (after coughing again)
    So then, I see I must resolve to yield;
    I must consent to grant you everything,
    And cannot hope to give full satisfaction
    Or win full confidence, at lesser cost.
135   No doubt 'tis very hard to come to this;
    'Tis quite against my will I go so far;
    But since I must be forced to it, since nothing
    That can be said suffices for belief,
    Since more convincing proof is still demanded,
140   I must make up my mind to humour people.
    If my consent give reason for offence,
    So much the worse for him who forced me to it;
    The fault can surely not be counted mine.
TARTUFFE: It need not, madam; and the thing itself . . .
ELMIRE: Open the door, I pray you, and just see
    Whether my husband's not there, in the hall.
TARTUFFE: Why take such care for him? Between ourselves,
    He is a man to lead round by the nose.
    He's capable of glorying in our meetings;
150   I've fooled him so, he'd see all, and deny it.
ELMIRE: No matter; go, I beg you, look about,
    And carefully examine every corner.

SCENE VI

Orgon, Elmire

ORGON: (crawling out from under the table)
    That is, I own, a man . . . abominable!
    I can't get over it; the whole thing floors me.
ELMIRE: What? You come out so soon? You cannot mean it!
5   Get back under the table; 'tis not time yet;
    Wait till the end, to see, and make quite certain,
    And don't believe a thing on mere conjecture.
ORGON: Nothing more wicked e'er came out of Hell.
ELMIRE: Dear me! Don't go and credit things too lightly.
10   No, let yourself be thoroughly convinced;
    Don't yield too soon, for fear you'll be mistaken.
    (As Tartuffe enters, she makes her husband stand behind her.)

SCENE VII

Tartuffe, Elmire, Orgon

TARTUFFE: (not seeing Orgon)
    All things conspire toward my satisfaction,
    Madam, I've searched the whole apartment through.
    There's no one here; and now my ravished soul . . .
ORGON: (stopping him)
    Softly! You are too eager in your amours;
    You needn't be so passionate. Ah ha!

My holy man! You want to put it on me!
How is your soul abandoned to temptation!
10   Marry my daughter, eh?—and want my wife, too?
I doubted long enough if this was earnest,
Expecting all the time the tone would change;
But now the proof's been carried far enough;
I'm satisfied, and ask no more, for my part.

ELMIRE: (to Tartuffe)
'Twas quite against my character to play
This part; but I was forced to treat you so.

TARTUFFE: What? You believe . . . ?

ORGON: Come, now, no protestations.
20   Get out from here, and make no fuss about it.

TARTUFFE: But my intent . . .

ORGON: That talk is out of season.
You leave my house this instant.

TARTUFFE: You're the one
25   To leave it, you who play the master here!
This house belongs to me, I'll have you know,
And show you plainly it's no use to turn
To these low tricks, to pick a quarrel with me,
And that you can't insult me at your pleasure,
30   For I have wherewith to confound your lies,
Avenge offended Heaven, and compel
Those to repent who talk to me of leaving.

SCENE VIII

Elmire, Orgon

ELMIRE: What sort of speech is this? What can it mean?

ORGON: My faith, I'm dazed. This is no laughing matter.

ELMIRE: What?

ORGON: From his words I see my great mistake;
5   The deed of gift is one thing troubles me.

ELMIRE: The deed of gift . . .

ORGON: Yes, that is past recall.
But I've another thing to make me anxious.

ELMIRE: What's that?

ORGON: You shall know all. Let's see at once
Whether a certain box is still upstairs.

ACT V

SCENE I

Orgon, Cleante

CLEANTE: Whither away so fast?

ORGON: How should I know?

CLEANTE: Methinks we should begin by taking counsel
To see what can be done to meet the case.

ORGON: I'm all worked up about that wretched box.
        More than all else it drives me to despair.
CLEANTE: That box must hide some mighty mystery?
ORGON: Argas, my friend who is in trouble, brought it
        Himself, most secretly, and left it with me.
10   He chose me, in his exile, for this trust;
        And on these documents, from what he said,
        I judge his life and property depend.
CLEANTE: How could you trust them to another's hands?
ORGON: By reason of a conscientious scruple.
15   I went straight to my traitor, to confide
        In him; his sophistry made me believe
        That I must give the box to him to keep,
        So that, in case of search, I might deny
        My having it at all, and still, by favour
20   Of this evasion, keep my conscience clear
        Even in taking oath against the truth.
CLEANTE: Your case is bad, so far as I can see;
        This deed of gift, this trusting of the secret
        To him, were both—to state my frank opinion—
25   Steps that you took too lightly; he can lead you
        To any length, with these for hostages;
        And since he holds you at such disadvantage,
        You'd be still more imprudent, to provoke him;
        So you must go some gentler way about.
ORGON: What! Can a soul so base, a heart so false,
        Hide neath the semblance of such touching fervour?
        I took him in, a vagabond, a beggar! . . .
        'Tis too much! No more pious folk for me!
        I shall abhor them utterly forever,
35   And henceforth treat them worse than any devil.
CLEANTE: So! There you go again, quite off the handle!
        In nothing do you keep an even temper.
        You never know what reason is, but always
        Jump first to one extreme, and then the other.
40   You see your error, and you recognise
        That you've been cozened by a feigned zeal;
        But to make up for't, in the name of reason,
        Why should you plunge into a worse mistake,
        And find no difference in character
45   Between a worthless scamp, and all good people?
        What! Just because a rascal boldly duped you
        With pompous show of false austerity,
        Must you needs have it everybody's like him,
        And no one's truly pious nowadays?
50   Leave such conclusions to mere infidels;
        Distinguish virtue from its counterfeit,
        Don't give esteem too quickly, at a venture,
        But try to keep, in this, the golden mean.

If you can help it, don't uphold imposture;
55   But do not rail at true devoutness, either;
And if you must fall into one extreme,
Then rather err again the other way.

SCENE II

Damis, Orgon, Cleante

DAMIS: What! father, can the scoundrel threaten you,
Forget the many benefits received,
And in his base abominable pride
Make of your very favours arms against you?
ORGON: Too true, my son. It tortures me to think on't.
DAMIS: Let me alone, I'll chop his ears off for him.
We must deal roundly with his insolence;
'Tis I must free you from him at a blow;
'Tis I, to set things right, must strike him down.
CLEANTE: Spoke like a true young man. Now just calm down,
And moderate your towering tantrums, will you?
We live in such an age, with such a king,
That violence can not advance our cause.

SCENE III

Madame Pernelle, Orgon, Elmire, Cleante, Mariane, Damis, Dorine

MADAME PERNELLE: What's this? I hear of fearful mysteries!
ORGON: Strange things indeed, for my own eyes to witness;
You see how I'm requited for my kindness,
I zealously receive a wretched beggar,
5   I lodge him, entertain him like my brother,
Load him with benefactions every day,
Give him my daughter, give him all my fortune:
And he meanwhile, the villain, rascal, wretch,
Tries with black treason to suborn my wife,
10   And not content with such a foul design,
He dares to menace me with my own favours,
And would make use of those advantages
Which my too foolish kindness armed him with,
To ruin me, to take my fortune from me,
15   And leave me in the state I saved him from.
DORINE: Poor man!
MADAME PERNELLE: My son, I cannot possibly
Believe he could intend so black a deed.
ORGON: What?
MADAME PERNELLE: Worthy men are still the sport of envy.
ORGON: Mother, what do you mean by such a speech?
MADAME PERNELLE: There are strange goings-on about your house,
And everybody knows your people hate him.
ORGON: What's that to do with what I tell you now?
MADAME PERNELLE: I always said, my son, when you were little:

That virtue here below is hated ever;
The envious may die, but envy never.
ORGON: What's that fine speech to do with present facts?
MADAME PERNELLE: Be sure, they've forged a hundred silly lies . . .
ORGON: I've told you once, I saw it all myself.
MADAME PERNELLE: For slanderers abound in calumnies . . .
ORGON: Mother, you'd make me damn my soul. I tell you
　　　I saw with my own eyes his shamelessness.
MADAME PERNELLE: Their tongues for spitting venom never lack,
35　　There's nothing here below they'll not attack.
ORGON: Your speech has not a single grain of sense.
　　　I saw it, harkee, saw it, with these eyes
　　　I saw—d'ye know what saw means?—must I say it
　　　A hundred times, and din it in your ears?
MADAME PERNELLE: My dear, appearances are oft deceiving,
　　　And seeing shouldn't always be believing.
ORGON: I'll go mad.
MADAME PERNELLE: False suspicions may delude,
　　　And good to evil oft is misconstrued.
ORGON: Must I construe as Christian charity
　　　The wish to kiss my wife!
MADAME PERNELLE: You must, at least,
　　　Have just foundation for accusing people,
　　　And wait until you see a thing for sure.
ORGON: The devil! How could I see any surer?
　　　Should I have waited till, before my eyes,
　　　He . . . No, you'll make me say things quite improper.
MADAME PERNELLE: In short, 'tis known too pure a zeal inflames him;
　　　And so, I cannot possibly conceive
55　　That he should try to do what's charged against him.
ORGON: If you were not my mother, I should say
　　　Such things! . . . I know not what, I'm so enraged!
DORINE: (to Orgon)
　　　Fortune has paid you fair, to be so doubted;
60　　You flouted our report, now yours is flouted.
CLEANTE: We're wasting time here in the merest trifling,
　　　Which we should rather use in taking measures
　　　To guard ourselves against the scoundrel's threats.
DAMIS: You think his impudence could go far?
ELMIRE: For one, I can't believe it possible;
　　　Why, his ingratitude would be too patent.
CLEANTE: Don't trust to that; he'll find abundant warrant
　　　To give good colour to his acts against you;
　　　And for less cause than this, a strong cabal
70　　Can make one's life a labyrinth of troubles.
　　　I tell you once again: armed as he is
　　　You never should have pushed him quite so far.
ORGON: True; yet what could I do? The rascal's pride
　　　Made me lose all control of my resentment.

CLEANTE: I wish with all my heart that some pretence
            Of peace could be patched up between you two
ELMIRE: If I had known what weapons he was armed with,
            I never should have raised such an alarm,
            And my . . .
ORGON: (to Dorine, seeing Mr. Loyal come in)
            Who's coming now? Go quick, find out.
            I'm in a fine state to receive a visit!

                    SCENE IV

        Orgon, Madame Pernelle, Elmire, Martiane, Cleante, Damis, Dorine, Mr. Loyal

MR. LOYAL: (to Dorine, at the back of the stage)
            Good day, good sister. Pray you, let me see
            The master of the house.
DORINE: He's occupied;
5   I think he can see nobody at present.
MR. LOYAL: I'm not by way of being unwelcome here.
            My coming can, I think, nowise displease him;
            My errand will be found to his advantage.
DORINE: Your name, then?
MR. LOYAL: Tell him simply that his friend
            Mr. Tartuffe has sent me, for his goods . . .
DORINE: (to Orgon)
            It is a man who comes, with civil manners,
            Sent by Tartuffe, he says, upon an errand
15   That you'll be pleased with.
CLEANTE: (to Orgon)
            Surely you must see him,
            And find out who he is, and what he wants.
ORGON: (to Cleante)
20   Perhaps he's come to make it up between us:
            How shall I treat him?
CLEANTE: You must not get angry;
            And if he talks of reconciliation
            Accept it.
MR. LOYAL: (to Orgon)
            Sir, good-day. And Heaven send
            Harm to your enemies, favour to you.
ORGON: (aside to Cleante)
            This mild beginning suits with my conjectures
30   And promises some compromise already.
MR. LOYAL: All of your house has long been dear to me;
            I had the honour, sir, to serve your father.
ORGON: Sir, I am much ashamed, and ask your pardon
            For not recalling now your face or name.
MR. LOYAL: My name is Loyal. I'm from Normandy.
            My office is court-bailiff, in despite
            Of envy; and for forty years, thank Heaven,

It's been my fortune to perform that office
With honour. So I've come, sir, by your leave
40   To render service of a certain writ . . .
ORGON: What, you are here to . . .
MR. LOYAL: Pray, sir, don't be angry.
      'Tis nothing, sir, but just a little summons: —
      Order to vacate, you and yours, this house,
45   Move out your furniture, make room for others,
      And that without delay or putting off,
      As needs must be . . .
ORGON: I? Leave this house?
MR. LOYAL: Yes, please, sir
50   The house is now, as you well know, of course,
      Mr. Tartuffe's. And he, beyond dispute,
      Of all your goods is henceforth lord and master
      By virtue of a contract here attached,
      Drawn in due form, and unassailable.
DAMIS: (to Mr. Loyal)
      Your insolence is monstrous, and astounding!
MR. LOYAL: (to Damis)
      I have no business, sir, that touches you;
      (Pointing to Orgon)
60   This is the gentleman. He's fair and courteous,
      And knows too well a gentleman's behaviour
      To wish in any wise to question justice.
ORGON: But . . .
MR. LOYAL: Sir, I know you would not for a million
65   Wish to rebel; like a good citizen
      You'll let me put in force the court's decree.
DAMIS: Your long black gown may well, before you know it,
      Mister Court-bailiff, get a thorough beating.
MR. LOYAL: (to Orgon)
70   Sir, make your son be silent or withdraw.
      I should be loath to have to set things down,
      And see your names inscribed in my report.
DORINE: (aside)
      This Mr. Loyal's looks are most disloyal.
MR. LOYAL: I have much feeling for respectable
      And honest folk like you, sir, and consented
      To serve these papers, only to oblige you,
      And thus prevent the choice of any other
      Who, less possessed of zeal for you than I am
80   Might order matters in less gentle fashion.
ORGON: And how could one do worse than order people
      Out of their house?
MR. LOYAL: Why, we allow you time;
      And even will suspend until to-morrow
85   The execution of the order, sir.
      I'll merely, without scandal, quietly,

Come here and spend the night, with half a score
Of officers; and just for form's sake, please,
You'll bring your keys to me, before retiring.
90   I will take care not to disturb your rest,
And see there's no unseemly conduct here.
But by to-morrow, and at early morning,
You must make haste to move your least belongings;
My men will help you—I have chosen strong ones
95   To serve you, sir, in clearing out the house.
No one could act more generously, I fancy,
And, since I'm treating you with great indulgence,
I beg you'll do as well by me, and see
I'm not disturbed in my discharge of duty.
ORGON: I'd give this very minute, and not grudge it,
The hundred best gold louis I have left,
If I could just indulge myself, and land
My fist, for one good square one, on his snout.
CLEANTE: (aside to Orgon)
105   Careful!—don't make things worse.
DAMIS: Such insolence!
I hardly can restrain myself. My hands
Are itching to be at him.
DORINE: By my faith,
110   With such a fine broad back, good Mr. Loyal,
A little beating would become you well.
MR. LOYAL: My girl, such infamous words are actionable.
And warrants can be issued against women.
CLEANTE: (to Mr. Loyal)
115   Enough of this discussion, sir; have done.
Give us the paper, and then leave us, pray.
MR. LOYAL: Then "au revoir". Heaven keep you from disaster!
ORGON: May Heaven confound you both, you and your master!

SCENE V

Orgon, Madame Pernelle, Elmire, Cleante, Mariane, Damis, Dorine

ORGON: Well, mother, am I right or am I not?
This writ may help you now to judge the matter.
Or don't you see his treason even yet?
MADAME PERNELLE: I'm all amazed, befuddled, and beflustered!
DORINE: (to Orgon)
You are quite wrong, you have no right to blame him;
This action only proves his good intentions.
Love for his neighbour makes his virtue perfect;
And knowing money is a root of evil,
10   In Christian charity, he'd take away
Whatever things may hinder your salvation.
ORGON: Be still. You always need to have that told you.
CLEANTE: (to Orgon)
Come, let us see what course you are to follow.

ELMIRE: Go and expose his bold ingratitude.
   Such action must invalidate the contract;
   His perfidy must now appear too black
   To bring him the success that he expects.

S C E N E   V I

Valere, Orgon, Madame Pernelle, Elmire, Cleante, Mariane, Damis, Dorine

VALERE: 'Tis with regret, sir, that I bring bad news;
   But urgent danger forces me to do so.
   A close and intimate friend of mine, who knows
   The interest I take in what concerns you,
5 Has gone so far, for my sake, as to break
   The secrecy that's due to state affairs,
   And sent me word but now, that leaves you only
   The one expedient of sudden flight.
   The villain who so long imposed upon you,
10 Found means, an hour ago, to see the prince,
   And to accuse you (among other things)
   By putting in his hands the private strong-box
   Of a state-criminal, whose guilty secret,
   You, failing in your duty as a subject,
15 (He says) have kept. I know no more of it
   Save that a warrant's drawn against you, sir,
   And for the greater surety, that same rascal
   Comes with the officer who must arrest you.
CLEANTE: His rights are armed; and this is how the scoundrel
20 Seeks to secure the property he claims.
ORGON: Man is a wicked animal, I'll own it!
VALERE: The least delay may still be fatal, sir.
   I have my carriage, and a thousand louis,
   Provided for your journey, at the door.
25 Let's lose no time; the bolt is swift to strike,
   And such as only flight can save you from.
   I'll be your guide to seek a place of safety,
   And stay with you until you reach it, sir.
ORGON: How much I owe to your obliging care!
30 Another time must serve to thank you fitly;
   And I pray Heaven to grant me so much favour
   That I may some day recompense your service.
   Good-bye; see to it, all of you . . .
CLEANTE: Come hurry;
35 We'll see to everything that's needful, brother.

S C E N E   V I I

Tartuffe, an officer, Madame Pernelle, Orgon, Elmire, Cleante,
Mariane, Valere, Damis, Dorine

TARTUFFE: (stopping Orgon)
   Softly, sir, softly; do not run so fast;

You haven't far to go to find your lodging;
By order of the prince, we here arrest you.
ORGON: Traitor! You saved this worst stroke for the last;
This crowns your perfidies, and ruins me.
TARTUFFE: I shall not be embittered by your insults,
For Heaven has taught me to endure all things.
CLEANTE: Your moderation, I must own, is great.
DAMIS: How shamelessly the wretch makes bold with Heaven!
TARTUFFE: Your ravings cannot move me; all my thought
Is but to do my duty.
MARIANE: You must claim
Great glory from this honourable act.
TARTUFFE: The act cannot be aught but honourable,
Coming from that high power which sends me here.
ORGON: Ungrateful wretch, do you forget 'twas I
That rescued you from utter misery?
TARTUFFE: I've not forgot some help you may have given;
20   But my first duty now is toward my prince.
The higher power of that most sacred claim
Must stifle in my heart all gratitude;
And to such puissant ties I'd sacrifice
My friend, my wife, my kindred, and myself.
ELMIRE: The hypocrite!
DORINE: How well he knows the trick
Of cloaking him with what we most revere!
CLEANTE: But if the motive that you make parade of
Is perfect as you say, why should it wait
30   To show itself, until the day he caught you
Soliciting his wife? How happens it
You have not thought to go inform against him
Until his honour forces him to drive you
Out of his house? And though I need not mention
35   That he'd just given you his whole estate,
Still, if you meant to treat him now as guilty,
How could you then consent to take his gift?
TARTUFFE: (to the Officer)
Pray, sir, deliver me from all this clamour;
40   Be good enough to carry out your order.
THE OFFICER: Yes, I've too long delayed its execution;
'Tis very fitting you should urge me to it;
So therefore, you must follow me at once
To prison, where you'll find your lodging ready.
TARTUFFE: Who? I, sir?
THE OFFICER: You.
TARTUFFE: By why to prison?
THE OFFICER: You
Are not the one to whom I owe account.
50   You, sir (to Orgon), recover from your hot alarm.
Our prince is not a friend to double dealing,

His eyes can read men's inmost hearts, and all
The art of hypocrites cannot deceive him.
His sharp discernment sees things clear and true;
55 His mind cannot too easily be swayed,
For reason always holds the balance even.
He honours and exalts true piety,
But knows the false, and views it with disgust.
This fellow was by no means apt to fool him,
60 Far subtler snares have failed against his wisdom,
And his quick insight pierced immediately
The hidden baseness of this tortuous heart.
Accusing you, the knave betrayed himself,
And by true recompense of Heaven's justice
65 He stood revealed before our monarch's eyes
A scoundrel known before by other names,
Whose horrid crimes, detailed at length, might fill
A long-drawn history of many volumes.
Our monarch—to resolve you in a word—
70 Detesting his ingratitude and baseness,
Added this horror to his other crimes,
And sent me hither under his direction
To see his insolence out-top itself,
And force him then to give you satisfaction.
75 Your papers, which the traitor says are his,
I am to take from him, and give you back;
The deed of gift transferring your estate
Our monarch's sovereign will makes null and void;
And for the secret personal offence
80 Your friend involved you in, he pardons you:
Thus he rewards your recent zeal, displayed
In helping to maintain his rights, and shows
How well his heart, when it is least expected,
Knows how to recompense a noble deed,
85 And will not let true merit miss its due,
Remembering always rather good than evil.

DORINE: Now Heaven be praised!

MADAME PERNELLE: At last I breathe again.

ELMIRE: A happy outcome!

MARIANE: Who'd have dared to hope it?

ORGON: (to Tartuffe, who is being led by the officer)
There traitor! Now you're . . .

Scene VIII

Madame Pernelle, Orgon, Elmire, Mariane, Cleante, Valere, Damis, Dorine

CLEANTE: Brother, hold!—and don't
Descend to such indignities, I beg you.
Leave the poor wretch to his unhappy fate,
And let remorse oppress him, but not you.
5 Hope rather that his heart may now return

To virtue, hate his vice, reform his ways,
And win the pardon of our glorious prince;
While you must straightway go, and on your knees
Repay with thanks his noble generous kindness.
ORGON: Well said! We'll go, and at his feet kneel down,
With joy to thank him for his goodness shown;
And this first duty done, with honours due,
We'll then attend upon another, too.
With wedded happiness reward Valere,
15   And crown a lover noble and sincere.

Jean Baptiste Racine
Phaedra

Translated by Robert Bruce Boswell

INTRODUCTORY NOTE

JEAN BAPTISTE RACINE, the younger contemporary of Corneille, and his rival for supremacy in French classical tragedy, was born at Ferte-Milon, December 21, 1639. He was educated at the College of Beauvais, at the great Jansenist school at Port Royal, and at the College d'Harcourt. He attracted notice by an ode written for the marriage of Louis XIV in 1660, and made his first really great dramatic success with his "Andromaque." His tragic masterpieces include "Britannicus," "Berenice," "Bajazet," "Mithridate," "Iphigenie," and "Phaedre," all written between 1669 and 1677. Then for some years he gave up dramatic composition, disgusted by the intrigues of enemies who sought to injure his career by exalting above him an unworthy rival. In 1689 he resumed his work under the persuasion of Mme. de Maintenon, and produced "Esther" and "Athalie," the latter ranking among his finest productions, although it did not receive public recognition until some time after his death in 1699. Besides his tragedies, Racine wrote one comedy, "Les Plaideurs," four hymns of great beauty, and a history of Port Royal.

The external conventions of classical tragedy which had been established by Corneille, Racine did not attempt to modify. His study of the Greek tragedians and his own taste led him to submit willingly to the rigor and simplicity of form which were the fundamental marks of the classical ideal. It was in his treatment of character that he differed most from his predecessor; for whereas, as we have seen, Corneille represented his leading figures as heroically subduing passion by force of will, Racine represents his as driven by almost uncontrollable passion. Thus his creations appeal to the modern reader as more warmly human; their speech, if less exalted, is simpler and more natural; and he succeeds more brilliantly with his portraits of women than with those of men.

All these characteristics are exemplified in "Phaedre," the tragedy of Racine which has made an appeal to the widest audience. To the legend as treated by Euripides, Racine added the love of Hippolytus for Aricia, and thus supplied a motive for Phaedra's jealousy, and at the same time he made the nurse instead of Phaedra the calumniator of his son to Theseus.

PHAEDRA

Characters

THESEUS, *son of Aegeus and King of Athens.*
PHAEDRA, *wife of Theseus and Daughter of Minos and Pasiphae.*
HIPPOLYTUS, *son of Theseus and Antiope, Queen of the Amazons.*
ARICIA, *Princess of the Blood Royal of Athens.*
OENONE, *nurse of Phaedra.*
THERAMENES, *tutor of Hippolytus.*
ISMEME, *bosom friend of Aricia.*
PANOPE, *waiting-woman of Phaedra.*
GUARDS.

The scene is laid at Troezen, a town of the Peloponnesus.

ACT I

SCENE I

Hippolytus, Theramenes

HIPPOLYTUS: My mind is settled, dear Theramenes,
And I can stay no more in lovely Troezen.
In doubt that racks my soul with mortal anguish,
I grow ashamed of such long idleness.
5   Six months and more my father has been gone,
And what may have befallen one so dear
I know not, nor what corner of the earth
Hides him.
THERAMENES: And where, prince, will you look for him?
10   Already, to content your just alarm,
Have I not cross'd the seas on either side
Of Corinth, ask'd if aught were known of Theseus
Where Acheron is lost among the Shades,
Visited Elis, doubled Toenarus,
15   And sail'd into the sea that saw the fall
Of Icarus? Inspired with what new hope,
Under what favour'd skies think you to trace
His footsteps? Who knows if the King, your father,
Wishes the secret of his absence known?
20   Perchance, while we are trembling for his life,
The hero calmly plots some fresh intrigue,
And only waits till the deluded fair—
HIPPOLYTUS: Cease, dear Theramenes, respect the name
Of Theseus. Youthful errors have been left
25   Behind, and no unworthy obstacle
Detains him. Phaedra long has fix'd a heart
Inconstant once, nor need she fear a rival.
In seeking him I shall but do my duty,
And leave a place I dare no longer see.

THERAMENES: Indeed! When, prince, did you begin to dread
　　　　　These peaceful haunts, so dear to happy childhood,
　　　　　Where I have seen you oft prefer to stay,
　　　　　Rather than meet the tumult and the pomp
　　　　　Of Athens and the court? What danger shun you,
35　　　Or shall I say what grief?
HIPPOLYTUS: That happy time
　　　　　Is gone, and all is changed, since to these shores
　　　　　The gods sent Phaedra.
THERAMENES: I perceive the cause
40　　　Of your distress. It is the queen whose sight
　　　　　Offends you. With a step-dame's spite she schemed
　　　　　Your exile soon as she set eyes on you.
　　　　　But if her hatred is not wholly vanish'd,
　　　　　It has at least taken a milder aspect.
45　　　Besides, what danger can a dying woman,
　　　　　One too who longs for death, bring on your head?
　　　　　Can Phaedra, sick'ning of a dire disease
　　　　　Of which she will not speak, weary of life
　　　　　And of herself, form any plots against you?
HIPPOLYTUS: It is not her vain enmity I fear,
　　　　　Another foe alarms Hippolytus.
　　　　　I fly, it must be own'd, from young Aricia,
　　　　　The sole survivor of an impious race.
THERAMENES: What! You become her persecutor too!
55　　　The gentle sister of the cruel sons
　　　　　Of Pallas shared not in their perfidy;
　　　　　Why should you hate such charming innocence?
HIPPOLYTUS: I should not need to fly, if it were hatred.
THERAMENES: May I, then, learn the meaning of your flight?
60　　　Is this the proud Hippolytus I see,
　　　　　Than whom there breathed no fiercer foe to love
　　　　　And to that yoke which Theseus has so oft
　　　　　Endured? And can it be that Venus, scorn'd
　　　　　So long, will justify your sire at last?
65　　　Has she, then, setting you with other mortals,
　　　　　Forced e'en Hippolytus to offer incense
　　　　　Before her? Can you love?
HIPPOLYTUS: Friend, ask me not.
　　　　　You, who have known my heart from infancy
70　　　And all its feelings of disdainful pride,
　　　　　Spare me the shame of disavowing all
　　　　　That I profess'd. Born of an Amazon,
　　　　　The wildness that you wonder at I suck'd
　　　　　With mother's milk. When come to riper age,
75　　　Reason approved what Nature had implanted.
　　　　　Sincerely bound to me by zealous service,
　　　　　You told me then the story of my sire,
　　　　　And know how oft, attentive to your voice,

I kindled when I heard his noble acts,
80   As you described him bringing consolation
To mortals for the absence of Alcides,
The highways clear'd of monsters and of robbers,
Procrustes, Cercyon, Sciro, Sinnis slain,
The Epidaurian giant's bones dispersed,
85   Crete reeking with the blood of Minotaur.
But when you told me of less glorious deeds,
Troth plighted here and there and everywhere,
Young Helen stolen from her home at Sparta,
And Periboea's tears in Salamis,
90   With many another trusting heart deceived
Whose very names have 'scaped his memory,
Forsaken Ariadne to the rocks
Complaining, last this Phaedra, bound to him
By better ties,—you know with what regret
95   I heard and urged you to cut short the tale,
Happy had I been able to erase
From my remembrance that unworthy part
Of such a splendid record. I, in turn,
Am I too made the slave of love, and brought
100   To stoop so low? The more contemptible
That no renown is mine such as exalts
The name of Theseus, that no monsters quell'd
Have given me a right to share his weakness.
And if my pride of heart must needs be humbled,
105   Aricia should have been the last to tame it.
Was I beside myself to have forgotten
Eternal barriers of separation
Between us? By my father's stern command
Her brethren's blood must ne'er be reinforced
110   By sons of hers; he dreads a single shoot
From stock so guilty, and would fain with her
Bury their name, that, even to the tomb
Content to be his ward, for her no torch
Of Hymen may be lit. Shall I espouse
115   Her rights against my sire, rashly provoke
His wrath, and launch upon a mad career—
THERAMENES: The gods, dear prince, if once your hour is come,
Care little for the reasons that should guide us.
Wishing to shut your eyes, Theseus unseals them;
120   His hatred, stirring a rebellious flame
Within you, lends his enemy new charms.
And, after all, why should a guiltless passion
Alarm you? Dare you not essay its sweetness,
But follow rather a fastidious scruple?
125   Fear you to stray where Hercules has wander'd?
What heart so stout that Venus has not vanquish'd?
Where would you be yourself, so long her foe,

Had your own mother, constant in her scorn
Of love, ne'er glowed with tenderness for Theseus?
130   What boots it to affect a pride you feel not?
Confess it, all is changed; for some time past
You have been seldom seen with wild delight
Urging the rapid car along the strand,
Or, skilful in the art that Neptune taught,
135   Making th' unbroken steed obey the bit;
Less often have the woods return'd our shouts;
A secret burden on your spirits cast
Has dimm'd your eye. How can I doubt you love?
Vainly would you conceal the fatal wound.
140   Has not the fair Aricia touch'd your heart?
HIPPOLYTUS: Theramenes, I go to find my father.
THERAMENES: Will you not see the queen before you start,
     My prince?
HIPPOLYTUS: That is my purpose: you can tell her.
145   Yes, I will see her; duty bids me do it.
But what new ill vexes her dear Oenone?

SCENE II

Hippolytus, Oenone, Theramenes

OENONE: Alas, my lord, what grief was e'er like mine?
The queen has almost touch'd the gates of death.
Vainly close watch I keep by day and night,
E'en in my arms a secret malady
5   Slays her, and all her senses are disorder'd.
Weary yet restless from her couch she rises,
Pants for the outer air, but bids me see
That no one on her misery intrudes.
She comes.
HIPPOLYTUS: Enough. She shall not be disturb'd,
Nor be confronted with a face she hates.

SCENE III

Phaedra, Oenone

PHAEDRA: We have gone far enough. Stay, dear Oenone;
Strength fails me, and I needs must rest awhile.
My eyes are dazzled with this glaring light
So long unseen, my trembling knees refuse
5   Support. Ah me!
OENONE: Would Heaven that our tears
     Might bring relief!
PHAEDRA: Ah, how these cumbrous gauds,
These veils oppress me! What officious hand
10   Has tied these knots, and gather'd o'er my brow
These clustering coils? How all conspires to add
To my distress!
OENONE: What is one moment wish'd,

The next, is irksome. Did you not just now,

15   Sick of inaction, bid us deck you out,
      And, with your former energy recall'd,
      Desire to go abroad, and see the light
      Of day once more? You see it, and would fain
      Be hidden from the sunshine that you sought.

PHAEDRA: Thou glorious author of a hapless race,
      Whose daughter 'twas my mother's boast to be,
      Who well may'st blush to see me in such plight,
      For the last time I come to look on thee,
      O Sun!

OENONE: What! Still are you in love with death?
      Shall I ne'er see you, reconciled to life,
      Forego these cruel accents of despair?

PHAEDRA: Would I were seated in the forest's shade!
      When may I follow with delighted eye,

30   Thro' glorious dust flying in full career,
      A chariot—

OENONE: Madam?

PHAEDRA: Have I lost my senses?
      What said I? and where am I? Whither stray

35   Vain wishes? Ah! The gods have made me mad.
      I blush, Oenone, and confusion covers
      My face, for I have let you see too clearly
      The shame of grief that, in my own despite,
      O'erflows these eyes of mine.

OENONE: If you must blush,
      Blush at a silence that inflames your woes.
      Resisting all my care, deaf to my voice,
      Will you have no compassion on yourself,
      But let your life be ended in mid course?

45   What evil spell has drain'd its fountain dry?
      Thrice have the shades of night obscured the heav'ns
      Since sleep has enter'd thro' your eyes, and thrice
      The dawn has chased the darkness thence, since food
      Pass'd your wan lips, and you are faint and languid.

50   To what dread purpose is your heart inclined?
      How dare you make attempts upon your life,
      And so offend the gods who gave it you,
      Prove false to Theseus and your marriage vows,
      Ay, and betray your most unhappy children,

55   Bending their necks yourself beneath the yoke?
      That day, be sure, which robs them of their mother,
      Will give high hopes back to the stranger's son,
      To that proud enemy of you and yours,
      To whom an Amazon gave birth, I mean

60   Hippolytus—

PHAEDRA: Ye gods!

OENONE: Ah, this reproach

Moves you!

PHAEDRA: Unhappy woman, to what name

65   Gave your mouth utterance?

OENONE: Your wrath is just.

'Tis well that that ill-omen'd name can rouse
Such rage. Then live. Let love and duty urge
Their claims. Live, suffer not this son of Scythia,

70   Crushing your children 'neath his odious sway,
To rule the noble offspring of the gods,
The purest blood of Greece. Make no delay;
Each moment threatens death; quickly restore
Your shatter'd strength, while yet the torch of life

75   Holds out, and can be fann'd into a flame.

PHAEDRA: Too long have I endured its guilt and shame!

OENONE: Why? What remorse gnaws at your heart? What crime
Can have disturb'd you thus? Your hands are not
Polluted with the blood of innocence?

PHAEDRA: Thanks be to Heav'n, my hands are free from stain.
Would that my soul were innocent as they!

OENONE: What awful project have you then conceived,
Whereat your conscience should be still alarm'd?

PHAEDRA: Have I not said enough? Spare me the rest.

85   I die to save myself a full confession.

OENONE: Die then, and keep a silence so inhuman;
But seek some other hand to close your eyes.
Tho' but a spark of life remains within you,
My soul shall go before you to the Shades.

90   A thousand roads are always open thither;
Pain'd at your want of confidence, I'll choose
The shortest. Cruel one, when has my faith
Deceived you! Think how in my arms you lay
New born. For you, my country and my children

95   I have forsaken. Do you thus repay
My faithful service?

PHAEDRA: What do you expect
From words so bitter? Were I to break silence
Horror would freeze your blood.

OENONE: What can you say
To horrify me more than to behold
You die before my eyes?

PHAEDRA: When you shall know
My crime, my death will follow none the less,

105   But with the added stain of guilt.

OENONE: Dear Madam,
By all the tears that I have shed for you,
By these weak knees I clasp, relieve my mind
From torturing doubt.

PHAEDRA: It is your wish. Then rise.

OENONE: I hear you. Speak.

PHAEDRA: Heav'ns! How shall I begin?

OENONE: Dismiss vain fears, you wound me with distrust.

PHAEDRA: O fatal animosity of Venus!

115   Into what wild distractions did she cast
         My mother!

OENONE: Be they blotted from remembrance,
         And for all time to come buried in silence.

PHAEDRA: My sister Ariadne, by what love

120   Were you betray'd to death, on lonely shores
         Forsaken!

OENONE: Madam, what deep-seated pain
         Prompts these reproaches against all your kin?

PHAEDRA: It is the will of Venus, and I perish,

125   Last, most unhappy of a family
         Where all were wretched.

OENONE: Do you love?

PHAEDRA: I feel
         All its mad fever.

OENONE: Ah! For whom?

PHAEDRA: Hear now
         The crowning horror. Yes, I love—my lips
         Tremble to say his name.

OENONE: Whom?

PHAEDRA: Know you him,
         Son of the Amazon, whom I've oppress'd
         So long?

OENONE: Hippolytus? Great gods!

PHAEDRA: 'Tis you

140   Have named him.

OENONE: All my blood within my veins
         Seems frozen. O despair! O cursed race!
         Ill-omen'd journey! Land of misery!
         Why did we ever reach thy dangerous shores?

PHAEDRA: My wound is not so recent. Scarcely had I
         Been bound to Theseus by the marriage yoke,
         And happiness and peace seem'd well secured,
         When Athens show'd me my proud enemy.
         I look'd, alternately turn'd pale and blush'd

150   To see him, and my soul grew all distraught;
         A mist obscured my vision, and my voice
         Falter'd, my blood ran cold, then burn'd like fire;
         Venus I felt in all my fever'd frame,
         Whose fury had so many of my race

155   Pursued. With fervent vows I sought to shun
         Her torments, built and deck'd for her a shrine,
         And there, 'mid countless victims did I seek
         The reason I had lost; but all for naught,
         No remedy could cure the wounds of love!

160   In vain I offer'd incense on her altars;

When I invoked her name my heart adored
Hippolytus, before me constantly;
And when I made her altars smoke with victims,
'Twas for a god whose name I dared not utter.
165 I fled his presence everywhere, but found him—
O crowning horror!—in his father's features.
Against myself, at last, I raised revolt,
And stirr'd my courage up to persecute
The enemy I loved. To banish him
170 I wore a step-dame's harsh and jealous carriage,
With ceaseless cries I clamour'd for his exile,
Till I had torn him from his father's arms.
I breathed once more, Oenone; in his absence
My days flow'd on less troubled than before,
175 And innocent. Submissive to my husband,
I hid my grief, and of our fatal marriage
Cherish'd the fruits. Vain caution! Cruel Fate!
Brought hither by my spouse himself, I saw
Again the enemy whom I had banish'd,
180 And the old wound too quickly bled afresh.
No longer is it love hid in my heart,
But Venus in her might seizing her prey.
I have conceived just terror for my crime;
I hate my life, and hold my love in horror.
185 Dying I wish'd to keep my fame unsullied,
And bury in the grave a guilty passion;
But I have been unable to withstand
Tears and entreaties, I have told you all;
Content, if only, as my end draws near,
190 You do not vex me with unjust reproaches,
Nor with vain efforts seek to snatch from death
The last faint lingering sparks of vital breath.

Scene IV

Phaedra, Oenone, Panope

PANOPE: Fain would I hide from you tidings so sad,
But 'tis my duty, Madam, to reveal them.
The hand of death has seized your peerless husband,
And you are last to hear of this disaster.
OENONE: What say you, Panope?
PANOPE: The queen, deceived
By a vain trust in Heav'n, begs safe return
For Theseus, while Hippolytus his son
Learns of his death from vessels that are now
10 In port.
PHAEDRA: Ye gods!
PANOPE: Divided counsels sway
The choice of Athens; some would have the prince,
Your child, for master; others, disregarding

15   The laws, dare to support the stranger's son.
        'Tis even said that a presumptuous faction
        Would crown Aricia and the house of Pallas.
        I deem'd it right to warn you of this danger.
        Hippolytus already is prepared
20   To start, and should he show himself at Athens,
        'Tis to be fear'd the fickle crowd will all
        Follow his lead.
OENONE: Enough. The queen, who hears you,
        By no means will neglect this timely warning.

SCENE V

Phaedra, Oenone

OENONE: Dear lady, I had almost ceased to urge
        The wish that you should live, thinking to follow
        My mistress to the tomb, from which my voice
        Had fail'd to turn you; but this new misfortune
5   Alters the aspect of affairs, and prompts
        Fresh measures. Madam, Theseus is no more,
        You must supply his place. He leaves a son,
        A slave, if you should die, but, if you live,
        A King. On whom has he to lean but you?
10   No hand but yours will dry his tears. Then live
        For him, or else the tears of innocence
        Will move the gods, his ancestors, to wrath
        Against his mother. Live, your guilt is gone,
        No blame attaches to your passion now.
15   The King's decease has freed you from the bonds
        That made the crime and horror of your love.
        Hippolytus no longer need be dreaded,
        Him you may see henceforth without reproach.
        It may be, that, convinced of your aversion,
20   He means to head the rebels. Undeceive him,
        Soften his callous heart, and bend his pride.
        King of this fertile land, in Troezen here
        His portion lies; but as he knows, the laws
        Give to your son the ramparts that Minerva
25   Built and protects. A common enemy
        Threatens you both, unite them to oppose
        Aricia.
PHAEDRA: To your counsel I consent.
        Yes, I will live, if life can be restored,
30   If my affection for a son has pow'r
        To rouse my sinking heart at such a dangerous hour.

ACT II

SCENE I

Aricia, Ismene

ARICIA: Hippolytus request to see me here!
　　　　Hippolytus desire to bid farewell!
　　　　Is't true, Ismene? Are you not deceived?
ISMENE: This is the first result of Theseus' death.
5　　　 Prepare yourself to see from every side.
　　　　Hearts turn towards you that were kept away
　　　　By Theseus. Mistress of her lot at last,
　　　　Aricia soon shall find all Greece fall low,
　　　　To do her homage.
ARICIA: 'Tis not then, Ismene,
　　　　An idle tale? Am I no more a slave?
　　　　Have I no enemies?
ISMENE: The gods oppose
　　　　Your peace no longer, and the soul of Theseus
15　　　 Is with your brothers.
ARICIA: Does the voice of fame
　　　　Tell how he died?
ISMENE: Rumours incredible
　　　　Are spread. Some say that, seizing a new bride,
20　　　 The faithless husband by the waves was swallow'd.
　　　　Others affirm, and this report prevails,
　　　　That with Pirithous to the world below
　　　　He went, and saw the shores of dark Cocytus,
　　　　Showing himself alive to the pale ghosts;
25　　　 But that he could not leave those gloomy realms,
　　　　Which whoso enters there abides for ever.
ARICIA: Shall I believe that ere his destined hour
　　　　A mortal may descend into the gulf
　　　　Of Hades? What attraction could o'ercome
30　　　 Its terrors?
ISMENE: He is dead, and you alone
　　　　Doubt it. The men of Athens mourn his loss.
　　　　Troezen already hails Hippolytus
　　　　As King. And Phaedra, fearing for her son,
35　　　 Asks counsel of the friends who share her trouble,
　　　　Here in this palace.
ARICIA: Will Hippolytus,
　　　　Think you, prove kinder than his sire, make light
　　　　My chains, and pity my misfortunes?
ISMENE: Yes,
　　　　I think so, Madam.
ARICIA: Ah, you know him not
　　　　Or you would never deem so hard a heart
　　　　Can pity feel, or me alone except
45　　　 From the contempt in which he holds our sex.

Has he not long avoided every spot
Where we resort?

ISMENE: I know what tales are told
Of proud Hippolytus, but I have seen
50   Him near you, and have watch'd with curious eye
How one esteem'd so cold would bear himself.
Little did his behavior correspond
With what I look'd for; in his face confusion
Appear'd at your first glance, he could not turn
55   His languid eyes away, but gazed on you.
Love is a word that may offend his pride,
But what the tongue disowns, looks can betray.

ARICIA: How eagerly my heart hears what you say,
Tho' it may be delusion, dear Ismene!
60   Did it seem possible to you, who know me,
That I, sad sport of a relentless Fate,
Fed upon bitter tears by night and day,
Could ever taste the maddening draught of love?
The last frail offspring of a royal race,
65   Children of Earth, I only have survived
War's fury. Cut off in the flow'r of youth,
Mown by the sword, six brothers have I lost,
The hope of an illustrious house, whose blood
Earth drank with sorrow, near akin to his
70   Whom she herself produced. Since then, you know
How thro' all Greece no heart has been allow'd
To sigh for me, lest by a sister's flame
The brothers' ashes be perchance rekindled.
You know, besides, with what disdain I view'd
75   My conqueror's suspicions and precautions,
And how, oppos'd as I have ever been
To love, I often thank'd the King's injustice
Which happily confirm'd my inclination.
But then I never had beheld his son.
80   Not that, attracted merely by the eye, I
love him for his beauty and his grace,
Endowments which he owes to Nature's bounty,
Charms which he seems to know not or to scorn.
I love and prize in him riches more rare,
85   The virtues of his sire, without his faults.
I love, as I must own, that generous pride
Which ne'er has stoop'd beneath the amorous yoke.
Phaedra reaps little glory from a lover
So lavish of his sighs; I am too proud
90   To share devotion with a thousand others,
Or enter where the door is always open.
But to make one who ne'er has stoop'd before
Bend his proud neck, to pierce a heart of stone,
To bind a captive whom his chains astonish,

95   Who vainly 'gainst a pleasing yoke rebels,—
That piques my ardour, and I long for that.
'Twas easier to disarm the god of strength
Than this Hippolytus, for Hercules
Yielded so often to the eyes of beauty,
100   As to make triumph cheap. But, dear Ismene,
I take too little heed of opposition
Beyond my pow'r to quell, and you may hear me,
Humbled by sore defeat, upbraid the pride
I now admire. What! Can he love? and I
105   Have had the happiness to bend—
ISMENE: He comes
Yourself shall hear him.

SCENE II

Hippolytus, Aricia, Ismene

HIPPOLYTUS: Lady, ere I go
My duty bids me tell you of your change
Of fortune. My worst fears are realized;
My sire is dead. Yes, his protracted absence
5   Was caused as I foreboded. Death alone,
Ending his toils, could keep him from the world
Conceal'd so long. The gods at last have doom'd
Alcides' friend, companion, and successor.
I think your hatred, tender to his virtues,
10   Can hear such terms of praise without resentment,
Knowing them due. One hope have I that soothes
My sorrow: I can free you from restraint.
Lo, I revoke the laws whose rigour moved
My pity; you are at your own disposal,
15   Both heart and hand; here, in my heritage,
In Troezen, where my grandsire Pittheus reign'd
Of yore and I am now acknowledged King,
I leave you free, free as myself,—and more.
ARICIA: Your kindness is too great, 'tis overwhelming.
20   Such generosity, that pays disgrace
With honour, lends more force than you can think
To those harsh laws from which you would release me.
HIPPOLYTUS: Athens, uncertain how to fill the throne
Of Theseus, speaks of you, anon of me,
25   And then of Phaedra's son.
ARICIA: Of me, my lord?
HIPPOLYTUS: I know myself excluded by strict law:
Greece turns to my reproach a foreign mother.
But if my brother were my only rival,
30   My rights prevail o'er his clearly enough
To make me careless of the law's caprice.
My forwardness is check'd by juster claims:
To you I yield my place, or, rather, own

That it is yours by right, and yours the sceptre,
35   As handed down from Earth's great son, Erechtheus.
Adoption placed it in the hands of Aegeus:
Athens, by him protected and increased,
Welcomed a king so generous as my sire,
And left your hapless brothers in oblivion.
40   Now she invites you back within her walls;
Protracted strife has cost her groans enough,
Her fields are glutted with your kinsmen's blood
Fatt'ning the furrows out of which it sprung
At first. I rule this Troezen; while the son
45   Of Phaedra has in Crete a rich domain.
Athens is yours. I will do all I can
To join for you the votes divided now
Between us.
ARICIA: Stunn'd at all I hear, my lord,
50   I fear, I almost fear a dream deceives me.
Am I indeed awake? Can I believe
Such generosity? What god has put it
Into your heart? Well is the fame deserved
That you enjoy! That fame falls short of truth!
55   Would you for me prove traitor to yourself?
Was it not boon enough never to hate me,
So long to have abstain'd from harbouring
The enmity—
HIPPOLYTUS: To hate you? I, to hate you?
60   However darkly my fierce pride was painted,
Do you suppose a monster gave me birth?
What savage temper, what envenom'd hatred
Would not be mollified at sight of you?
Could I resist the soul-bewitching charm—
ARICIA: Why, what is this, Sir?
HIPPOLYTUS: I have said too much
Not to say more. Prudence in vain resists
The violence of passion. I have broken
Silence at last, and I must tell you now
70   The secret that my heart can hold no longer.
You see before you an unhappy instance
Of hasty pride, a prince who claims compassion
I, who, so long the enemy of Love,
Mock'd at his fetters and despised his captives,
75   Who, pitying poor mortals that were shipwreck'd,
In seeming safety view'd the storms from land,
Now find myself to the same fate exposed,
Toss'd to and fro upon a sea of troubles!
My boldness has been vanquish'd in a moment,
80   And humbled is the pride wherein I boasted.
For nearly six months past, ashamed, despairing,
Bearing where'er I go the shaft that rends

My heart, I struggle vainly to be free
From you and from myself; I shun you, present;
85   Absent, I find you near; I see your form
In the dark forest depths; the shades of night,
Nor less broad daylight, bring back to my view
The charms that I avoid; all things conspire
To make Hippolytus your slave. For fruit
90   Of all my bootless sighs, I fail to find
My former self. My bow and javelins
Please me no more, my chariot is forgotten,
With all the Sea God's lessons; and the woods
Echo my groans instead of joyous shouts
95   Urging my fiery steeds.

Hearing this tale
Of passion so uncouth, you blush perchance
At your own handiwork. With what wild words
I offer you my heart, strange captive held
100   By silken jess! But dearer in your eyes
Should be the offering, that this language comes
Strange to my lips; reject not vows express'd
So ill, which but for you had ne'er been form'd.

S C E N E   I I I

Hippolytus, Aricia, Theramenes, Ismene

THERAMENES: Prince, the Queen comes. I herald her approach.
        'Tis you she seeks.
HIPPOLYTUS: Me?
THERAMENES: What her thought may be
5   I know not. But I speak on her behalf.
        She would converse with you ere you go hence.
HIPPOLYTUS: What shall I say to her? Can she expect—
ARICIA: You cannot, noble Prince, refuse to hear her,
        Howe'er convinced she is your enemy,
10   Some shade of pity to her tears is due.
HIPPOLYTUS: Shall we part thus? and will you let me go,
        Not knowing if my boldness has offended
        The goddess I adore? Whether this heart,
        Left in your hands—
ARICIA: Go, Prince, pursue the schemes
        Your generous soul dictates, make Athens own
        My sceptre. All the gifts you offer me
        Will I accept, but this high throne of empire
        Is not the one most precious in my sight.

S C E N E   I V

Hippolytus, Theramenes

HIPPOLYTUS: Friend, is all ready?
        But the Queen approaches.

Go, see the vessel in fit trim to sail.
Haste, bid the crew aboard, and hoist the signal:
5   Then soon return, and so deliver me
From interview most irksome.

Scene V

Phaedra, Hippolytus, Oenone

PHAEDRA: (To Oenone)
There I see him!
My blood forgets to flow, my tongue to speak
What I am come to say.
OENONE: Think of your son,
How all his hopes depend on you.
PHAEDRA: I hear
You leave us, and in haste. I come to add
My tears to your distress, and for a son
10   Plead my alarm. No more has he a father,
And at no distant day my son must witness
My death. Already do a thousand foes
Threaten his youth. You only can defend him
But in my secret heart remorse awakes,
15   And fear lest I have shut your ears against
His cries. I tremble lest your righteous anger
Visit on him ere long the hatred earn'd
By me, his mother.
HIPPOLYTUS: No such base resentment,
20   Madam, is mine.
PHAEDRA: I could not blame you, Prince,
If you should hate me. I have injured you:
So much you know, but could not read my heart.
T' incur your enmity has been mine aim.
25   The self-same borders could not hold us both;
In public and in private I declared
Myself your foe, and found no peace till seas
Parted us from each other. I forbade
Your very name to be pronounced before me.
30   And yet if punishment should be proportion'd
To the offence, if only hatred draws
Your hatred, never woman merited
More pity, less deserved your enmity.
HIPPOLYTUS: A mother jealous of her children's rights
35   Seldom forgives the offspring of a wife
Who reign'd before her. Harassing suspicions
Are common sequels of a second marriage.
Of me would any other have been jealous
No less than you, perhaps more violent.
PHAEDRA: Ah, Prince, how Heav'n has from the general law
Made me exempt, be that same Heav'n my witness!
Far different is the trouble that devours me!

HIPPOLYTUS: This is no time for self-reproaches, Madam.
　　　　　It may be that your husband still beholds
45　　　The light, and Heav'n may grant him safe return,
　　　　　In answer to our prayers. His guardian god
　　　　　Is Neptune, ne'er by him invoked in vain.
PHAEDRA: He who has seen the mansions of the dead
　　　　　Returns not thence. Since to those gloomy shores
50　　　Theseus is gone, 'tis vain to hope that Heav'n
　　　　　May send him back. Prince, there is no release
　　　　　From Acheron's greedy maw. And yet, methinks,
　　　　　He lives, and breathes in you. I see him still
　　　　　Before me, and to him I seem to speak;
55　　　My heart—
　　　　　Oh! I am mad; do what I will,
　　　　　I cannot hide my passion.
HIPPOLYTUS: Yes, I see
　　　　　The strange effects of love. Theseus, tho' dead,
60　　　Seems present to your eyes, for in your soul
　　　　　There burns a constant flame.
PHAEDRA: Ah, yes for Theseus
　　　　　I languish and I long, not as the Shades
　　　　　Have seen him, of a thousand different forms
65　　　The fickle lover, and of Pluto's bride
　　　　　The would-be ravisher, but faithful, proud
　　　　　E'en to a slight disdain, with youthful charms
　　　　　Attracting every heart, as gods are painted,
　　　　　Or like yourself. He had your mien, your eyes,
70　　　Spoke and could blush like you, when to the isle
　　　　　Of Crete, my childhood's home, he cross'd the waves,
　　　　　Worthy to win the love of Minos' daughters.
　　　　　What were you doing then? Why did he gather
　　　　　The flow'r of Greece, and leave Hippolytus?
75　　　Oh, why were you too young to have embark'd
　　　　　On board the ship that brought thy sire to Crete?
　　　　　At your hands would the monster then have perish'd,
　　　　　Despite the windings of his vast retreat.
　　　　　To guide your doubtful steps within the maze
80　　　My sister would have arm'd you with the clue.
　　　　　But no, therein would Phaedra have forestall'd her,
　　　　　Love would have first inspired me with the thought;
　　　　　And I it would have been whose timely aid
　　　　　Had taught you all the labyrinth's crooked ways.
85　　　What anxious care a life so dear had cost me!
　　　　　No thread had satisfied your lover's fears:
　　　　　I would myself have wish'd to lead the way,
　　　　　And share the peril you were bound to face;
　　　　　Phaedra with you would have explored the maze,
90　　　With you emerged in safety, or have perish'd.
HIPPOLYTUS: Gods! What is this I hear? Have you forgotten
　　　　　That Theseus is my father and your husband?

PHAEDRA: Why should you fancy I have lost remembrance
      Thereof, and am regardless of mine honour?
HIPPOLYTUS: Forgive me, Madam. With a blush I own
      That I misconstrued words of innocence.
      For very shame I cannot bear your sight
      Longer. I go—
PHAEDRA: Ah! cruel Prince, too well
100   You understood me. I have said enough
      To save you from mistake. I love. But think not
      That at the moment when I love you most
      I do not feel my guilt; no weak compliance
      Has fed the poison that infects my brain.
105   The ill-starr'd object of celestial vengeance,
      I am not so detestable to you
      As to myself. The gods will bear me witness,
      Who have within my veins kindled this fire,
      The gods, who take a barbarous delight
110   In leading a poor mortal's heart astray.
      Do you yourself recall to mind the past:
      'Twas not enough for me to fly, I chased you
      Out of the country, wishing to appear
      Inhuman, odious; to resist you better,
115   I sought to make you hate me. All in vain!
      Hating me more I loved you none the less:
      New charms were lent to you by your misfortunes.
      I have been drown'd in tears, and scorch'd by fire;
      Your own eyes might convince you of the truth,
120   If for one moment you could look at me.
      What is't I say? Think you this vile confession
      That I have made is what I meant to utter?
      Not daring to betray a son for whom
      I trembled, 'twas to beg you not to hate him
125   I came. Weak purpose of a heart too full
      Of love for you to speak of aught besides!
      Take your revenge, punish my odious passion;
      Prove yourself worthy of your valiant sire,
      And rid the world of an offensive monster!
130   Does Theseus' widow dare to love his son?
      The frightful monster! Let her not escape you!
      Here is my heart. This is the place to strike.
      Already prompt to expiate its guilt,
      I feel it leap impatiently to meet
135   Your arm. Strike home. Or, if it would disgrace you
      To steep your hand in such polluted blood,
      If that were punishment too mild to slake
      Your hatred, lend me then your sword, if not
      Your arm. Quick, give't.
OENONE: What, Madam, will you do?
      Just gods! But someone comes. Go, fly from shame,
      You cannot 'scape if seen by any thus.

Scene VI

Hippolytus, Theramenes

THERAMINES: Is that the form of Phaedra that I see
      Hurried away? What mean these signs of sorrow?
      Where is your sword? Why are you pale, confused?
HIPPOLYTUS: Friend, let us fly. I am, indeed, confounded
5   With horror and astonishment extreme.
      Phaedra—but no; gods, let this dreadful secret
      Remain for ever buried in oblivion.
THERAMENES: The ship is ready if you wish to sail.
      But Athens has already giv'n her vote;
10   Their leaders have consulted all her tribes;
      Your brother is elected, Phaedra wins.
HIPPOLYTUS: Phaedra?
THERAMENES: A herald, charged with a commission
      From Athens, has arrived to place the reins
15   Of power in her hands. Her son is King.
HIPPOLYTUS: Ye gods, who know her, do ye thus reward
      Her virtue?
THERAMENES: A faint rumour meanwhile whispers
      That Theseus is not dead, but in Epirus
20   Has shown himself. But, after all my search,
      I know too well—
HIPPOLYTUS: Let nothing be neglected.
      This rumour must be traced back to its source.
      If it be found unworthy of belief,
25   Let us set sail, and cost whate'er it may,
      To hands deserving trust the sceptre's sway.

Act III

Scene I

Phaedra, Oenone

PHAEDRA: Ah! Let them take elsewhere the worthless honours
      They bring me. Why so urgent I should see them?
      What flattering balm can soothe my wounded heart?
      Far rather hide me: I have said too much.
5   My madness has burst forth like streams in flood,
      And I have utter'd what should ne'er have reach'd
      His ear. Gods! How he heard me! How reluctant
      To catch my meaning, dull and cold as marble,
      And eager only for a quick retreat!
10   How oft his blushes made my shame the deeper!
      Why did you turn me from the death I sought?
      Ah! When his sword was pointed to my bosom,
      Did he grow pale, or try to snatch it from me?
      That I had touch'd it was enough for him
15   To render it for ever horrible,
      Leaving defilement on the hand that holds it.

OENONE: Thus brooding on your bitter disappointment,
        You only fan a fire that must be stifled.
        Would it not be more worthy of the blood
20   Of Minos to find peace in nobler cares,
        And, in defiance of a wretch who flies
        From what he hates, reign, mount the proffer'd throne?
PHAEDRA: I reign! Shall I the rod of empire sway,
        When reason reigns no longer o'er myself?
25   When I have lost control of all my senses?
        When 'neath a shameful yoke I scarce can breathe?
        When I am dying?
OENONE: Fly.
PHAEDRA: I cannot leave him.
OENONE: Dare you not fly from him you dared to banish?
PHAEDRA: The time for that is past. He knows my frenzy.
        I have o'erstepp'd the bounds of modesty,
        And blazon'd forth my shame before his eyes.
        Hope stole into my heart against my will.
35   Did you not rally my declining pow'rs?
        Was it not you yourself recall'd my soul
        When fluttering on my lips, and with your counsel,
        Lent me fresh life, and told me I might love him?
OENONE: Blame me or blame me not for your misfortunes,
40   Of what was I incapable, to save you?
        But if your indignation e'er was roused
        By insult, can you pardon his contempt?
        How cruelly his eyes, severely fix'd,
        Survey'd you almost prostrate at his feet!
45   How hateful then appear'd his savage pride!
        Why did not Phaedra see him then as I
        Beheld him?
PHAEDRA: This proud mood that you resent
        May yield to time. The rudeness of the forests
50   Where he was bred, inured to rigorous laws,
        Clings to him still; love is a word he ne'er
        Had heard before. It may be his surprise
        Stunn'd him, and too much vehemence was shown
        In all I said.
OENONE: Remember that his mother
        Was a barbarian.
PHAEDRA: Scythian tho' she was,
        She learned to love.
OENONE: He has for all the sex
60   Hatred intense.
PHAEDRA: Then in his heart no rival
        Shall ever reign. Your counsel comes too late
        Oenone, serve my madness, not my reason.
        His heart is inaccessible to love.
65   Let us attack him where he has more feeling.

The charms of sovereignty appear'd to touch him;
He could not hide that he was drawn to Athens;
His vessels' prows were thither turn'd already,
All sail was set to scud before the breeze.
70   Go you on my behalf, to his ambition
Appeal, and let the prospect of the crown
Dazzle his eyes. The sacred diadem
Shall deck his brow, no higher honour mine
Than there to bind it. His shall be the pow'r
75   I cannot keep; and he shall teach my son
How to rule men. It may be he will deign
To be to him a father. Son and mother
He shall control. Try ev'ry means to move him;
Your words will find more favour than can mine.
80   Urge him with groans and tears; show Phaedra dying.
Nor blush to use the voice of supplication.
In you is my last hope; I'll sanction all
You say; and on the issue hangs my fate.

Scene II

PHAEDRA: (alone)
Venus implacable, who seest me shamed
And sore confounded, have I not enough
Been humbled? How can cruelty be stretch'd
5   Farther? Thy shafts have all gone home, and thou
Hast triumph'd. Would'st thou win a new renown?
Attack an enemy more contumacious:
Hippolytus neglects thee, braves thy wrath,
Nor ever at thine altars bow'd the knee.
10   Thy name offends his proud, disdainful ears.
Our interests are alike: avenge thyself,
Force him to love—
But what is this? Oenone
Return'd already? He detests me then,
15   And will not hear you.

Scene III

Phaedra, Oenone

OENONE: Madam, you must stifle
A fruitless love. Recall your former virtue:
The king who was thought dead will soon appear
Before your eyes, Theseus has just arrived,
5   Theseus is here. The people flock to see him
With eager haste. I went by your command
To find the prince, when with a thousand shouts
The air was rent—
PHAEDRA: My husband is alive,
10   That is enough, Oenone. I have own'd

A passion that dishonours him. He lives:
I ask to know no more.

OENONE: What?

PHAEDRA: I foretold it,

15   But you refused to hear. Your tears prevail'd
Over my just remorse. Dying this morn,
I had deserved compassion; your advice
I took, and die dishonour'd.

OENONE: Die?

PHAEDRA: Just Heav'ns!
What have I done to-day? My husband comes,
With him his son: and I shall see the witness
Of my adulterous flame watch with what face
I greet his father, while my heart is big

25   With sighs he scorn'd, and tears that could not move him
Moisten mine eyes. Think you that his respect
For Theseus will induce him to conceal
My madness, nor disgrace his sire and king?
Will he be able to keep back the horror

30   He has for me? His silence would be vain.
I know my treason, and I lack the boldness
Of those abandon'd women who can taste
Tranquillity in crime, and show a forehead
All unabash'd. I recognize my madness,

35   Recall it all. These vaulted roofs, methinks,
These walls can speak, and, ready to accuse me,
Wait but my husband's presence to reveal
My perfidy. Death only can remove
This weight of horror. Is it such misfortune

40   To cease to live? Death causes no alarm
To misery. I only fear the name
That I shall leave behind me. For my sons
How sad a heritage! The blood of Jove
Might justly swell the pride that boasts descent

45   From Heav'n, but heavy weighs a mother's guilt
Upon her offspring. Yes, I dread the scorn
That will be cast on them, with too much truth,
For my disgrace. I tremble when I think
That, crush'd beneath that curse, they'll never dare

50   To raise their eyes.

OENONE: Doubt not I pity both;
Never was fear more just than yours. Why, then,
Expose them to this ignominy? Why
Will you accuse yourself? You thus destroy

55   The only hope that's left; it will be said
That Phaedra, conscious of her perfidy,
Fled from her husband's sight. Hippolytus
Will be rejoiced that, dying, you should lend
His charge support. What can I answer him?

60   He'll find it easy to confute my tale,
        And I shall hear him with an air of triumph
        To every open ear repeat your shame.
        Sooner than that may fire from heav'n consume me!
        Deceive me not. Say, do you love him still?
65   How look you now on this contemptuous prince?
PHAEDRA: As on a monster frightful to mine eyes.
OENONE: Why yield him, then, an easy victory?
        You fear him? Venture to accuse him first,
        As guilty of the charge which he may bring
70   This day against you. Who can say 'tis false?
        All tells against him: in your hands his sword
        Happily left behind, your present trouble,
        Your past distress, your warnings to his father,
        His exile which your earnest pray'rs obtain'd.
PHAEDRA: What! Would you have me slander innocence?
OENONE: My zeal has need of naught from you but silence.
        Like you I tremble, and am loath to do it;
        More willingly I'd face a thousand deaths,
        But since without this bitter remedy
80   I lose you, and to me your life outweighs
        All else, I'll speak. Theseus, howe'er enraged
        Will do no worse than banish him again.
        A father, when he punishes, remains
        A father, and his ire is satisfied
85   With a light sentence. But if guiltless blood
        Should flow, is not your honour of more moment?
        A treasure far too precious to be risk'd?
        You must submit, whatever it dictates;
        For, when our reputation is at stake,
90   All must be sacrificed, conscience itself.
        But someone comes. 'Tis Theseus.
PHAEDRA: And I see
        Hippolytus, my ruin plainly written
        In his stern eyes. Do what you will; I trust
95   My fate to you. I cannot help myself.

Scene IV

Theseus, Hippolytus, Phaedra, Oenone, Theramenes

THESEUS: Fortune no longer fights against my wishes,
        Madam, and to your arms restores—
PHAEDRA: Stay, Theseus!
        Do not profane endearments that were once
5   So sweet, but which I am unworthy now
        To taste. You have been wrong'd. Fortune has proved
        Spiteful, nor in your absence spared your wife.
        I am unfit to meet your fond caress,
        How I may bear my shame my only care
10   Henceforth.

S CENE   V

Theseus, Hippolytus, Theramenes

THESEUS: Strange welcome for your father, this!
      What does it mean, my son?
HIPPOLYTUS: Phaedra alone
      Can solve this mystery. But if my wish
5   Can move you, let me never see her more;
      Suffer Hippolytus to disappear
      For ever from the home that holds your wife.
THESEUS: You, my son! Leave me?
HIPPOLYTUS: 'Twas not I who sought her:
10   'Twas you who led her footsteps to these shores.
      At your departure you thought meet, my lord,
      To trust Aricia and the Queen to this
      Troezenian land, and I myself was charged
      With their protection. But what cares henceforth
15   Need keep me here? My youth of idleness
      Has shown its skill enough o'er paltry foes
      That range the woods. May I not quit a life
      Of such inglorious ease, and dip my spear
      In nobler blood? Ere you had reach'd my age
20   More than one tyrant, monster more than one
      Had felt the weight of your stout arm. Already,
      Successful in attacking insolence,
      You had removed all dangers that infested
      Our coasts to east and west. The traveller fear'd
25   Outrage no longer. Hearing of your deeds,
      Already Hercules relied on you,
      And rested from his toils. While I, unknown
      Son of so brave a sire, am far behind
      Even my mother's footsteps. Let my courage
30   Have scope to act, and if some monster yet
      Has 'scaped you, let me lay the glorious spoils
      Down at your feet; or let the memory
      Of death faced nobly keep my name alive,
      And prove to all the world I was your son.
THESEUS: Why, what is this? What terror has possess'd
      My family to make them fly before me?
      If I return to find myself so fear'd,
      So little welcome, why did Heav'n release me
      From prison? My sole friend, misled by passion,
40   Was bent on robbing of his wife the tyrant
      Who ruled Epirus. With regret I lent
      The lover aid, but Fate had made us blind,
      Myself as well as him. The tyrant seized me
      Defenceless and unarm'd. Pirithous
45   I saw with tears cast forth to be devour'd
      By savage beasts that lapp'd the blood of men.

Myself in gloomy caverns he inclosed,
Deep in the bowels of the earth, and nigh
To Pluto's realms. Six months I lay ere Heav'n
50   Had pity, and I 'scaped the watchful eyes
That guarded me. Then did I purge the world
Of a foul foe, and he himself has fed
His monsters. But when with expectant joy
To all that is most precious I draw near
55   Of what the gods have left me, when my soul
Looks for full satisfaction in a sight
So dear, my only welcome is a shudder,
Embrace rejected, and a hasty flight.
Inspiring, as I clearly do, such terror,
60   Would I were still a prisoner in Epirus!
Phaedra complains that I have suffer'd outrage.
Who has betray'd me? Speak. Why was I not
Avenged? Has Greece, to whom mine arm so oft
Brought useful aid, shelter'd the criminal?
65   You make no answer. Is my son, mine own
Dear son, confederate with mine enemies?
I'll enter. This suspense is overwhelming.
I'll learn at once the culprit and the crime,
And Phaedra must explain her troubled state.

SCENE VI

Hippolytus, Theramenes

HIPPOLYTUS: What do these words portend, which seem'd to freeze
My very blood? Will Phaedra, in her frenzy
Accuse herself, and seal her own destruction?
What will the King say? Gods! What fatal poison
5   Has love spread over all his house! Myself,
Full of a fire his hatred disapproves,
How changed he finds me from the son he knew!
With dark forebodings in my mind alarm'd,
But innocence has surely naught to fear.
10   Come, let us go, and in some other place
Consider how I best may move my sire
To tenderness, and tell him of a flame
Vex'd but not vanquish'd by a father's blame.

ACT IV

SCENE I

Theseus, Oenone

THESEUS: Ah! What is this I hear? Presumptuous traitor!
And would he have disgraced his father's honour?
With what relentless footsteps Fate pursues me!
Whither I go I know not, nor where know
5   I am. O kind affection ill repaid!

Audacious scheme! Abominable thought!
To reach the object of his foul desire
The wretch disdain'd not to use violence.
I know this sword that served him in his fury,
10   The sword I gave him for a nobler use.
Could not the sacred ties of blood restrain him?
And Phaedra,—was she loath to have him punish'd?
She held her tongue. Was that to spare the culprit?
OENONE: Nay, but to spare a most unhappy father.
15   O'erwhelm'd with shame that her eyes should have kindled
So infamous a flame and prompted him
To crime so heinous, Phaedra would have died.
I saw her raise her arm, and ran to save her.
To me alone you owe it that she lives;
20   And, in my pity both for her and you,
Have I against my will interpreted
Her tears.
THESEUS: The traitor! He might well turn pale.
'Twas fear that made him tremble when he saw me.
25   I was astonish'd that he show'd no pleasure;
His frigid greeting chill'd my tenderness.
But was this guilty passion that devours him
Declared already ere I banish'd him
From Athens?
OENONE: Sire, remember how the Queen
Urged you. Illicit love caused all her hatred.
THESEUS: And then this fire broke out again at Troezen?
OENONE: Sire, I have told you all. Too long the Queen
Has been allow'd to bear her grief alone
35   Let me now leave you and attend to her.

SCENE II

Theseus, Hippolytus

THESEUS: Ah! There he is. Great gods! That noble mien
Might well deceive an eye less fond than mine!
Why should the sacred stamp of virtue gleam
Upon the forehead of an impious wretch?
5   Ought not the blackness of a traitor's heart
To show itself by sure and certain signs?
HIPPOLYTUS: My father, may I ask what fatal cloud
Has troubled your majestic countenance?
Dare you not trust this secret to your son?
THESEUS: Traitor, how dare you show yourself before me?
Monster, whom Heaven's bolts have spared too long!
Survivor of that robber crew whereof
I cleansed the earth. After your brutal lust
Scorn'd even to respect my marriage bed,
15   You venture—you, my hated foe—to come
Into my presence, here, where all is full

Of your foul infamy, instead of seeking
Some unknown land that never heard my name.
Fly, traitor, fly! Stay not to tempt the wrath
20   That I can scarce restrain, nor brave my hatred.
Disgrace enough have I incurr'd for ever
In being father of so vile a son,
Without your death staining indelibly
The glorious record of my noble deeds.
25   Fly, and unless you wish quick punishment
To add you to the criminals cut off
By me, take heed this sun that lights us now
Ne'er sees you more set foot upon this soil.
I tell you once again,—fly, haste, return not,
30   Rid all my realms of your atrocious presence.
To thee, to thee, great Neptune, I appeal
If erst I clear'd thy shores of foul assassins
Recall thy promise to reward those efforts,
Crown'd with success, by granting my first pray'r.
35   Confined for long in close captivity,
I have not yet call'd on thy pow'rful aid,
Sparing to use the valued privilege
Till at mine utmost need. The time is come
I ask thee now. Avenge a wretched father!
40   I leave this traitor to thy wrath; in blood
Quench his outrageous fires, and by thy fury
Theseus will estimate thy favour tow'rds him.
HIPPOLYTUS: Phaedra accuses me of lawless passion!
This crowning horror all my soul confounds;
45   Such unexpected blows, falling at once,
O'erwhelm me, choke my utterance, strike me dumb.
THESEUS: Traitor, you reckon'd that in timid silence
Phaedra would bury your brutality.
You should not have abandon'd in your flight
50   The sword that in her hands helps to condemn you;
Or rather, to complete your perfidy,
You should have robb'd her both of speech and life.
HIPPOLYTUS: Justly indignant at a lie so black
I might be pardon'd if I told the truth;
55   But it concerns your honour to conceal it.
Approve the reverence that shuts my mouth;
And, without wishing to increase your woes,
Examine closely what my life has been.
Great crimes are never single, they are link'd
60   To former faults. He who has once transgress'd
May violate at last all that men hold
Most sacred; vice, like virtue, has degrees
Of progress; innocence was never seen
To sink at once into the lowest depths
65   Of guilt. No virtuous man can in a day

Turn traitor, murderer, an incestuous wretch.
The nursling of a chaste, heroic mother,
I have not proved unworthy of my birth.
Pittheus, whose wisdom is by all esteem'd,
70   Deign'd to instruct me when I left her hands.
It is no wish of mine to vaunt my merits,
But, if I may lay claim to any virtue,
I think beyond all else I have display'd
Abhorrence of those sins with which I'm charged.
75   For this Hippolytus is known in Greece,
So continent that he is deem'd austere.
All know my abstinence inflexible:
The daylight is not purer than my heart.
How, then, could I, burning with fire profane—
THESEUS: Yes, dastard, 'tis that very pride condemns you.
I see the odious reason of your coldness
Phaedra alone bewitch'd your shameless eyes;
Your soul, to others' charms indifferent,
Disdain'd the blameless fires of lawful love.
HIPPOLYTUS: No, father, I have hidden it too long,
This heart has not disdain'd a sacred flame.
Here at your feet I own my real offence:
I love, and love in truth where you forbid me;
Bound to Aricia by my heart's devotion,
90   The child of Pallas has subdued your son.
A rebel to your laws, her I adore,
And breathe forth ardent sighs for her alone.
THESEUS: You love her? Heav'ns!
But no, I see the trick.
95   You feign a crime to justify yourself.
HIPPOLYTUS: Sir, I have shunn'd her for six months, and still
Love her. To you yourself I came to tell it,
Trembling the while. Can nothing clear your mind
Of your mistake? What oath can reassure you?
100   By heav'n and earth and all the pow'rs of nature—
THESEUS: The wicked never shrink from perjury.
Cease, cease, and spare me irksome protestations,
If your false virtue has no other aid.
HIPPOLYTUS: Tho' it to you seem false and insincere,
105   Phaedra has secret cause to know it true.
THESEUS: Ah! how your shamelessness excites my wrath!
HIPPOLYTUS: What is my term and place of banishment?
THESEUS: Were you beyond the Pillars of Alcides,
Your perjured presence were too near me yet.
HIPPOLYTUS: What friends will pity me, when you forsake
And think me guilty of a crime so vile?
THESEUS: Go, look you out for friends who hold in honour
Adultery and clap their hands at incest,
Low, lawless traitors, steep'd in infamy,
115   The fit protectors of a knave like you.

HIPPOLYTUS: Are incest and adultery the words
        You cast at me? I hold my tongue. Yet think
        What mother Phaedra had; too well you know
        Her blood, not mine, is tainted with those horrors.
THESEUS: What! Does your rage before my eyes lose all
        Restraint? For the last time,—out of my sight!
        Hence, traitor! Wait not till a father's wrath
        Force thee away 'mid general execration.

S C E N E   I I I

THESEUS: (alone)
        Wretch! Thou must meet inevitable ruin.
        Neptune has sworn by Styx—to gods themselves
        A dreadful oath,—and he will execute
5   His promise. Thou canst not escape his vengeance.
        I loved thee; and, in spite of thine offence,
        My heart is troubled by anticipation
        For thee. But thou hast earn'd thy doom too well.
        Had father ever greater cause for rage?
10   Just gods, who see the grief that overwhelms me,
        Why was I cursed with such a wicked son?

S C E N E   I V

Phaedra, Theseus

PHAEDRA: My lord, I come to you, fill'd with just dread.
        Your voice raised high in anger reach'd mine ears,
        And much I fear that deeds have follow'd threats.
        Oh, if there yet is time, spare your own offspring.
5   Respect your race and blood, I do beseech you.
        Let me not hear that blood cry from the ground;
        Save me the horror and perpetual pain
        Of having caused his father's hand to shed it.
THESEUS: No, Madam, from that stain my hand is free.
10   But, for all that, the wretch has not escaped me.
        The hand of an Immortal now is charged
        With his destruction. 'Tis a debt that Neptune
        Owes me, and you shall be avenged.
PHAEDRA: A debt
15   Owed you? Pray'rs made in anger—
THESEUS: Never fear
        That they will fail. Rather join yours to mine
        In all their blackness paint for me his crimes,
        And fan my tardy passion to white heat.
20   But yet you know not all his infamy;
        His rage against you overflows in slanders;
        Your mouth, he says, is full of all deceit,
        He says Aricia has his heart and soul,
        That her alone he loves.

PHAEDRA: Aricia?

THESEUS: Aye,

>He said it to my face! an idle pretext!
>A trick that gulls me not! Let us hope Neptune
>Will do him speedy justice. To his altars
30   I go, to urge performance of his oaths.

SCENE V

PHAEDRA: (alone)

>Ah, he is gone! What tidings struck mine ears?
>What fire, half smother'd, in my heart revives?
>What fatal stroke falls like a thunderbolt?
5   Stung by remorse that would not let me rest,
>I tore myself out of Oenone's arms,
>And flew to help Hippolytus with all
>My soul and strength. Who knows if that repentance
>Might not have moved me to accuse myself?
10   And, if my voice had not been choked with shame,
>Perhaps I had confess'd the frightful truth.
>Hippolytus can feel, but not for me!
>Aricia has his heart, his plighted troth.
>Ye gods, when, deaf to all my sighs and tears,
15   He arm'd his eye with scorn, his brow with threats,
>I deem'd his heart, impregnable to love,
>Was fortified 'gainst all my sex alike.
>And yet another has prevail'd to tame
>His pride, another has secured his favour.
20   Perhaps he has a heart easily melted;
>I am the only one he cannot bear!
>And shall I charge myself with his defence?

SCENE VI

Phaedra, Oenone

PHAEDRA: Know you, dear Nurse, what I have learn'd just now?

OENONE: No; but I come in truth with trembling limbs.

>I dreaded with what purpose you went forth,
>The fear of fatal madness made me pale.

PHAEDRA: Who would have thought it, Nurse? I had a rival.

OENONE: A rival?

PHAEDRA: Yes, he loves. I cannot doubt it.

>This wild untamable Hippolytus,
>Who scorn'd to be admired, whom lovers' sighs
10   Wearied, this tiger, whom I fear'd to rouse,
>Fawns on a hand that has subdued his pride:
>Aricia has found entrance to his heart.

OENONE: Aricia?

PHAEDRA: Ah! anguish as yet untried!

15   For what new tortures am I still reserved?

All I have undergone, transports of passion,
Longings and fears, the horrors of remorse,
The shame of being spurn'd with contumely,
Were feeble foretastes of my present torments.

20 They love each other! By what secret charm
Have they deceived me? Where, and when, and how
Met they? You knew it all. Why was I cozen'd?
You never told me of those stolen hours
Of amorous converse. Have they oft been seen

25 Talking together? Did they seek the shades
Of thickest woods? Alas! full freedom had they
To see each other. Heav'n approved their sighs;
They loved without the consciousness of guilt;
And every morning's sun for them shone clear,

30 While I, an outcast from the face of Nature,
Shunn'd the bright day, and sought to hide myself.
Death was the only god whose aid I dared
To ask: I waited for the grave's release.
Water'd with tears, nourish'd with gall, my woe

35 Was all too closely watch'd; I did not dare
To weep without restraint. In mortal dread
Tasting this dangerous solace, I disguised
My terror 'neath a tranquil countenance,
And oft had I to check my tears, and smile.

OENONE: What fruit will they enjoy of their vain love?
They will not see each other more.

PHAEDRA: That love
Will last for ever. Even while I speak,
Ah, fatal thought, they laugh to scorn the madness

45 Of my distracted heart. In spite of exile
That soon must part them, with a thousand oaths
They seal yet closer union. Can I suffer
A happiness, Oenone, which insults me?
I crave your pity. She must be destroy'd.

50 My husband's wrath against a hateful stock
Shall be revived, nor must the punishment
Be light: the sister's guilt passes the brothers'.
I will entreat him in my jealous rage.
What am I saying? Have I lost my senses?

55 Is Phaedra jealous, and will she implore
Theseus for help? My husband lives, and yet
I burn. For whom? Whose heart is this I claim
As mine? At every word I say, my hair
Stands up with horror. Guilt henceforth has pass'd

60 All bounds. Hypocrisy and incest breathe
At once thro' all. My murderous hands are ready
To spill the blood of guileless innocence.
Do I yet live, wretch that I am, and dare
To face this holy Sun from whom I spring?

65 My father's sire was king of all the gods;
My ancestors fill all the universe.
Where can I hide? In the dark realms of Pluto?
But there my father holds the fatal urn;
His hand awards th' irrevocable doom:
70 Minos is judge of all the ghosts in hell.
Ah! how his awful shade will start and shudder
When he shall see his daughter brought before him,
Forced to confess sins of such varied dye,
Crimes it may be unknown to hell itself!
75 What wilt thou say, my father, at a sight
So dire? I think I see thee drop the urn,
And, seeking some unheard-of punishment,
Thyself become my executioner.
Spare me! A cruel goddess has destroy'd
80 Thy race; and in my madness recognize
Her wrath. Alas! My aching heart has reap'd
No fruit of pleasure from the frightful crime
The shame of which pursues me to the grave,
And ends in torment life-long misery.

OENONE: Ah, Madam, pray dismiss a groundless dread:
Look less severely on a venial error.
You love. We cannot conquer destiny.
You were drawn on as by a fatal charm.
Is that a marvel without precedent
90 Among us? Has love triumph'd over you,
And o'er none else? Weakness is natural
To man. A mortal, to a mortal's lot
Submit. You chafe against a yoke that others
Have long since borne. The dwellers in Olympus,
95 The gods themselves, who terrify with threats
The sins of men, have burn'd with lawless fires.

PHAEDRA: What words are these I hear? What counsel this
You dare to give me? Will you to the end
Pour poison in mine ears? You have destroy'd me.
100 You brought me back when I should else have quitted
The light of day, made me forget my duty
And see Hippolytus, till then avoided.
What hast thou done? Why did your wicked mouth
With blackest lies slander his blameless life?
105 Perhaps you've slain him, and the impious pray'r
Of an unfeeling father has been answer'd.
No, not another word! Go, hateful monster;
Away, and leave me to my piteous fate.
May Heav'n with justice pay you your deserts!
110 And may your punishment for ever be
A terror to all those who would, like you,
Nourish with artful wiles the weaknesses
Of princes, push them to the brink of ruin

To which their heart inclines, and smooth the path
115   Of guilt. Such flatterers doth the wrath of Heav'n
Bestow on kings as its most fatal gift.

OENONE: (alone)

O gods! to serve her what have I not done?
This is the due reward that I have won.

ACT V

SCENE I

Hippolytus, Aricia

ARICIA: Can you keep silent in this mortal peril?
Your father loves you. Will you leave him thus
Deceived? If in your cruel heart you scorn
My tears, content to see me nevermore,
5   Go, part from poor Aricia; but at least,
Going, secure the safety of your life.
Defend your honor from a shameful stain,
And force your father to recall his pray'rs.
There yet is time. Why out of mere caprice
10   Leave the field free to Phaedra's calumnies?
Let Theseus know the truth.

HIPPOLYTUS: Could I say more,
Without exposing him to dire disgrace?
How should I venture, by revealing all,
15   To make a father's brow grow red with shame?
The odious mystery to you alone
Is known. My heart has been outpour'd to none
Save you and Heav'n. I could not hide from you
(Judge if I love you), all I fain would hide
20   E'en from myself. But think under what seal
I spoke. Forget my words, if that may be;
And never let so pure a mouth disclose
This dreadful secret. Let us trust to Heav'n
My vindication, for the gods are just;
25   For their own honour will they clear the guiltless;
Sooner or later punish'd for her crime,
Phaedra will not escape the shame she merits.
I ask no other favour than your silence;
In all besides I give my wrath free scope.
30   Make your escape from this captivity,
Be bold to bear me company in flight;
Linger not here on this accursed soil,
Where virtue breathes a pestilential air.
To cover your departure take advantage
35   Of this confusion, caused by my disgrace.
The means of flight are ready, be assured;
You have as yet no other guards than mine.

Pow'rful defenders will maintain our quarrel;
Argos spreads open arms, and Sparta calls us.
40   Let us appeal for justice to our friends,
Nor suffer Phaedra, in a common ruin
Joining us both, to hunt us from the throne,
And aggrandise her son by robbing us.
Embrace this happy opportunity:
45   What fear restrains? You seem to hesitate.
Your interest alone prompts me to urge
Boldness. When I am all on fire, how comes it
That you are ice? Fear you to follow then
A banish'd man?
ARICIA: Ah, dear to me would be
Such exile! With what joy, my fate to yours
United, could I live, by all the world
Forgotten! but not yet has that sweet tie
Bound us together. How then can I steal
55   Away with you? I know the strictest honour
Forbids me not out of your father's hands
To free myself; this is no parent's home,
And flight is lawful when one flies from tyrants.
But you, Sir, love me; and my virtue shrinks—
HIPPOLYTUS: No, no, your reputation is to me
As dear as to yourself. A nobler purpose
Brings me to you. Fly from your foes, and follow
A husband. Heav'n, that sends us these misfortunes,
Sets free from human instruments the pledge
65   Between us. Torches do not always light
The face of Hymen.
At the gates of Troezen,
'Mid ancient tombs where princes of my race
Lie buried, stands a temple, ne'er approach'd
70   By perjurers, where mortals dare not make
False oaths, for instant punishment befalls
The guilty. Falsehood knows no stronger check
Than what is present there—the fear of death
That cannot be avoided. Thither then
75   We'll go, if you consent, and swear to love
For ever, take the guardian god to witness
Our solemn vows, and his paternal care
Entreat. I will invoke the name of all
The holiest Pow'rs; chaste Dian, and the Queen
80   Of Heav'n, yea all the gods who know my heart
Will guarantee my sacred promises.
ARICIA: The King draws near. Depart,—make no delay.
To mask my flight, I linger yet one moment.
Go you; and leave with me some trusty guide,
85   To lead my timid footsteps to your side.

Scene II

Theseus, Aricia, Ismene

THESEUS: Ye gods, throw light upon my troubled mind,
    Show me the truth which I am seeking here.
ARICIA: (aside to Ismene)
    Get ready, dear Ismene, for our flight.

Scene III

Theseus, Aricia

THESEUS: Your colour comes and goes, you seem confused,
    Madame! What business had my son with you?
ARICIA: Sire, he was bidding me farewell for ever.
THESEUS: Your eyes, it seems, can tame that stubborn pride;
5   And the first sighs he breathes are paid to you.
ARICIA: I can't deny the truth; he has not, Sire,
    Inherited your hatred and injustice;
    He did not treat me like a criminal.
THESEUS: That is to say, he swore eternal love.
10   Do not rely on that inconstant heart;
    To others has he sworn as much before.
ARICIA: He, Sire?
THESEUS: You ought to check his roving taste.
    How could you bear a partnership so vile?
ARICIA: And how can you endure that vilest slanders
    Should make a life so pure as black as pitch?
    Have you so little knowledge of his heart?
    Do you so ill distinguish between guilt
    And innocence? What mist before your eyes
20   Blinds them to virtue so conspicuous?
    Ah! 'tis too much to let false tongues defame him.
    Repent; call back your murderous wishes, Sire;
    Fear, fear lest Heav'n in its severity
    Hate you enough to hear and grant your pray'rs.
25   Oft in their wrath the gods accept our victims,
    And oftentimes chastise us with their gifts.
THESEUS: No, vainly would you cover up his guilt.
    Your love is blind to his depravity.
    But I have witness irreproachable:
30   Tears have I seen, true tears, that may be trusted.
ARICIA: Take heed, my lord. Your hands invincible
    Have rid the world of monsters numberless;
    But all are not destroy'd, one you have left
    Alive—Your son forbids me to say more.
35   Knowing with what respect he still regards you,
    I should too much distress him if I dared
    Complete my sentence. I will imitate
    His reverence, and, to keep silence, leave you.

S c e n e   I V

THESEUS: (alone)

40   What is there in her mind? What meaning lurks
       In speech begun but to be broken short?
       Would both deceive me with a vain pretence?
       Have they conspired to put me to the torture?
       And yet, despite my stern severity,
45   What plaintive voice cries deep within my heart?
       A secret pity troubles and alarms me.
       Oenone shall be questioned once again,
       I must have clearer light upon this crime.
       Guards, bid Oenone come, and come alone.

S c e n e   V

Theseus, Panope

PANOPE: I know not what the Queen intends to do,
       But from her agitation dread the worst.
       Fatal despair is painted on her features;
       Death's pallor is already in her face.
5   Oenone, shamed and driven from her sight,
       Has cast herself into the ocean depths.
       None knows what prompted her to deed so rash;
       And now the waves hide her from us for ever.
THESEUS: What say you?
PANOPE: Her sad fate seems to have added
       Fresh trouble to the Queen's tempestuous soul.
       Sometimes, to soothe her secret pain, she clasps
       Her children close, and bathes them with her tears;
       Then suddenly, the mother's love forgotten,
15   She thrusts them from her with a look of horror,
       She wanders to and fro with doubtful steps;
       Her vacant eye no longer knows us. Thrice
       She wrote, and thrice did she, changing her mind,
       Destroy the letter ere 'twas well begun.
20   Vouchsafe to see her, Sire: vouchsafe to help her.
THESEUS: Heav'ns! Is Oenone dead, and Phaedra bent
       On dying too? Oh, call me back my son!
       Let him defend himself, and I am ready
       To hear him. Be not hasty to bestow
25   Thy fatal bounty, Neptune; let my pray'rs
       Rather remain ever unheard. Too soon
       I lifted cruel hands, believing lips
       That may have lied! Ah! What despair may follow!

S c e n e   V I

Theseus, Theramenes

THESEUS: Theramenes, is't thou? Where is my son?
       I gave him to thy charge from tenderest childhood.

But whence these tears that overflow thine eyes?
How is it with my son?

THERAMENES: Concern too late!
Affection vain! Hippolytus is dead.

THESEUS: Gods!

THERAMENES: I have seen the flow'r of all mankind
Cut off, and I am bold to say that none
10   Deserved it less.

THESEUS: What! My son dead! When I
Was stretching out my arms to him, has Heav'n
Hasten'd his end? What was this sudden stroke?

THERAMENES: Scarce had we pass'd out of the gates of Troezen,
15   He silent in his chariot, and his guards
Downcast and silent too, around him ranged;
To the Mycenian road he turn'd his steeds,
Then, lost in thought, allow'd the reins to lie
Loose on their backs. His noble chargers, erst
20   So full of ardour to obey his voice,
With head depress'd and melancholy eye
Seem'd now to mark his sadness and to share it.
A frightful cry, that issues from the deep,
With sudden discord rends the troubled air;
25   And from the bosom of the earth a groan
Is heard in answer to that voice of terror.
Our blood is frozen at our very hearts;
With bristling manes the list'ning steeds stand still.
Meanwhile upon the watery plain there rises
30   A mountain billow with a mighty crest
Of foam, that shoreward rolls, and, as it breaks
Before our eyes vomits a furious monster.
With formidable horns its brow is arm'd,
And all its body clothed with yellow scales,
35   In front a savage bull, behind a dragon
Turning and twisting in impatient rage.
Its long continued bellowings make the shore
Tremble; the sky seems horror-struck to see it;
The earth with terror quakes; its poisonous breath
40   Infects the air. The wave that brought it ebbs
In fear. All fly, forgetful of the courage
That cannot aid, and in a neighbouring temple
Take refuge—all save bold Hippolytus.
A hero's worthy son, he stays his steeds,
45   Seizes his darts, and, rushing forward, hurls
A missile with sure aim that wounds the monster
Deep in the flank. With rage and pain it springs
E'en to the horses' feet, and, roaring, falls,
Writhes in the dust, and shows a fiery throat
50   That covers them with flames, and blood, and smoke.
Fear lends them wings; deaf to his voice for once,

And heedless of the curb, they onward fly.
Their master wastes his strength in efforts vain;
With foam and blood each courser's bit is red.
55 Some say a god, amid this wild disorder,
Was seen with goads pricking their dusty flanks.
O'er jagged rocks they rush urged on by terror;
Crash! goes the axle-tree. Th' intrepid youth
Sees his car broken up, flying to pieces;
60 He falls himself entangled in the reins.
Pardon my grief. That cruel spectacle
Will be for me a source of endless tears.
I saw thy hapless son, I saw him, Sire,
Drag'd by the horses that his hands had fed,
65 Pow'rless to check their fierce career, his voice
But adding to their fright, his body soon
One mass of wounds. Our cries of anguish fill
The plain. At last they slacken their swift pace,
Then stop, not far from those old tombs that mark
70 Where lie the ashes of his royal sires.
Panting I thither run, and after me
His guard, along the track stain'd with fresh blood
That reddens all the rocks; caught in the briers
Locks of his hair hang dripping, gory spoils!
75 I come, I call him. Stretching forth his hand,
He opens his dying eyes, soon closed again.
"The gods have robb'd me of a guiltless life,"
I hear him say: "Take care of sad Aricia
When I am dead. Dear friend, if e'er my father
80 Mourn, undeceived, his son's unhappy fate
Falsely accused; to give my spirit peace,
Tell him to treat his captive tenderly,
And to restore—" With that the hero's breath
Fails, and a mangled corpse lies in my arms,
85 A piteous object, trophy of the wrath
Of Heav'n—so changed, his father would not know him.
THESEUS: Alas, my son! Dear hope for ever lost!
The ruthless gods have served me but too well.
For what a life of anguish and remorse
90 Am I reserved!
THERAMENES: Aricia at that instant,
Flying from you, comes timidly, to take him
For husband, there, in presence of the gods.
Thus drawing nigh, she sees the grass all red
95 And reeking, sees (sad sight for lover's eye!)
Hippolytus stretch'd there, pale and disfigured.
But, for a time doubtful of her misfortune,
Unrecognized the hero she adores,
She looks, and asks—"Where is Hippolytus?"
100 Only too sure at last that he lies there

Before her, with sad eyes that silently
Reproach the gods, she shudders, groans, and falls
Swooning and all but lifeless, at his feet.
Ismene, all in tears, kneels down beside her,
105   And calls her back to life—life that is naught
But sense of pain. And I, to whom this light
Is darkness now, come to discharge the duty
The hero has imposed on me, to tell thee
His last request—a melancholy task.
110   But hither comes his mortal enemy.

Scene VII

Thesus, Phaedra, Theramenes, Panope, Guards

THESEUS: Madame, you've triumph'd, and my son is kill'd!
Ah, but what room have I for fear! How justly
Suspicion racks me that in blaming him
I err'd! But he is dead; accept your victim;
5   Rightly or wrongly slain, let your heart leap
For joy. My eyes shall be for ever blind:
Since you accuse him, I'll believe him guilty.
His death affords me cause enough for tears,
Without a foolish search for further light
10   Which, pow'rless to restore him to my grief,
Might only serve to make me more unhappy,
Far from this shore and far from you I'll fly,
For here the image of my mangled son
Would haunt my memory and drive me mad.
15   From the whole world I fain would banish me,
For all the world seems to rise up in judgment
Against me; and my very glory weights
My punishment; for, were my name less known
'Twere easier to hide me. All the favours
20   The gods have granted me I mourn and hate,
Nor will I importune them with vain pray'rs
Henceforth for ever. Give me what they may,
What they have taken will all else outweigh.
PHAEDRA: Theseus, I cannot hear you and keep silence:
25   I must repair the wrong that he has suffer'd—
Your son was innocent.
THESEUS: Unhappy father!
And it was on your word that I condemn'd him!
Think you such cruelty can be excused—
PHAEDRA: Moments to me are precious; hear me, Theseus.
'Twas I who cast an eye of lawless passion
On chaste and dutiful Hippolytus.
Heav'n in my bosom kindled baleful fire,
And vile Oenone's cunning did the rest.
35   She fear'd Hippolytus, knowing my madness,
Would make that passion known which he regarded

With horror; so advantage of my weakness
She took, and hasten'd to accuse him first.
For that she has been punish'd, tho' too mildly;
40   Seeking to shun my wrath she cast herself
Beneath the waves. The sword ere now had cut
My thread of life, but slander'd innocence
Made its cry heard, and I resolved to die
In a more lingering way, confessing first
45   My penitence to you. A poison, brought
To Athens by Medea, runs thro' my veins.
Already in my heart the venom works,
Infusing there a strange and fatal chill;
Already as thro' thickening mists I see
50   The spouse to whom my presence is an outrage;
Death, from mine eyes veiling the light of heav'n,
Restores its purity that they defiled.
PHAEDRA: She dies my lord!
THESEUS: Would that the memory
55   Of her disgraceful deed could perish with her!
Ah, disabused too late! Come, let us go,
And with the blood of mine unhappy son
Mingle our tears, clasping his dear remains,
In deep repentance for a pray'r detested.
60   Let him be honour'd as he well deserves;
And, to appease his sore offended ghost,
Be her near kinsmen's guilt whate'er it may,
Aricia shall be held my daughter from to-day.

William Blake
Introduction to Songs of Innocence

Piping down the valleys wild,
Piping songs of pleasant glee,
On a cloud I saw a child,
And he laughing said to me:

5   "Pipe a song about a Lamb!"
So I piped with merry cheer.
"Piper, pipe that song again;"
So I piped: he wept to hear.

"Drop thy pipe, thy happy pipe;
10 Sing thy songs of happy cheer!"
So I sung the same again,
While he wept with joy to hear.

"Piper, sit thee down and write
In a book, that all may read."
15 So he vanished from my sight,
And I plucked a hollow reed,

And I made a rural pen,
And I stained the water clear,
And I wrote my happy songs
20 Every child may joy to hear.

—William Blake

The Lamb

Little Lamb, who made thee?
Dost thou know who made thee?
Gave thee life, and bid thee feed,
By the stream and o'er the mead;
5   Gave thee clothing of delight,
Softest clothing, woolly, bright;
Gave thee such a tender voice,
Making all the vales rejoice?
Little Lamb, who made thee?
10   Dost thou know who made thee?

Little Lamb, I'll tell thee,
Little Lamb, I'll tell thee.
He is called by thy name,
For He calls Himself a Lamb.
15   He is meek, and He is mild;
He became a little child.
I a child, and thou a lamb,
We are called by His name.
Little Lamb, God bless thee!
20   Little Lamb, God bless thee!

—William Blake

The Little Black Boy

MY mother bore me in the southern wild,
    And I am black, but O, my soul is white!
White as an angel is the English child,
    But I am black, as if bereaved of light.

5   My mother taught me underneath a tree,
    And, sitting down before the heat of day,
She took me on her lap and kissèd me,
    And, pointing to the East, began to say:

'Look at the rising sun: there God does live,
10   And gives His light, and gives His heat away,
And flowers and trees and beasts and men receive
    Comfort in morning, joy in the noonday.

'And we are put on earth a little space,
    That we may learn to bear the beams of love;
15   And these black bodies and this sunburnt face
    Are but a cloud, and like a shady grove.

'For when our souls have learn'd the heat to bear,
    The cloud will vanish; we shall hear His voice,
Saying, "Come out from the grove, my love and care,
20   And round my golden tent like lambs rejoice."'

Thus did my mother say, and kissèd me,
    And thus I say to little English boy.
When I from black and he from white cloud free,
    And round the tent of God like lambs we joy,

25   I'll shade him from the heat till he can bear
    To lean in joy upon our Father's knee;
And then I'll stand and stroke his silver hair,
    And be like him, and he will then love me.

                —*William Blake*

The Chimney Sweeper

When my mother died I was very young,
And my father sold me while yet my tongue
Could scarcely cry "Weep! weep! weep! weep!"
So your chimneys I sweep, and in soot I sleep.

5   There's little Tom Dacre, who cried when his head,
That curled like a lamb's back, was shaved; so I said,
"Hush, Tom! never mind it, for, when your head's bare,
You know that the soot cannot spoil your white hair."

And so he was quiet, and that very night,
10   As Tom was a-sleeping, he had such a sight! —
That thousands of sweepers, Dick, Joe, Ned, and Jack,
Were all of them locked up in coffins of black.

And by came an angel, who had a bright key,
And he opened the coffins, and let them all free;
15   Then down a green plain, leaping, laughing, they run,
And wash in a river, and shine in the sun.

Then naked and white, all their bags left behind,
They rise upon clouds, and sport in the wind;
And the Angel told Tom, if he'd be a good boy,
20   He'd have God for his father, and never want joy.

And so Tom awoke, and we rose in the dark,
And got with our bags and our brushes to work.
Though the morning was cold, Tom was happy and warm:
So, if all do their duty, they need not fear harm.

—*William Blake*

The Tyger

Tyger! Tyger! burning bright
In the forests of the night,
What immortal hand or eye
Could frame thy fearful symmetry?

5   In what distant deeps or skies
Burnt the fire of thine eyes?
On what wings dare he aspire?
What the hand dare sieze the fire?

And what shoulder, & what art.
10   Could twist the sinews of thy heart?
And when thy heart began to beat,
What dread hand? & what dread feet?

What the hammer? what the chain?
In what furnace was thy brain?
15   What the anvil? what dread grasp
Dare its deadly terrors clasp?

When the stars threw down their spears,
And watered heaven with their tears,
Did he smile his work to see?
20   Did he who made the Lamb make thee?

Tyger! Tyger! burning bright
In the forests of the night,
What immortal hand or eye
Dare frame thy fearful symmetry?

—*William Blake*

The Sick Rose

O Rose, thou art sick!
The invisible worm
That flies in the night,
In the howling storm,

5   Has found out thy bed
Of crimson joy:
And his dark secret love
Does thy life destroy.

—William Blake

London (from *Songs of Experience*)

I wandered through each chartered street,
    Near where the chartered Thames does flow,
A mark in every face I meet,
    Marks of weakness, marks of woe.

5   In every cry of every man,
    In every infant's cry of fear,
In every voice, in every ban,
    The mind-forged manacles I hear:

How the chimney-sweeper's cry
10   Every blackening church appals,
And the hapless soldier's sigh
    Runs in blood down palace-walls.

But most, through midnight streets I hear
    How the youthful harlot's curse
15   Blasts the new-born infant's tear,
    And blights with plagues the marriage-hearse.

—William Blake

William Wordsworth
Composed a Few Miles Above Tintern Abbey, on Revisiting the Banks of the Wye During a Tour. July 13, 1798

FIVE years have past; five summers, with the length
Of five long winters! and again I hear
These waters, rolling from their mountain-springs
With a soft inland murmur.—Once again
5   Do I behold these steep and lofty cliffs,
That on a wild secluded scene impress
Thoughts of more deep seclusion; and connect
The landscape with the quiet of the sky.
The day is come when I again repose
10   Here, under this dark sycamore, and view
These plots of cottage-ground, these orchard-tufts,
Which at this season, with their unripe fruits,
Are clad in one green hue, and lose themselves
'Mid groves and copses. Once again I see
15   These hedge-rows, hardly hedge-rows, little lines
Of sportive wood run wild: these pastoral farms,
Green to the very door; and wreaths of smoke
Sent up, in silence, from among the trees!
With some uncertain notice, as might seem
20   Of vagrant dwellers in the houseless woods,
Or of some Hermit's cave, where by his fire
The Hermit sits alone.
                              These beauteous forms,
Through a long absence, have not been to me
25   As is a landscape to a blind man's eye:
But oft, in lonely rooms, and 'mid the din
Of towns and cities, I have owed to them
In hours of weariness, sensations sweet,
Felt in the blood, and felt along the heart;
30   And passing even into my purer mind,
With tranquil restoration:—feelings too
Of unremembered pleasure: such, perhaps,
As have no slight or trivial influence
On that best portion of a good man's life,
35   His little, nameless, unremembered, acts
Of kindness and of love. Nor less, I trust,

To them I may have owed another gift,
Of aspect more sublime; that blessed mood,
In which the burthen of the mystery,
40   In which the heavy and the weary weight
Of all this unintelligible world,
Is lightened:—that serene and blessed mood,
In which the affections gently lead us on,—
Until, the breath of this corporeal frame
45   And even the motion of our human blood
Almost suspended, we are laid asleep
In body, and become a living soul:
While with an eye made quiet by the power
Of harmony, and the deep power of joy,
50   We see into the life of things.
                              If this
Be but a vain belief, yet, oh! how oft—
In darkness and amid the many shapes
Of joyless daylight; when the fretful stir
55   Unprofitable, and the fever of the world,
Have hung upon the beatings of my heart—
How oft, in spirit, have I turned to thee,
O sylvan Wye! thou wanderer thro' the woods,
How often has my spirit turned to thee!
60   And now, with gleams of half-extinguished thought,
With many recognitions dim and faint,
And somewhat of a sad perplexity,
The picture of the mind revives again:
While here I stand, not only with the sense
65   Of present pleasure, but with pleasing thoughts
That in this moment there is life and food
For future years. And so I dare to hope,
Though changed, no doubt, from what I was when first
I came among these hills; when like a roe
70   I bounded o'er the mountains, by the sides
Of the deep rivers, and the lonely streams,
Wherever nature led: more like a man
Flying from something that he dreads, than one
Who sought the thing he loved. For nature then
75   (The coarser pleasures of my boyish days,
And their glad animal movements all gone by)
To me was all in all.—I cannot paint
What then I was. The sounding cataract
Haunted me like a passion: the tall rock,
80   The mountain, and the deep and gloomy wood,
Their colours and their forms, were then to me
An appetite; a feeling and a love,
That had no need of a remoter charm,
By thought supplied, nor any interest
85   Unborrowed from the eye.—That time is past,

And all its aching joys are now no more,
And all its dizzy raptures. Not for this
Faint I, nor mourn nor murmur, other gifts
Have followed; for such loss, I would believe,
90   Abundant recompence. For I have learned
To look on nature, not as in the hour
Of thoughtless youth; but hearing oftentimes
The still, sad music of humanity,
Nor harsh nor grating, though of ample power
95   To chasten and subdue. And I have felt
A presence that disturbs me with the joy
Of elevated thoughts; a sense sublime
Of something far more deeply interfused,
Whose dwelling is the light of setting suns,
100   And the round ocean and the living air,
And the blue sky, and in the mind of man;
A motion and a spirit, that impels
All thinking things, all objects of all thought,
And rolls through all things. Therefore am I still
105   A lover of the meadows and the woods,
And mountains; and of all that we behold
From this green earth; of all the mighty world
Of eye, and ear,—both what they half create,
And what perceive; well pleased to recognise
110   In nature and the language of the sense,
The anchor of my purest thoughts, the nurse,
The guide, the guardian of my heart, and soul
Of all my moral being.
                                    Nor perchance,
115   If I were not thus taught, should I the more
Suffer my genial spirits to decay:
For thou art with me here upon the banks
Of this fair river; thou my dearest Friend,
My dear, dear Friend; and in thy voice I catch
120   The language of my former heart, and read
My former pleasures in the shooting lights
Of thy wild eyes. Oh! yet a little while
May I behold in thee what I was once,
My dear, dear Sister! and this prayer I make,
125   Knowing that Nature never did betray
The heart that loved her; 'tis her privilege,
Through all the years of this our life, to lead
From joy to joy: for she can so inform
The mind that is within us, so impress
130   With quietness and beauty, and so feed
With lofty thoughts, that neither evil tongues,
Rash judgments, nor the sneers of selfish men,
Nor greetings where no kindness is, nor all
The dreary intercourse of daily life,

135   Shall e'er prevail against us, or disturb
     Our cheerful faith, that all which we behold
     Is full of blessings. Therefore let the moon
     Shine on thee in thy solitary walk;
     And let the misty mountain-winds be free
140   To blow against thee: and, in after years,
     When these wild ecstasies shall be matured
     Into a sober pleasure; when thy mind
     Shall be a mansion for all lovely forms,
     Thy memory be as a dwelling-place
145   For all sweet sounds and harmonies; oh! then,
     If solitude, or fear, or pain, or grief,
     Should be thy portion, with what healing thoughts
     Of tender joy wilt thou remember me,
     And these my exhortations! Nor, perchance—
150   If I should be where I no more can hear
     Thy voice, nor catch from thy wild eyes these gleams
     Of past existence—wilt thou then forget
     That on the banks of this delightful stream
     We stood together; and that I, so long
155   A worshipper of Nature, hither came
     Unwearied in that service: rather say
     With warmer love—oh! with far deeper zeal
     Of holier love. Nor wilt thou then forget,
     That after many wanderings, many years
160   Of absence, these steep woods and lofty cliffs,
     And this green pastoral landscape, were to me
     More dear, both for themselves and for thy sake!

—*William Wordsworth*

Ode

Intimations of Immortality from Recollections of Early Childhood

I

THERE was a time when meadow, grove, and stream,
The earth, and every common sight,
    To me did seem
    Apparelled in celestial light,
The glory and the freshness of a dream.
It is not now as it hath been of yore;—
    Turn wheresoe'er I may,
      By night or day,
The things which I have seen I now can see no more.

II

    The Rainbow comes and goes,
    And lovely is the Rose,
    The Moon doth with delight
Look round her when the heavens are bare,
    Waters on a starry night
    Are beautiful and fair;
  The sunshine is a glorious birth;
  But yet I know, where'er I go,
That there hath past away a glory from the earth.

III

Now, while the birds thus sing a joyous song,
    And while the young lambs bound
    As to the tabor's sound,
To me alone there came a thought of grief:
A timely utterance gave that thought relief,
    And I again am strong:
The cataracts blow their trumpets from the steep;
No more shall grief of mine the season wrong;
I hear the Echoes through the mountains throng,
The Winds come to me from the fields of sleep,
    And all the earth is gay;
      Land and sea

Give themselves up to jollity,
And with the heart of May
Doth every Beast keep holiday;—
Thou Child of Joy,
35   Shout round me, let me hear thy shouts, thou happy
Shepherd-boy!

IV

Ye blessed Creatures, I have heard the call
Ye to each other make; I see
The heavens laugh with you in your jubilee;
40   My heart is at your festival,
My head hath its coronal,
The fulness of your bliss, I feel—I feel it all.
Oh evil day! if I were sullen
While Earth herself is adorning,
45   This sweet May-morning,
And the Children are culling
On every side,
In a thousand valleys far and wide,
Fresh flowers; while the sun shines warm,
50   And the Babe leaps up on his Mother's arm:—
I hear, I hear, with joy I hear!
—But there's a Tree, of many, one,
A single Field which I have looked upon,
Both of them speak of something that is gone:
55   The Pansy at my feet
Doth the same tale repeat:
Whither is fled the visionary gleam?
Where is it now, the glory and the dream?

V

Our birth is but a sleep and a forgetting:
60   The Soul that rises with us, our life's Star,
Hath had elsewhere its setting,
And cometh from afar:
Not in entire forgetfulness,
And not in utter nakedness,
65   But trailing clouds of glory do we come
From God, who is our home:
Heaven lies about us in our infancy!
Shades of the prison-house begin to close
Upon the growing Boy,
70   But He beholds the light, and whence it flows,
He sees it in his joy;
The Youth, who daily farther from the east
Must travel, still is Nature's Priest,
And by the vision splendid

75   Is on his way attended;
    At length the Man perceives it die away,
    And fade into the light of common day.

VI

    Earth fills her lap with pleasures of her own;
    Yearnings she hath in her own natural kind,
80   And, even with something of a Mother's mind,
        And no unworthy aim,
        The homely Nurse doth all she can
    To make her Foster-child, her Inmate Man,
        Forget the glories he hath known,
85   And that imperial palace whence he came.

VII

    Behold the Child among his new-born blisses,
    A six years' Darling of a pigmy size!
    See, where 'mid work of his own hand he lies,
    Fretted by sallies of his mother's kisses,
90   With light upon him from his father's eyes!
    See, at his feet, some little plan or chart,
    Some fragment from his dream of human life,
    Shaped by himself with newly-learned art;
        A wedding or a festival,
95   A mourning or a funeral;
            And this hath now his heart,
            And unto this he frames his song:
                Then will he fit his tongue
    To dialogues of business, love, or strife;
100   But it will not be long
            Ere this be thrown aside,
            And with new joy and pride
    The little Actor cons another part;
    Filling from time to time his "humorous stage"
105   With all the Persons, down to palsied Age,
    That Life brings with her in her equipage;
        As if his whole vocation
        Were endless imitation.

VIII

    Thou, whose exterior semblance doth belie
110   Thy Soul's immensity;
    Thou best Philosopher, who yet dost keep
    Thy heritage, thou Eye among the blind,
    That, deaf and silent, read'st the eternal deep,
    Haunted for ever by the eternal mind,—
115   Mighty Prophet! Seer blest!
            On whom those truths do rest,

Which we are toiling all our lives to find,
In darkness lost, the darkness of the grave;
Thou, over whom thy Immortality
120 Broods like the Day, a Master o'er a Slave,
A Presence which is not to be put by;
Thou little Child, yet glorious in the might
Of heaven-born freedom on thy being's height,
Why with such earnest pains dost thou provoke
125 The years to bring the inevitable yoke,
Thus blindly with thy blessedness at strife?
Full soon thy Soul shall have her earthly freight,
And custom lie upon thee with a weight
Heavy as frost, and deep almost as life!

IX

130   O joy! that in our embers
        Is something that doth live,
        That nature yet remembers
          What was so fugitive!
The thought of our past years in me doth breed
135 Perpetual benediction: not indeed
For that which is most worthy to be blest—
Delight and liberty, the simple creed
Of Childhood, whether busy or at rest,
With new-fledged hope still fluttering in his breast:—
140   Not for these I raise
        The song of thanks and praise;
      But for those obstinate questionings
        Of sense and outward things,
        Fallings from us, vanishings;
145   Blank misgivings of a Creature
Moving about in worlds not realised,
High instincts before which our mortal Nature
Did tremble like a guilty Thing surprised:
        But for those first affections,
150   Those shadowy recollections,
      Which, be they what they may,
Are yet the fountain light of all our day,
Are yet a master light of all our seeing;
      Uphold us, cherish, and have power to make
155 Our noisy years seem moments in the being
Of the eternal Silence: truths that wake,
        To perish never;
Which neither listlessness, nor mad endeavour,
        Nor Man nor Boy,
160 Nor all that is at enmity with joy,
Can utterly abolish or destroy!
        Hence in a season of calm weather
        Though inland far we be,

Our Souls have sight of that immortal sea
165   Which brought us hither,
          Can in a moment travel thither,
And see the Children sport upon the shore,
And hear the mighty waters rolling evermore.

                    X

Then sing, ye Birds, sing, sing a joyous song!
170   And let the young Lambs bound
          As to the tabor's sound!
We in thought will join your throng,
          Ye that pipe and ye that play,
          Ye that through your hearts to-day
175   Feel the gladness of the May!
What though the radiance which was once so bright
Be now for ever taken from my sight,
          Though nothing can bring back the hour
Of splendour in the grass, of glory in the flower;
180   We will grieve not, rather find
          Strength in what remains behind;
          In the primal sympathy
          Which having been must ever be;
          In the soothing thoughts that spring
185   Out of human suffering;
          In the faith that looks through death,
In years that bring the philosophic mind.

                    XI

And O, ye Fountains, Meadows, Hills, and Groves,
Forebode not any severing of our loves!
190   Yet in my heart of hearts I feel your might;
I only have relinquished one delight
To live beneath your more habitual sway.
I love the Brooks which down their channels fret,
Even more than when I tripped lightly as they;
195   The innocent brightness of a new-born Day
               Is lovely yet;
The Clouds that gather round the setting sun
Do take a sober colouring from an eye
That hath kept watch o'er man's mortality;
200   Another race hath been, and other palms are won.
Thanks to the human heart by which we live,
Thanks to its tenderness, its joys, and fears,
To me the meanest flower that blows can give
Thoughts that do often lie too deep for tears.

                    —William Wordsworth

Composed Upon Westminster Bridge, Sept. 3, 1802

EARTH has not anything to show more fair:
Dull would he be of soul who could pass by
A sight so touching in its majesty:
This City now doth, like a garment, wear
The beauty of the morning; silent, bare,
Ships, towers, domes, theatres, and temples lie
Open unto the fields, and to the sky;
All bright and glittering in the smokeless air.
Never did sun more beautifully steep
In his first splendour, valley, rock, or hill;
Ne'er saw I, never felt, a calm so deep!
The river glideth at his own sweet will:
Dear God! the very houses seem asleep;
And all that mighty heart is lying still!

—*William Wordsworth*

. . .The World Is Too Much with Us; Late and Soon. . .

THE world is too much with us; late and soon,
Getting and spending, we lay waste our powers:
Little we see in Nature that is ours;
We have given our hearts away, a sordid boon!
5   The Sea that bares her bosom to the moon;
The winds that will be howling at all hours,
And are up-gathered now like sleeping flowers;
For this, for everything, we are out of tune;
It moves us not.—Great God! I'd rather be
10   A Pagan suckled in a creed outworn;
So might I, standing on this pleasant lea,
Have glimpses that would make me less forlorn;
Have sight of Proteus rising from the sea;
Or hear old Triton blow his wreathed horn.

—William Wordsworth

Samuel Taylor Coleridge
Kubla Khan

In Xanadu did Kubla Khan
    A stately pleasure-dome decree:
        Where Alph, the sacred river, ran
            Through caverns measureless to man
5   Down to a sunless sea.
So twice five miles of fertile ground
With walls and towers were girdled round:
And here were gardens bright with sinuous rills
Where blossomed many an incense-bearing tree;
10 And here were forests ancient as the hills,
Enfolding sunny spots of greenery.
But oh! that deep romantic chasm which slanted
Down the green hill athwart a cedarn cover!
A savage place! as holy and enchanted
15 As e'er beneath a waning moon was haunted
By woman wailing for her demon-lover!

And from this chasm, with ceaseless turmoil seething,
As if this earth in fast thick pants were breathing,
A mighty fountain momently was forced;
20 Amid whose swift half-intermitted burst
Huge fragments vaulted like rebounding hail,
Or chaffy grain beneath the thresher's flail:
And 'mid these dancing rocks at once and ever
It flung up momently the sacred river.
25 Five miles meandering with a mazy motion
Through wood and dale the sacred river ran,
Then reached the caverns measureless to man,
And sank in tumult to a lifeless ocean:
And 'mid this tumult Kubla heard from far
30 Ancestral voices prophesying war!

The shadow of the dome of pleasure
    Floated midway on the waves:
Where was heard the mingled measure
    From the fountain and the caves.
35 It was a miracle of rare device,
A sunny pleasure-dome with caves of ice!
    A damsel with a dulcimer
    In a vision once I saw:

It was an Abyssinian maid,
40 And on her dulcimer she played,
Singing of Mount Abora.
Could I revive within me
Her symphony and song,
To such a deep delight 't would win me
45 That with music loud and long,
I would build that dome in air,
That sunny dome! those caves of ice!
And all who heard should see them there,
And all should cry, Beware! Beware!
50 His flashing eyes, his floating hair!
Weave a circle round him thrice,
And close your eyes with holy dread,
For he on honey-dew hath fed,
And drunk the milk of Paradise.

—*Samuel Taylor Coleridge*

John Keats
On First Looking Into Chapman's Homer

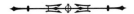

Much have I travell'd in the realms of gold,
And many goodly states and kingdoms seen;
Round many western islands have I been
Which bards in fealty to Apollo hold.
5   Oft of one wide expanse had I been told
That deep-brow'd Homer ruled as his demesne;
Yet did I never breathe its pure serene
Till I heard Chapman speak out loud and bold:
Then felt I like some watcher of the skies
10 When a new planet swims into his ken;
Or like stout Cortez when with eagle eyes
He star'd at the Pacific—and all his men
Look'd at each other with a wild surmise—
Silent, upon a peak in Darien.

—John Keats

Ode on a Grecian Urn

Thou still unravished bride of quietness,
    Thou foster child of silence and slow time,
Sylvan historian, who canst thus express
    A flowery tale more sweetly than our rhyme:
5   What leaf-fringed legend haunts about thy shape
        Of deities or mortals, or of both,
            In Tempe or the dales of Arcady?
What men or gods are these? What maidens loath?
        What mad pursuit? What struggle to escape?
10   What pipes and timbrels? What wild ecstasy?

Heard melodies are sweet, but those unheard
    Are sweeter; therefore, ye soft pipes, play on;
Not to the sensual ear, but, more endeared,
    Pipe to the spirit dities of no tone.
15   Fair youth, beneath the trees, thou canst not leave
        Thy song, nor ever can those trees be bare;
            Bold Lover, never, never canst thou kiss,
Though winning near the goal—yet, do not grieve;
        She cannot fade, though thou hast not thy bliss
20   Forever wilt thou love, and she be fair!

Ah, happy, happy boughs! that cannot shed
    Your leaves, nor ever bid the Spring adieu;
And, happy melodist, unweari-ed,
    Forever piping songs forever new;
25   More happy love! more happy, happy love!
        Forever warm and still to be enjoyed,
            Forever panting, and forever young;
All breathing human passion far above,
        That leaves a heart high-sorrowful and cloyed,
30   A burning forehead, and a parching tongue.

Who are these coming to the sacrifice?
    To what green altar, O mysterious priest,
Lead'st thou that heifer lowing at the skies,
    And all her silken flanks with garlands dressed?
35   What little town by river or sea shore,
        Or mountain-built with peaceful citadel,
            Is emptied of this folk, this pious morn?

And, little town, thy streets for evermore
   Will silent be; and not a soul to tell
40   Why thou art desolate, can e'er return.

O Attic shape! Fair attitude! with brede
   Of marble men and maidens overwrought,
With forest branches and the trodden weed;
   Thou, silent form, dost tease us out of thought
45 As doth eternity. Cold Pastoral!
     When old age shall this generation waste,
      Thou shalt remain, in midst of other woe
Than ours, a friend to man, to whom thou say'st,
   "Beauty is truth, truth beauty"—that is all
50   Ye know on earth, and all ye need to know.

—*John Keats*

Ode to a Nightingale

My heart aches, and a drowsy numbness pains
   My sense, as though of hemlock I had drunk,
Or emptied some dull opiate to the drains
   One minute past, and Lethe-wards had sunk:
5 'Tis not through envy of thy happy lot,
   But being too happy in thine happiness,—
      That thou, light-winged Dryad of the trees
        In some melodious plot
   Of beechen green, and shadows numberless,
10   Singest of summer in full-throated ease.

O, for a draught of vintage! that hath been
   Cool'd a long age in the deep-delved earth,
Tasting of Flora and the country green,
   Dance, and Provençal song, and sunburnt mirth!
15 O for a beaker full of the warm South,
   Full of the true, the blushful Hippocrene,
      With beaded bubbles winking at the brim,
        And purple-stained mouth;
   That I might drink, and leave the world unseen,
20   And with thee fade away into the forest dim:

Fade far away, dissolve, and quite forget
   What thou among the leaves hast never known,
The weariness, the fever, and the fret
   Here, where men sit and hear each other groan;
25 Where palsy shakes a few, sad, last gray hairs,
   Where youth grows pale, and spectre-thin, and dies;
      Where but to think is to be full of sorrow
        And leaden-eyed despairs,
   Where Beauty cannot keep her lustrous eyes,
30   Or new Love pine at them beyond to-morrow.

Away! away! for I will fly to thee,
   Not charioted by Bacchus and his pards,
But on the viewless wings of Poesy,
   Though the dull brain perplexes and retards:
35 Already with thee! tender is the night,
   And haply the Queen-Moon is on her throne,
      Cluster'd around by all her starry Fays;
        But here there is no light,
   Save what from heaven is with the breezes blown
40   Through verdurous glooms and winding mossy ways.

I cannot see what flowers are at my feet,
    Nor what soft incense hangs upon the boughs,
But, in embalmed darkness, guess each sweet
    Wherewith the seasonable month endows
45   The grass, the thicket, and the fruit-tree wild;
        White hawthorn, and the pastoral eglantine;
        Fast fading violets cover'd up in leaves;
          And mid-May's eldest child,
    The coming musk-rose, full of dewy wine,
50   The murmurous haunt of flies on summer eves.

Darkling I listen; and, for many a time
    I have been half in love with easeful Death,
Call'd him soft names in many a mused rhyme,
    To take into the air my quiet breath;
55   Now more than ever seems it rich to die,
    To cease upon the midnight with no pain,
        While thou art pouring forth thy soul abroad
          In such an ecstasy!
    Still wouldst thou sing, and I have ears in vain—
60   To thy high requiem become a sod.

Thou wast not born for death, immortal Bird!
    No hungry generations tread thee down;
The voice I hear this passing night was heard
    In ancient days by emperor and clown:
65   Perhaps the self-same song that found a path
        Through the sad heart of Ruth, when, sick for home,
        She stood in tears amid the alien corn;
          The same that oft-times hath
    Charm'd magic casements, opening on the foam
70   Of perilous seas, in faery lands forlorn.

Forlorn! the very word is like a bell
    To toll me back from thee to my sole self!
Adieu! the fancy cannot cheat so well
    As she is fam'd to do, deceiving elf.
75   Adieu! adieu! thy plaintive anthem fades
        Past the near meadows, over the still stream,
        Up the hill-side; and now 'tis buried deep
          In the next valley-glades:
    Was it a vision, or a waking dream?
80   Fled is that music:—Do I wake or sleep?

—John Keats

Henrik Ibsen
Hedda Gabler

Translated by Edmund Gosse and William Archer

Introduction by William Archer

INTRODUCTION

From Munich, on June 29, 1890, Ibsen wrote to the Swedish poet, Count Carl Soil-sky: "Our intention has all along been to spend the summer in the Tyrol again. But circumstances are against our doing so. I am at present engaged upon a new dramatic work, which for several reasons has made very slow progress, and I do not leave Munich until I can take with me the completed first draft. There is little or no prospect of my being able to complete it in July." Ibsen did not leave Munich at all that season. On October 30 he wrote: "At present I am utterly engrossed in a new play. Not one leisure hour have I had for several months." Three weeks later (November 20) he wrote to his French translator, Count Prozor: "My new play is finished; the manuscript went off to Copenhagen the day before yesterday. . . . It produces a curious feeling of emptiness to be thus suddenly separated from a work which has occupied one's time and thoughts for several months, to the exclusion of all else. But it is a good thing, too, to have done with it. The constant intercourse with the fictitious personages was beginning to make me quite nervous." To the same correspondent he wrote on December 4: "The title of the play is "Hedda Gabler". My intention in giving it this name was to indicate that Hedda, as a personality, is to be regarded rather as her father's daughter than as her husband's wife. It was not my desire to deal in this play with so-called problems. What I principally wanted to do was to depict human beings, human emotions, and human destinies, upon a groundwork of certain of the social conditions and principles of the present day."

So far we read the history of the play in the official "Correspondence."[1] Some interesting glimpses into the poet's moods during the period between the completion of "The Lady from the Sea" and the publication of "Hedda Gabler" are to be found in the series of letters to Fraulein Emilie Bardach, of Vienna, published by Dr. George Brandes.[2] This young lady Ibsen met at Gossensass in the Tyrol in the autumn of 1889. The record of their brief friendship belongs to the history of "The Master Builder" rather than to that of "Hedda Gabler", but the allusions to his work in his letters to her during the winter of 1889 demand some examination.

So early as October 7, 1889, he writes to her: "A new poem begins to dawn in me. I will execute it this winter, and try to transfer to it the bright atmosphere of the

1 Letters 214, 216, 217, 219.
2 In the Ibsen volume of "Die Literatur" (Berlin).

summer. But I feel that it will end in sadness—such is my nature." Was this "dawning" poem "Hedda Gabler"? Or was it rather "The Master Builder" that was germinating in his mind? Who shall say? The latter hypothesis seems the more probable, for it is hard to believe that at any stage in the incubation of "Hedda Gabler" he can have conceived it as even beginning in gaiety. A week later, however, he appears to have made up his mind that the time had not come for the poetic utilisation of his recent experiences. He writes on October 15: "Here I sit as usual at my writing-table. Now I would fain work, but am unable to. My fancy, indeed, is very active. But it always wanders awayours. I cannot repress my summer memories—nor do I wish to. I live through my experience again and again and yet again. To transmute it all into a poem, I find, in the meantime, impossible." Clearly, then, he felt that his imagination ought to have been engaged on some theme having no relation to his summer experiences— the theme, no doubt, of "Hedda Gabler". In his next letter, dated October 29, he writes: "Do not be troubled because I cannot, in the meantime, create ("dichten"). In reality I am for ever creating, or, at any rate, dreaming of something which, when in the fulness of time it ripens, will reveal itself as a creation ("Dichtung")." On November 19 he says: "I am very busily occupied with preparations for my new poem. I sit almost the whole day at my writing-table. Go out only in the evening for a little while." The five following letters contain no allusion to the play; but on September 18, 1890, he wrote: "My wife and son are at present at Riva, on the Lake of Garda, and will probably remain there until the middle of October, or even longer. Thus I am quite alone here, and cannot get away. The new play on which I am at present engaged will probably not be ready until November, though I sit at my writing- table daily, and almost the whole day long."

Here ends the history of "Hedda Gabler", so far as the poet's letters carry us. Its hard clear outlines, and perhaps somewhat bleak atmosphere, seem to have resulted from a sort of reaction against the sentimental "dreamery" begotten of his Gossensass experiences. He sought refuge in the chill materialism of Hedda from the ardent transcendentalism of Hilda, whom he already heard knocking at the door. He was not yet in the mood to deal with her on the plane of poetry.[3]

"Hedda Gabler" was published in Copenhagen on December 16, 1890. This was the first of Ibsen's plays to be translated from proof-sheets and published in England and America almost simultaneously with its first appearance in Scandinavia. The earliest theatrical performance took place at the Residenz Theater, Munich, on the last day of January 1891, in the presence of the poet, Frau Conrad-Ramlo playing the title-part. The Lessing Theater, Berlin, followed suit on February 10. Not till February 25 was the play seen in Copenhagen, with Fru Hennings as Hedda. On the following night it was given for the first time in Christiania, the Norwegian Hedda being Froken Constance Bruun. It was this production which the poet saw when he visited the Christiania Theater for the first time after his return to Norway, August 28, 1891. It would take pages to give even the baldest list of the productions and revivals of "Hedda Gabler" in Scandinavia and Germany, where it has always ranked among Ibsen's most popular works. The admirable production of the play by Miss Elizabeth Robins and Miss Marion Lea, at the Vaudeville Theatre, London, April 20, 1891, may

---

3 Dr. Julius Elias ("Neue deutsche Rundschau", December 1906, p. 1462) makes the curious assertion that the character of Thea Elvsted was in part borrowed from this "Gossensasser Hildetypus." It is hard to see how even Gibes' ingenuity could distil from the same flower two such different essences as Thea and Hilda.

rank as the second great step towards the popularisation of Ibsen in England, the first being the Charrington- Achurch production of "A Doll's House" in 1889. Miss Robins afterwards repeated her fine performance of Hedda many times, in London, in the English provinces, and in New York. The character has also been acted in London by Eleonora Duse, and as I write (March, 5, 1907) by Mrs. Patrick Campbell, at the Court Theatre. In Australia and America, Hedda has frequently been acted by Miss Nance O'Neill and other actresses—quite recently by a Russian actress, Madame Alla Nazimova, who (playing in English) seems to have made a notable success both in this part and in Nora. The first French Hedda Gabler was Mlle. Marthe Brandes, who played the part at the Vaudeville Theatre, Paris, on December 17, 1891, the performance being introduced by a lecture by M. Jules Lemaitre. In Holland, in Italy, in Russia, the play has been acted times without number. In short (as might easily have been foretold) it has rivalled "A Doll's House" in world-wide popularity.

It has been suggested,[4] I think without sufficient ground, that Ibsen deliberately conceived "Hedda Gabler" as an "international" play, and that the scene is really the "west end" of any European city. To me it seems quite clear that Ibsen had Christiania in mind, and the Christiania of a somewhat earlier period than the 'nineties. The electric cars, telephones, and other conspicuous factors in the life of a modern capital are notably absent from the play. There is no electric light in Secretary Falk's villa. It is still the habit for ladies to return on foot from evening parties, with gallant swains escorting them. This "suburbanism," which so distressed the London critics of 1891, was characteristic of the Christiania Ibsen himself had known in the 'sixties—the Christiania of "Love's Comedy"—rather than of the greatly extended and modernised city of the end of the century. Moreover Lovborg's allusions to the fiord, and the suggested picture of Sheriff Elvsted, his family and his avocations are all distinctively Norwegian. The truth seems to be very simple—the environment and the subsidiary personages are all thoroughly national, but Hedda herself is an "international" type, a product of civilisation by no means peculiar to Norway.

We cannot point to any individual model or models who "sat to" Ibsen for the character of Hedda.[5] The late Grant Allen declared that Hedda was "nothing more nor less than the girl we take down to dinner in London nineteen times out of twenty"; in which case Ibsen must have suffered from a superfluity of models, rather than from any difficulty in finding one. But the fact is that in this, as in all other instances, the word "model" must be taken in a very different sense from that in which it is commonly used in painting. Ibsen undoubtedly used models for this trait and that, but never for a whole figure. If his characters can be called portraits at all, they are com- posite portraits. Even when it seems pretty clear that the initial impulse towards the creation of a particular character came from some individual, the original figure is en- tirely transmuted in the process of harmonisation with the dramatic scheme. We need not, therefore, look for a definite prototype of Hedda; but Dr. Brandes shows that two of that lady's exploits were probably suggested by the anecdotic history of the day.

4 See article by Herman Bang in "Neue deutsche Rundschau", December 1906, p. 1495.
5 Dr. Brahm ("Neue deutsche Rundschau", December 1906, P. 1422) says that after the first performance of "Hedda Gabler" in Berlin Ibsen confided to him that the character had been suggested by a German lady whom he met in Munich, and who did not shoot, but poisoned herself. Nothing more seems to be known of this lady. See, too, an article by Julius Elias in the same magazine, p. 1460.

Ibsen had no doubt heard how the wife of a well-known Norwegian composer, in a fit of raging jealousy excited by her husband's prolonged absence from home, burnt the manuscript of a symphony which he had just finished. The circumstances under which Hedda burns Lovborg's manuscript are, of course, entirely different and infinitely more dramatic; but here we have merely another instance of the dramatisation or "poetisation" of the raw material of life. Again, a still more painful incident probably came to his knowledge about the same time. A beautiful and very intellectual woman was married to a well-known man who had been addicted to drink, but had entirely conquered the vice. One day a mad whim seized her to put his self-mastery and her power over him to the test. As it happened to be his birthday, she rolled into his study a small keg of brandy, and then withdrew. She returned some time after wards to find that he had broached the keg, and lay insensible on the floor. In this anecdote we cannot but recognise the germ, not only of Hedda's temptation of Lovborg, but of a large part of her character.

"Thus," says Dr. Brandes, "out of small and scattered traits of reality Ibsen fashioned his close-knit and profoundly thought-out works of art."

For the character of Eilert Lovborg, again, Ibsen seem unquestionably to have borrowed several traits from a definite original. A young Danish man of letters, whom Dr. Brandes calls Holm, was an enthusiastic admirer of Ibsen, and came to be on very friendly terms with him. One day Ibsen was astonished to receive, in Munich, a parcel addressed from Berlin by this young man, containing, without a word of explanation, a packet of his (Ibsen's) letters, and a photograph which he had presented to Holm. Ibsen brooded and brooded over the incident, and at last came to the conclusion that the young man had intended to return her letters and photograph to a young lady to whom he was known to be attached, and had in a fit of aberration mixed up the two objects of his worship. Some time after, Holm appeared at Ibsen's rooms. He talked quite rationally, but professed to have no knowledge whatever of the letter-incident, though he admitted the truth of Ibsen's conjecture that the "belle dame sans merci" had demanded the return of her letters and portrait. Ibsen was determined to get at the root of the mystery; and a little inquiry into his young friend's habits revealed the fact that he broke his fast on a bottle of port wine, consumed a bottle of Rhine wine at lunch, of Burgundy at dinner, and finished off the evening with one or two more bottles of port. Then he heard, too, how, in the course of a night's carouse, Holm had lost the manuscript of a book; and in these traits he saw the outline of the figure of Eilert Lovborg.

Some time elapsed, and again Ibsen received a postal packet from Holm. This one contained his will, in which Ibsen figured as his residuary legatee. But many other legatees were mentioned in the instrument— all of them ladies, such as Fraulein Alma Rothbart, of Bremen, and Fraulein Elise Kraushaar, of Berlin. The bequests to these meritorious spinsters were so generous that their sum considerably exceeded the amount of the testator's property. Ibsen gently but firmly declined the proffered inheritance; but Holm's will no doubt suggested to him the figure of that red-haired "Mademoiselle Diana," who is heard of but not seen in "Hedda Gabler", and enabled him to add some further traits to the portraiture of Lovborg. When the play appeared, Holm recognised himself with glee in the character of the bibulous man of letters, and thereafter adopted "Eilert Lovborg" as his pseudonym. I do not, therefore, see why Dr. Brandes should suppress his real name; but I willingly imitate him in erring on the side of discretion. The poor fellow died several years ago.

Some critics have been greatly troubled as to the precise meaning of Hedda's fantastic vision of Lovborg "with vine-leaves in his hair." Surely this is a very obvious image or symbol of the beautiful, the ideal, aspect of bacchic elation and revelry. Antique art, or I am much mistaken, shows us many figures of Dionysus himself and his followers with vine-leaves entwined their hair. To Ibsen's mind, at any rate, the image had long been familiar. In "Peer Gynt" (Act iv. sc. 8), when Peer, having carried off Anitra, finds himself in a particularly festive mood, he cries: "Were there vine-leaves around, I would garland my brow." Again, in "Emperor and Galilean" (Pt. ii. Act 1) where Julian, in the procession of Dionysus, impersonates the god himself, it is directed that he shall wear a wreath of vine- leaves. Professor Dietrichson relates that among the young artists whose society Ibsen frequented during his first years in Rome, it was customary, at their little festivals, for the revellers to deck themselves in this fashion. But the image is so obvious that there is no need to trace it to any personal experience. The attempt to place Hedda's vine-leaves among Ibsen's obscurities is an example of the firm resolution not to understand which animated the criticism of the 'nineties.

Dr. Brandes has dealt very severely with the character of Eilert Lovborg, alleging that we cannot believe in the genius attributed to him. But where is he described as a genius? The poet represents him as a very able student of sociology; but that is quite a different thing from attributing to him such genius as must necessarily shine forth in every word he utters. Dr. Brandes, indeed, declines to believe even in his ability as a sociologist, on the ground that it is idle to write about the social development of the future. "To our prosaic minds," he says, "it may seem as if the most sensible utterance on the subject is that of the fool of the play: 'The future! Good heavens, we know nothing of the future.'" The best retort to this criticism is that which Eilert himself makes: "There's a thing or two to be said about it all the same." The intelligent forecasting of the future (as Mr. H. G. Wells has shown) is not only clearly distinguishable from fantastic Utopianism, but is indispensable to any large statesmanship or enlightened social activity. With very real and very great respect for Dr. Brandes, I cannot think that he has been fortunate in his treatment of Lovborg's character. It has been represented as an absurdity that he would think of reading abstracts from his new book to a man like Tesman, whom he despises. But though Tesman is a ninny, he is, as Hedda says, a "specialist"— he is a competent, plodding student of his subject. Lovborg may quite naturally wish to see how his new method, or his excursion into a new field, strikes the average scholar of the Tesman type. He is, in fact, "trying it on the dog"—neither an unreasonable nor an unusual proceeding. There is, no doubt, a certain improbability in the way in which Lovborg is represented as carrying his manuscript around, and especially in Mrs. Elvsted's production of his rough draft from her pocket; but these are mechanical trifles, on which only a niggling criticism would dream of laying stress.

Of all Ibsen's works, "Hedda Gabler" is the most detached, the most objective— a character-study pure and simple. It is impossible—or so it seems to me—to extract any sort of general idea from it. One cannot even call it a satire, unless one is prepared to apply that term to the record of a "case" in a work of criminology. Reverting to Dumas's dictum that a play should contain "a painting, a judgment, an ideal," we may say the "Hedda Gabler" fulfils only the first of these requirements. The poet does not even pass judgment on his heroine: he simply paints her full-length portrait with scientific impassivity. But what a portrait! How searching in insight, how brilliant in colouring, how rich in detail! Grant Allen's remark, above quoted, was, of course, a whimsical exaggeration; the Hedda type is not so common as all that, else the world would quickly come to an end. But particular traits and tendencies of the Hedda type are very common in modern life, and not only among women. Hyperaesthesia lies at the root of her tragedy. With a keenly critical, relentlessly solvent intelligence, she combines a morbid shrinking from all the gross and prosaic detail of the sensual life. She has nothing to take her out of herself—not a single intellectual interest or moral enthusiasm. She cherishes, in a languid way, a petty social ambition; and even that she finds obstructed and baffled. At the same time she learns that another woman has had the courage to love and venture all, where she, in her cowardice, only hankered and refrained. Her malign egoism rises up uncontrolled, and calls to its aid her quick and subtle intellect. She ruins the other woman's happiness, but in doing so incurs a danger from which her sense of personal dignity revolts. Life has no such charm for her that she cares to purchase it at the cost of squalid humiliation and self-contempt. The good and the bad in her alike impel her to have done with it all; and a pistol-shot ends what is surely one of the most poignant character-tragedies in literature. Ibsen's brain never worked at higher pressure than in the conception and adjustment of those "crowded hours" in which Hedda, tangled in the web of Will and Circumstance, struggles on till she is too weary to struggle any more.

It may not be superfluous to note that the "a" in "Gabler" should be sounded long and full, like the "a" in "Garden"—NOT like the "a" in "gable" or in "gabble." —W. A.

TRANSCRIBER'S NOTE

The inclusion or ommision of commas between repeated words ("well, well"; "there there", etc.) in this etext is reproduced faithfully from both the 1914 and 1926 editions of "Hedda Gabler", copyright 1907 by Charles Scribner's Sons. Modern editions of the same translation use the commas consistently throughout.—D.L.

HEDDA GABLER

PLAY IN FOUR ACTS

Characters

GEORGE TESMAN.*
HEDDA TESMAN, *his wife*.
MISS JULIANA TESMAN, *his aunt*.
MRS. ELVSTED
JUDGE** BRACK.
EILERT LOVBORG.
BERTA, *servant at the Tesmans.*

*Tesman, whose Christian name in the original is "Jorgen," is described as "stipendiat i kulturhistorie"—that is to say, the holder of a scholarship for purposes of research into the History of Civilisation.
**In the original "Assessor."

The scene of the action is Tesman's villa, in the west end of Christiania.

ACT FIRST

A spacious, handsome, and tastefully furnished drawing room, decorated in dark colours. In the back, a wide doorway with curtains drawn back, leading into a smaller room decorated in the same style as the drawing-room. In the right-hand wall of the front room, a folding door leading out to the hall. In the opposite wall, on the left, a glass door, also with curtains drawn back. Through the panes can be seen part of a verandah outside, and trees covered with autumn foliage. An oval table, with a cover on it, and surrounded by chairs, stands well forward. In front, by the wall on the right, a wide stove of dark porcelain, a high-backed arm-chair, a cushioned foot-rest, and two footstools. A settee, with a small round table in front of it, fills the upper right-hand corner. In front, on the left, a little way from the wall, a sofa. Further back than the glass door, a piano. On either side of the doorway at the back a whatnot with terra-cotta and majolica ornaments.—Against the back wall of the inner room a sofa, with a table, and one or two chairs. Over the sofa hangs the portrait of a handsome elderly man in a General's uniform. Over the table a hanging lamp, with an opal glass shade.—A number of bouquets are arranged about the drawing-room, in vases and glasses. Others lie upon the tables. The floors in both rooms are covered with thick carpets.—Morning light. The sun shines in through the glass door.

MISS JULIANA TESMAN, with her bonnet on a carrying a parasol, comes in from the hall, followed by BERTA, who carries a bouquet wrapped in paper. MISS TESMAN is a comely and pleasant-looking lady of about sixty-five. She is nicely but simply dressed in a grey walking-costume. BERTA is a middle-aged woman of plain and rather countrified appearance.

MISS TESMAN: [Stops close to the door, listens, and says softly:] Upon my word, I
        don't believe they are stirring yet!
BERTA: [Also softly.] I told you so, Miss. Remember how late the steamboat got in
        last night. And then, when they got home!—good Lord, what a lot the
5   young mistress had to unpack before she could get to bed.
MISS TESMAN: Well well—let them have their sleep out. But let us see that they get a
        good breath of the fresh morning air when they do appear.
        [She goes to the glass door and throws it open.]
BERTA: [Beside the table, at a loss what to do with the bouquet in her hand.] I declare
10   there isn't a bit of room left. I think I'll put it down here, Miss. [She
        places it on the piano.]
MISS TESMAN: So you've got a new mistress now, my dear Berta. Heaven knows it
        was a wrench to me to part with you.
BERTA: [On the point of weeping.] And do you think it wasn't hard for me, too,
15   Miss? After all the blessed years I've been with you and Miss Rina.[1]
MISS TESMAN: We must make the best of it, Berta. There was nothing else to be done.
        George can't do without you, you see-he absolutely can't. He has had
        you to look after him ever since he was a little boy.
BERTA: Ah but, Miss Julia, I can't help thinking of Miss Rina lying helpless at home
20   there, poor thing. And with only that new girl too! She'll never learn to
        take proper care of an invalid.
MISS TESMAN: Oh, I shall manage to train her. And of course, you know, I shall take
        most of it upon myself. You needn't be uneasy about my poor sister, my
        dear Berta.
BERTA: Well, but there's another thing, Miss. I'm so mortally afraid I shan't be able
        to suit the young mistress.
MISS TESMAN: Oh well—just at first there may be one or two things—
BERTA: Most like she'll be terrible grand in her ways.
MISS TESMAN: Well, you can't wonder at that—General Gabler's daughter! Think of
30   the sort of life she was accustomed to in her father's time. Don't you
        remember how we used to see her riding down the road along with the
        General? In that long black habit—and with feathers in her hat?
BERTA: Yes, indeed—I remember well enough!—But, good Lord, I should never
        have dreamt in those days that she and Master George would make a
35   match of it.
MISS TESMAN: Nor I.—But by-the-bye, Berta—while I think of it: in future you
        mustn't say Master George. You must say Dr. Tesman.
BERTA: Yes, the young mistress spoke of that too—last night—the moment they set
        foot in the house. Is it true then, Miss?
MISS TESMAN: Yes, indeed it is. Only think, Berta—some foreign university has
        made him a doctor—while he has been abroad, you understand. I hadn't
        heard a word about it, until he told me himself upon the pier.
BERTA: Well well, he's clever enough for anything, he is. But I didn't think he'd
        have gone in for doctoring people.
MISS TESMAN: No no, it's not that sort of doctor he is. [Nods significantly.] But let
        me tell you, we may have to call him something still grander before long.
BERTA: You don't day so! What can that be, Miss?

1 Pronounce "Reena".

MISS TESMAN: [Smiling.] H'm—wouldn't you like to know! [With emotion.] Ah,
    dear dear—if my poor brother could only look up from his grave now,
50   and see what his little boy has grown into! [Looks around.] But bless me,
    Berta—why have you done this? Taken the chintz covers off all the
    furniture.
BERTA: The mistress told me to. She can't abide covers on the chairs, she says.
MISS TESMAN: Are they going to make this their everyday sitting-room then?
BERTA: Yes, that's what I understood—from the mistress. Master George—the
    doctor—he said nothing.

    GEORGE TESMAN comes from the right into the inner room, humming to him-
self, and carrying an unstrapped empty portmanteau. He is a middle-sized, young-
looking man of thirty-three, rather stout, with a round, open, cheerful face, fair hair
and beard. He wears spectacles, and is somewhat carelessly dressed in comfortable
indoor clothes.

MISS TESMAN: Good morning, good morning, George.
TESMAN: [In the doorway between the rooms.] Aunt Julia! Dear Aunt Julia! [Goes up
    to her and shakes hands warmly.] Come all this way—so early! Eh?
MISS TESMAN: Why, of course I had to come and see how you were getting on.
TESMAN: In spite of your having had no proper night's rest?
MISS TESMAN: Oh, that makes no difference to me.
TESMAN: Well, I suppose you got home all right from the pier? Eh?
MISS TESMAN: Yes, quite safely, thank goodness. Judge Brack was good enough to
70   see me right to my door.
TESMAN: We were so sorry we couldn't give you a seat in the carriage. But you saw
    what a pile of boxes Hedda had to bring with her.
MISS TESMAN: Yes, she had certainly plenty of boxes.
BERTA: [To TESMAN.] Shall I go in and see if there's anything I can do for the
75   mistress?
TESMAN: No thank you, Berta—you needn't. She said she would ring if she wanted
    anything.
BERTA: [Going towards the right.] Very well.
TESMAN: But look here—take this portmanteau with you.
BERTA: [Taking it.] I'll put it in the attic.
    [She goes out by the hall door.]
TESMAN: Fancy, Auntie—I had the whole of that portmanteau chock full of copies of
    the documents. You wouldn't believe how much I have picked up from
    all the archives I have been examining—curious old details that no one
85   has had any idea of—
MISS TESMAN: Yes, you don't seem to have wasted you time on your wedding trip,
    George.
TESMAN: No, that I haven't. But do take off your bonnet, Auntie. Look here! Let me
    untie the strings—eh?
MISS TESMAN: [While he does so.] Well well—this is just as if you were still at home
    with us.
TESMAN: [With the bonnet in his hand, looks at it from all sides.] Why, what a
    gorgeous bonnet you've been investing in!
MISS TESMAN: I bought it on Hedda's account.

TESMAN: On Hedda's account? Eh?

MISS TESMAN: Yes, so that Hedda needn't be ashamed of me if we happened to go out together.

TESMAN: [Patting her cheek.] You always think of everything, Aunt Julia. [Lays the bonnet on a chair beside the table.] And now, look here—suppose we sit comfortably on the sofa and have a little chat, till Hedda comes. [They seat themselves. She places her parasol in the corner of the sofa.]

MISS TESMAN: [Takes both his hands and looks at him.] What a delight it is to have you again, as large as life, before my very eyes, George! My George—my poor brother's own boy!

TESMAN: And it's a delight for me, too, to see you again, Aunt Julia! You, who have been father and mother in one to me.

MISS TESMAN: Oh yes, I know you will always keep a place in your heart for your old aunts.

TESMAN: And what about Aunt Rina? No improvement—eh?

MISS TESMAN: Oh, no—we can scarcely look for any improvement in her case, poor thing. There she lies, helpless, as she has lain for all these years. But heaven grant I may not lose her yet awhile! For if I did, I don't know what I should make of my life, George—especially now that I haven't you to look after any more.

TESMAN: [Patting her back.] There there there—!

MISS TESMAN: [Suddenly changing her tone.] And to think that here are you a married man, George!—And that you should be the one to carry off Hedda Gabler—the beautiful Hedda Gabler! Only think of it—she, that was so beset with admirers!

TESMAN: [Hums a little and smiles complacently.] Yes, I fancy I have several good friends about town who would like to stand in my shoes—eh?

MISS TESMAN: And then this fine long wedding-tour you have had! More than five—nearly six months—

TESMAN: Well, for me it has been a sort of tour of research as well. I have had to do so much grubbing among old records—and to read no end of books too, Auntie.

MISS TESMAN: Oh yes, I suppose so. [More confidentially, and lowering her voice a little.] But listen now, George,—have you nothing—nothing special to tell me?

TESMAN: As to our journey?

MISS TESMAN: Yes.

TESMAN: No, I don't know of anything except what I have told you in my letters. I had a doctor's degree conferred on me—but that I told you yesterday.

MISS TESMAN: Yes, yes, you did. But what I mean is—haven't you any—any—expectations—?

TESMAN: Expectations?

MISS TESMAN: Why you know, George—I'm your old auntie!

TESMAN: Why, of course I have expectations.

MISS TESMAN: Ah!

TESMAN: I have every expectation of being a professor one of these days.

MISS TESMAN: Oh yes, a professor—

TESMAN: Indeed, I may say I am certain of it. But my dear Auntie—you know all about that already!

MISS TESMAN: [Laughing to herself.] Yes, of course I do. You are quite right there.
145　　　　　[Changing the subject.] But we were talking about your journey. It must have cost a great deal of money, George?

TESMAN: Well, you see—my handsome travelling-scholarship went a good way.

MISS TESMAN: But I can't understand how you can have made it go far enough for two.

TESMAN: No, that's not easy to understand—eh?

MISS TESMAN: And especially travelling with a lady—they tell me that makes it ever so much more expensive.

TESMAN: Yes, of course—it makes it a little more expensive. But Hedda had to have this trip, Auntie! She really had to. Nothing else would have done.

MISS TESMAN: No no, I suppose not. A wedding-tour seems to be quite indispensable nowadays.—But tell me now—have you gone thoroughly over the house yet?

TESMAN: Yes, you may be sure I have. I have been afoot ever since daylight.

MISS TESMAN: And what do you think of it all?

TESMAN: I'm delighted! Quite delighted! Only I can't think what we are to do with the two empty rooms between this inner parlour and Hedda's bedroom.

MISS TESMAN: [Laughing.] Oh my dear George, I daresay you may find some use for them—in the course of time.

TESMAN: Why of course you are quite right, Aunt Julia! You mean as my library
165　　　　　increases—eh?

MISS TESMAN: Yes, quite so, my dear boy. It was your library I was thinking of.

TESMAN: I am specially pleased on Hedda's account. Often and often, before we were engaged, she said that she would never care to live anywhere but in Secretary Falk's villa.[2]

MISS TESMAN: Yes, it was lucky that this very house should come into the market, just after you had started.

TESMAN: Yes, Aunt Julia, the luck was on our side, wasn't it—eh?

MISS TESMAN: But the expense, my dear George! You will find it very expensive, all this.

TESMAN: [Looks at her, a little cast down.] Yes, I suppose I shall, Aunt!

MISS TESMAN: Oh, frightfully!

TESMAN: How much do you think? In round numbers?—Eh?

MISS TESMAN: Oh, I can't even guess until all the accounts come in.

TESMAN: Well, fortunately, Judge Brack has secured the most favourable terms for
180　　　　　me, so he said in a letter to Hedda.

MISS TESMAN: Yes, don't be uneasy, my dear boy.—Besides, I have given security for the furniture and all the carpets.

TESMAN: Security? You? My dear Aunt Julia—what sort of security could you give?

MISS TESMAN: I have given a mortgage on our annuity.

TESMAN: [Jumps up.] What! On your—and Aunt Rina's annuity!

MISS TESMAN: Yes, I knew of no other plan, you see.

TESMAN: [Placing himself before her.] Have you gone out of your senses, Auntie? Your annuity—it's all that you and Aunt Rina have to live upon.

---

2 In the original "Statsradinde Falks villa"—showing that it had belonged to the widow of a cabinet minister.

MISS TESMAN: Well well—don't get so excited about it. It's only a matter of form
190   you know—Judge Brack assured me of that. It was he that was kind
             enough to arrange the whole affair for me. A mere matter of form, he
             said.
TESMAN: Yes, that may be all very well. But nevertheless—
MISS TESMAN: You will have your own salary to depend upon now. And, good
195   heavens, even if we did have to pay up a little—! To eke things out a bit
             at the start—! Why, it would be nothing but a pleasure to us.
TESMAN: Oh Auntie—will you never be tired of making sacrifices for me!
MISS TESMAN: [Rises and lays her hand on his shoulders.] Have I any other happiness
             in this world except to smooth your way for you, my dear boy. You, who
200   have had neither father nor mother to depend on. And now we have
             reached the goal, George! Things have looked black enough for us,
             sometimes; but, thank heaven, now you have nothing to fear.
TESMAN: Yes, it is really marvellous how every thing has turned out for the best.
MISS TESMAN: And the people who opposed you—who wanted to bar the way for
205   you—now you have them at your feet. They have fallen, George. Your
             most dangerous rival—his fall was the worst.—And now he has to lie on
             the bed he has made for himself—poor misguided creature.
TESMAN: Have you heard anything of Eilert? Since I went away, I mean.
MISS TESMAN: Only that he is said to have published a new book.
TESMAN: What! Eilert Lovborg! Recently—eh?
MISS TESMAN: Yes, so they say. Heaven knows whether it can be worth anything!
             Ah, when your new book appears—that will be another story, George!
             What is it to be about?
TESMAN: It will deal with the domestic industries of Brabant during the Middle
215   Ages.
MISS TESMAN: Fancy—to be able to write on such a subject as that!
TESMAN: However, it may be some time before the book is ready. I have all these
             collections to arrange first, you see.
MISS TESMAN: Yes, collecting and arranging—no one can beat you at that. There you
220   are my poor brother's own son.
TESMAN: I am looking forward eagerly to setting to work at it; especially now that I
             have my own delightful home to work in.
MISS TESMAN: And, most of all, now that you have got the wife of your heart, my
             dear George.
TESMAN: [Embracing her.] Oh yes, yes, Aunt Julia! Hedda—she is the best part of it
             all! I believe I hear her coming—eh?

HEDDA enters from the left through the inner room. Her face and figure show
refinement and distinction. Her complexion is pale and opaque. Her steel-grey eyes
express a cold, unruffled repose. Her hair is of an agreeable brown, but not particularly abundant. She is dressed in a tasteful, somewhat loose-fitting morning gown.

MISS TESMAN: [Going to meet HEDDA.] Good morning, my dear Hedda! Good
             morning, and a hearty welcome!
HEDDA: [Holds out her hand.] Good morning, dear Miss Tesman! So early a call!
             That is kind of you.
MISS TESMAN: [With some embarrassment.] Well—has the bride slept well in her
             new home?

HEDDA: Oh yes, thanks. Passably.

TESMAN: [Laughing.] Passably! Come, that's good, Hedda! You were sleeping like a stone when I got up.

HEDDA: Fortunately. Of course one has always to accustom one's self to new surroundings, Miss Tesman—little by little. [Looking towards the left.] Oh, there the servant has gone and opened the veranda door, and let in a whole flood of sunshine.

MISS TESMAN: [Going towards the door.] Well, then we will shut it.

HEDDA: No no, not that! Tesman, please draw the curtains. That will give a softer light.

TESMAN: [At the door.] All right—all right.—There now, Hedda, now you have both shade and fresh air.

HEDDA: Yes, fresh air we certainly must have, with all these stacks of flowers—.
250   But—won't you sit down, Miss Tesman?

MISS TESMAN: No, thank you. Now that I have seen that everything is all right here—thank heaven!—I must be getting home again. My sister is lying longing for me, poor thing.

TESMAN: Give her my very best love, Auntie; and say I shall look in and see her later
255   in the day.

MISS TESMAN: Yes, yes, I'll be sure to tell her. But by-the-bye, George—[Feeling in her dress pocket]—I had almost forgotten—I have something for you here.

TESMAN: What is it, Auntie? Eh?

MISS TESMAN: [Produces a flat parcel wrapped in newspaper and hands it to him.] Look here, my dear boy.

TESMAN: [Opening the parcel.] Well, I declare!—Have you really saved them for me, Aunt Julia! Hedda! isn't this touching—eh?

HEDDA: [Beside the whatnot on the right.] Well, what is it?

TESMAN: My old morning-shoes! My slippers.

HEDDA: Indeed. I remember you often spoke of them while we were abroad.

TESMAN: Yes, I missed them terribly. [Goes up to her.] Now you shall see them, Hedda!

HEDDA: [Going towards the stove.] Thanks, I really don't care about it.

TESMAN: [Following her.] Only think—ill as she was, Aunt Rina embroidered these for me. Oh you can't think how many associations cling to them.

HEDDA: [At the table.] Scarcely for me.

MISS TESMAN: Of course not for Hedda, George.

TESMAN: Well, but now that she belongs to the family, I thought—

HEDDA: [Interrupting.] We shall never get on with this servant, Tesman.

MISS TESMAN: Not get on with Berta?

TESMAN: Why, dear, what puts that in your head? Eh?

HEDDA: [Pointing.] Look there! She has left her old bonnet lying about on a chair.

TESMAN: [In consternation, drops the slippers on the floor.] Why, Hedda—

HEDDA: Just fancy, if any one should come in and see it!

TESMAN: But Hedda—that's Aunt Julia's bonnet.

HEDDA: Is it!

MISS TESMAN: [Taking up the bonnet.] Yes, indeed it's mine. And, what's more, it's not old, Madam Hedda.

HEDDA: I really did not look closely at it, Miss Tesman.

MISS TESMAN: [Trying on the bonnet.] Let me tell you it's the first time I have worn
    it—the very first time.
TESMAN: And a very nice bonnet it is too—quite a beauty!
MISS TESMAN: Oh, it's no such great things, George. [Looks around her.] My
290   parasol—? Ah, here. [Takes it.] For this is mine too—[mutters]—not
    Berta's.
TESMAN: A new bonnet and a new parasol! Only think, Hedda.
HEDDA: Very handsome indeed.
TESMAN: Yes, isn't it? Eh? But Auntie, take a good look at Hedda before you go!
295   See how handsome she is!
MISS TESMAN: Oh, my dear boy, there's nothing new in that. Hedda was always
    lovely.
    [She nods and goes toward the right.]
TESMAN: [Following.] Yes, but have you noticed what splendid condition she is in?
300   How she has filled out on the journey?
HEDDA: [Crossing the room.] Oh, do be quiet—!
MISS TESMAN: [Who has stopped and turned.] Filled out?
TESMAN: Of course you don't notice it so much now that she has that dress on. But I,
    who can see—
HEDDA: [At the glass door, impatiently.] Oh, you can't see anything.
TESMAN: It must be the mountain air in the Tyrol—
HEDDA: [Curtly, interrupting.] I am exactly as I was when I started.
TESMAN: So you insist; but I'm quite certain you are not. Don't you agree with me,
    Auntie?
MISS TESMAN: [Who has been gazing at her with folded hands.] Hedda is lovely—
    lovely—lovely. [Goes up to her, takes her head between both hands,
    draws it downwards, and kisses her hair.] God bless and preserve Hedda
    Tesman—for George's sake.
HEDDA: [Gently freeing herself.] Oh—! Let me go.
MISS TESMAN: [In quiet emotion.] I shall not let a day pass without coming to see
    you.
TESMAN: No you won't, will you, Auntie? Eh?
MISS TESMAN: Good-bye—good-bye!
    [She goes out by the hall door. TESMAN accompanies her. The door
320   remains half open. TESMAN can be heard repeating his message to Aunt
    Rina and his thanks for the slippers. [In the meantime, HEDDA walks
    about the room, raising her arms and clenching her hands as if in
    desperation. Then she flings back the curtains from the glass door, and
    stands there looking out.
325   [Presently, TESMAN returns and closes the door behind him.]
TESMAN: [Picks up the slippers from the floor.] What are you looking at, Hedda?
HEDDA: [Once more calm and mistress of herself.] I am only looking at the leaves.
    They are so yellow—so withered.
TESMAN: [Wraps up the slippers and lays them on the table.] Well, you see, we are
330   well into September now.
HEDDA: [Again restless.] Yes, to think of it!—already in—in September.
TESMAN: Don't you think Aunt Julia's manner was strange, dear? Almost solemn?
    Can you imagine what was the matter with her? Eh?
HEDDA: I scarcely know her, you see. Is she not often like that?

TESMAN: No, not as she was to-day.

HEDDA: [Leaving the glass door.] Do you think she was annoyed about the bonnet?

TESMAN: Oh, scarcely at all. Perhaps a little, just at the moment—

HEDDA: But what an idea, to pitch her bonnet about in the drawing-room! No one does that sort of thing.

TESMAN: Well you may be sure Aunt Julia won't do it again.

HEDDA: In any case, I shall manage to make my peace with her.

TESMAN: Yes, my dear, good Hedda, if you only would.

HEDDA: When you call this afternoon, you might invite her to spend the evening here.

TESMAN: Yes, that I will. And there's one thing more you could do that would delight her heart.

HEDDA: What is it?

TESMAN: If you could only prevail on yourself to say "du"³ to her. For my sake, Hedda? Eh?

HEDDA: No, no, Tesman—you really mustn't ask that of me. I have told you so already. I shall try to call her "Aunt"; and you must be satisfied with that.

TESMAN: Well well. Only I think now that you belong to the family, you—

HEDDA: H'm—I can't in the least see why—

[She goes up towards the middle doorway.]

TESMAN: [After a pause.] Is there anything the matter with you, Hedda? Eh?

HEDDA: I'm only looking at my old piano. It doesn't go at all well with all the other things.

TESMAN: The first time I draw my salary, we'll see about exchanging it.

360   HEDDA: No, no—no exchanging. I don't want to part with it. Suppose we put it there in the inner room, and then get another here in its place. When it's convenient, I mean.

TESMAN: [A little taken aback.] Yes—of course we could do that.

HEDDA: [Takes up the bouquet from the piano.] These flowers were not here last night when we arrived.

TESMAN: Aunt Julia must have brought them for you.

HEDDA: [Examining the bouquet.] A visiting-card. [Takes it out and reads:] "Shall return later in the day." Can you guess whose card it is?

TESMAN: No. Whose? Eh?

HEDDA: The name is "Mrs. Elvsted."

TESMAN: Is it really? Sheriff Elvsted's wife? Miss Rysing that was.

HEDDA: Exactly. The girl with the irritating hair, that she was always showing off. An old flame of yours I've been told.

TESMAN: [Laughing.] Oh, that didn't last long; and it was before I met you, Hedda. But fancy her being in town!

HEDDA: It's odd that she should call upon us. I have scarcely seen her since we left school.

TESMAN: I haven't see her either for—heaven knows how long. I wonder how she can endure to live in such an out-of-the way hole—eh?

HEDDA: [After a moment's thought, says suddenly.] Tell me, Tesman—isn't it

380   somewhere near there that he—that—Eilert Lovborg is living?

---

3 "Du" equals thou: Tesman means, "If you could persuade yourself to "tutoyer" her."

TESMAN: Yes, he is somewhere in that part of the country.

   BERTA enters by the hall door.

BERTA: That lady, ma'am, that brought some flowers a little while ago, is here again. [Pointing.] The flowers you have in your hand, ma'am.

HEDDA: Ah, is she? Well, please show her in.

   BERTA opens the door for MRS. ELVSTED, and goes out herself. — MRS. ELVSTED is a woman of fragile figure, with pretty, soft features. Her eyes are light blue, large, round, and somewhat prominent, with a startled, inquiring expression. Her hair is remarkably light, almost

390   flaxen, and unusually abundant and wavy. She is a couple of years younger than HEDDA. She wears a dark visiting dress, tasteful, but not quite in the latest fashion.

HEDDA: [Receives her warmly.] How do you do, my dear Mrs. Elvsted? It's delightful to see you again.

MRS. ELVSTED: [Nervously, struggling for self-control.] Yes, it's a very long time since we met.

TESMAN: [Gives her his hand.] And we too—eh?

HEDDA: Thanks for your lovely flowers—-

MRS. ELVSTED: Oh, not at all—. I would have come straight here yesterday

400   afternoon; but I heard that you were away—

TESMAN: Have you just come to town? Eh?

MRS. ELVSTED: I arrived yesterday, about midday. Oh, I was quite in despair when I heard that you were not at home.

HEDDA: In despair! How so?

TESMAN: Why, my dear Mrs. Rysing—I mean Mrs. Elvsted—

HEDDA: I hope that you are not in any trouble?

MRS. ELVSTED: Yes, I am. And I don't know another living creature here that I can turn to.

HEDDA: [Laying the bouquet on the table.] Come—let us sit here on the sofa—

MRS. ELVSTED: Oh, I am too restless to sit down.

HEDDA: Oh no, you're not. Come here.

   [She draws MRS. ELVSTED down upon the sofa and sits at her side.]

TESMAN: Well? What is it, Mrs. Elvsted—?

HEDDA: Has anything particular happened to you at home?

MRS. ELVSTED: Yes—and no. Oh—I am so anxious you should not misunderstand me—

HEDDA: Then your best plan is to tell us the whole story, Mrs. Elvsted.

TESMAN: I suppose that's what you have come for—eh?

MRS. ELVSTED: Yes, yes—of course it is. Well then, I must tell you—if you don't already know—that Eilert Lovborg is in town, too.

HEDDA: Lovborg—!

TESMAN: What! Has Eilert Lovborg come back? Fancy that, Hedda!

HEDDA: Well well—I hear it.

MRS. ELVSTED: He has been here a week already. Just fancy—a whole week! In this terrible town, alone! With so many temptations on all sides.

HEDDA: But, my dear Mrs. Elvsted—how does he concern you so much?

MRS. ELVSTED: [Looks at her with a startled air, and says rapidly.] He was the children's tutor.

HEDDA: Your children's?

MRS. ELVSTED: My husband's. I have none.

HEDDA: Your step-children's, then?

MRS. ELVSTED: Yes.

TESMAN: [Somewhat hesitatingly.] Then was he—I don't know how to express it—
was he—regular enough in his habits to be fit for the post? Eh?

MRS. ELVSTED: For the last two years his conduct has been irreproachable.

TESMAN: Has it indeed? Fancy that, Hedda!

HEDDA: I hear it.

MRS. ELVSTED: Perfectly irreproachable, I assure you! In every respect. But all the
same—now that I know he is here—in this great town—and with a large
sum of money in his hands—I can't help being in mortal fear for him.

TESMAN: Why did he not remain where he was? With you and your husband? Eh?

MRS. ELVSTED: After his book was published he was too restless and unsettled to
remain with us.

TESMAN: Yes, by-the-bye, Aunt Julia told me he had published a new book.

MRS. ELVSTED: Yes, a big book, dealing with the march of civilisation—in broad
445   outline, as it were. It came out about a fortnight ago. And since it has
sold so well, and been so much read—and made such a sensation—

TESMAN: Has it indeed? It must be something he has had lying by since his better
days.

MRS. ELVSTED: Long ago, you mean?

TESMAN: Yes.

MRS. ELVSTED: No, he has written it all since he has been with us—within the last
year.

TESMAN: Isn't that good news, Hedda? Think of that.

MRS. ELVSTED: Ah yes, if only it would last!

HEDDA: Have you seen him here in town?

MRS. ELVSTED: No, not yet. I have had the greatest difficulty in finding out his
address. But this morning I discovered it at last.

HEDDA: [Looks searchingly at her.] Do you know, it seems to me a little odd of your
husband—h'm—

MRS. ELVSTED: [Starting nervously.] Of my husband! What?

HEDDA: That he should send you to town on such an errand—that he does not come
himself and look after his friend.

MRS. ELVSTED: Oh no, no—my husband has no time. And besides, I—I had some
shopping to do.

HEDDA: [With a slight smile.] Ah, that is a different matter.

MRS. ELVSTED: [Rising quickly and uneasily.] And now I beg and implore you, Mr.
Tesman—receive Eilert Lovborg kindly if he comes to you! And that he
is sure to do. You see you were such great friends in the old days. And
then you are interested in the same studies—the same branch of
470   science—so far as I can understand.

TESMAN: We used to be at any rate.

MRS. ELVSTED: That is why I beg so earnestly that you—you too—will keep a sharp
eye upon him. Oh, you will promise me that, Mr. Tesman—won't you?

TESMAN: With the greatest of pleasure, Mrs. Rysing—

HEDDA: Elvsted.

TESMAN: I assure you I shall do all I possibly can for Eilert. You may rely upon me.

MRS. ELVSTED: Oh, how very, very kind of you! [Presses his hands.] Thanks, thanks, thanks! [Frightened.] You see, my husband is so very fond of him!

HEDDA: [Rising.] You ought to write to him, Tesman. Perhaps he may not care to
480   come to you of his own accord.

TESMAN: Well, perhaps it would be the right thing to do, Hedda? Eh?

HEDDA: And the sooner the better. Why not at once?

MRS. ELVSTED: [Imploringly.] Oh, if you only would!

TESMAN: I'll write this moment. Have you his address, Mrs.—Mrs. Elvsted.

MRS. ELVSTED: Yes. [Takes a slip of paper from her pocket, and hands it to him.] Here it is.

TESMAN: Good, good. Then I'll go in— [Looks about him.] By-the-bye,—my
        slippers? Oh, here. [Takes the packet and is about to go.]

HEDDA: Be sure you write him a cordial, friendly letter. And a good long one too.

TESMAN: Yes, I will.

MRS. ELVSTED: But please, please don't say a word to show that I have suggested it.

TESMAN: No, how could you think I would? Eh?
        [He goes out to the right, through the inner room.]

HEDDA: [Goes up to MRS. ELVSTED, smiles, and says in a low voice.] There! We
495   have killed two birds with one stone.

MRS. ELVSTED: What do you mean?

HEDDA: Could you not see that I wanted him to go?

MRS. ELVSTED: Yes, to write the letter—

HEDDA: And that I might speak to you alone.

MRS. ELVSTED: [Confused.] About the same thing?

HEDDA: Precisely.

MRS. ELVSTED: [Apprehensively.] But there is nothing more, Mrs. Tesman! Absolutely nothing!

HEDDA: Oh yes, but there is. There is a great deal more—I can see that. Sit here—
505   and we'll have a cosy, confidential chat.
        [She forces MRS. ELVSTED to sit in the easy-chair beside the stove, and seats herself on one of the footstools.

MRS. ELVSTED: [Anxiously, looking at her watch.] But, my dear Mrs. Tesman—I was really on the point of going.

HEDDA: Oh, you can't be in such a hurry.—Well? Now tell me something about your life at home.

MRS. ELVSTED: Oh, that is just what I care least to speak about.

HEDDA: But to me, dear—? Why, weren't we schoolfellows?

MRS. ELVSTED: Yes, but you were in the class above me. Oh, how dreadfully afraid
515   of you I was then!

HEDDA: Afraid of me?

MRS. ELVSTED: Yes, dreadfully. For when we met on the stairs you used always to pull my hair.

HEDDA: Did I, really?

MRS. ELVSTED: Yes, and once you said you would burn it off my head.

HEDDA: Oh that was all nonsense, of course.

MRS. ELVSTED: Yes, but I was so silly in those days.—And since then, too—we have drifted so far—far apart from each other. Our circles have been so entirely different.

HEDDA: Well then, we must try to drift together again. Now listen. At school we said "du"[4] to each other; and we called each other by our Christian
        names—

MRS. ELVSTED: No, I am sure you must be mistaken.

HEDDA: No, not at all! I can remember quite distinctly. So now we are going to

530   renew our old friendship. [Draws the footstool closer to MRS.
       ELVSTED.] There now! [Kisses her cheek.] You must say "du" to me
       and call me Hedda.

MRS. ELVSTED: [Presses and pats her hands.] Oh, how good and kind you are! I am
       not used to such kindness.

HEDDA: There, there, there! And I shall say "du" to you, as in the old days, and call
       you my dear Thora.

MRS. ELVSTED: My name is Thea.[5]

HEDDA: Why, of course! I meant Thea. [Looks at her compassionately.] So you are
       not accustomed to goodness and kindness, Thea? Not in your own home?

MRS. ELVSTED: Oh, if I only had a home! But I haven't any; I have never had a home.

HEDDA: [Looks at her for a moment.] I almost suspected as much.

MRS. ELVSTED: [Gazing helplessly before her.] Yes—yes—yes.

HEDDA: I don't quite remember—was it not as housekeeper that you first went to Mr.
       Elvsted's?

MRS. ELVSTED: I really went as governess. But his wife—his late wife—was an
       invalid,—and rarely left her room. So I had to look after the
       housekeeping as well.

HEDDA: And then—at last—you became mistress of the house.

MRS. ELVSTED: [Sadly.] Yes, I did.

HEDDA: Let me see—about how long ago was that?

MRS. ELVSTED: My marriage?

HEDDA: Yes.

MRS. ELVSTED: Five years ago.

HEDDA: To be sure; it must be that.

MRS. ELVSTED: Oh those five years—! Or at all events the last two or three of them!
       Oh, if you[6] could only imagine—

HEDDA: [Giving her a little slap on the hand.] De? Fie, Thea!

MRS. ELVSTED: Yes, yes, I will try—. Well, if—you could only imagine and
       understand—

HEDDA: [Lightly.] Eilert Lovborg has been in your neighbourhood about three years,
       hasn't he?

MRS. ELVSTED: [Looks at here doubtfully.] Eilert Lovborg? Yes—he has.

HEDDA: Had you known him before, in town here?

MRS. ELVSTED: Scarcely at all. I mean—I knew him by name of course.

HEDDA: But you saw a good deal of him in the country?

MRS. ELVSTED: Yes, he came to us every day. You see, he gave the children lessons;
       for in the long run I couldn't manage it all myself.

HEDDA: No, that's clear.—And your husband—? I suppose he is often away from
       home?

---

4 See previous note.
5 Pronounce "Tora" and "Taya".

6 Mrs. Elvsted here uses the formal pronoun "De",
whereupon Hedda rebukes her. In her next speech Mrs.
Elvsted says "du".

MRS. ELVSTED: Yes. Being sheriff, you know, he has to travel about a good deal in his district.

HEDDA: [Leaning against the arm of the chair.] Thea—my poor, sweet Thea— now you must tell me everything—exactly as it stands.

MRS. ELVSTED: Well, then you must question me.

HEDDA: What sort of a man is your husband, Thea? I mean—you know—in everyday life. Is he kind to you?

MRS. ELVSTED: [Evasively.] I am sure he means well in everything.

HEDDA: I should think he must be altogether too old for you. There is at least twenty years' difference between you, is there not?

MRS. ELVSTED: [Irritably.] Yes, that is true, too. Everything about him is repellent to me! We have not a thought in common. We have no single point of sympathy—he and I.

HEDDA: But is he not fond of you all the same? In his own way?

MRS. ELVSTED: Oh I really don't know. I think he regards me simply as a useful
585   property. And then it doesn't cost much to keep me. I am not expensive.

HEDDA: That is stupid of you.

MRS. ELVSTED: [Shakes her head.] It cannot be otherwise—not with him. I don't think he really cares for any one but himself—and perhaps a little for the children.

HEDDA: And for Eilert Lovborg, Thea?

MRS. ELVSTED: [Looking at her.] For Eilert Lovborg? What puts that into your head?

HEDDA: Well, my dear—I should say, when he sends you after him all the way to town— [Smiling almost imperceptibly.] And besides, you said so yourself, to Tesman.

MRS. ELVSTED: [With a little nervous twitch.] Did I? Yes, I suppose I did. [Vehemently, but not loudly.] No—I may just as well make a clean breast of it at once! For it must all come out in any case.

HEDDA: Why, my dear Thea—?

MRS. ELVSTED: Well, to make a long story short: My husband did not know that I
600   was coming.

HEDDA: What! Your husband didn't know it!

MRS. ELVSTED: No, of course not. For that matter, he was away from home himself— he was travelling. Oh, I could bear it no longer, Hedda! I couldn't indeed—so utterly alone as I should have been in future.

HEDDA: Well? And then?

MRS. ELVSTED: So I put together some of my things—what I needed most—as quietly as possible. And then I left the house.

HEDDA: Without a word?

MRS. ELVSTED: Yes—and took the train to town.

HEDDA: Why, my dear, good Thea—to think of you daring to do it!

MRS. ELVSTED: [Rises and moves about the room.] What else could I possibly do?

HEDDA: But what do you think your husband will say when you go home again?

MRS. ELVSTED: [At the table, looks at her.] Back to him?

HEDDA: Of course.

MRS. ELVSTED: I shall never go back to him again.

HEDDA: [Rising and going towards her.] Then you have left your home—for good and all?

MRS. ELVSTED: Yes. There was nothing else to be done.

HEDDA: But then—to take flight so openly.

MRS. ELVSTED: Oh, it's impossible to keep things of that sort secret.

HEDDA: But what do you think people will say of you, Thea?

MRS. ELVSTED: They may say what they like, for aught *I* care. [Seats herself wearily
        and sadly on the sofa.] I have done nothing but what I had to do.

HEDDA: [After a short silence.] And what are your plans now? What do you think of
625   doing.

MRS. ELVSTED: I don't know yet. I only know this, that I must live here, where Eilert
        Lovborg is—if I am to live at all.

HEDDA: [Takes a chair from the table, seats herself beside her, and strokes her
        hands.] My dear Thea—how did this—this friendship—between you and
630   Eilert Lovborg come about?

MRS. ELVSTED: Oh it grew up gradually. I gained a sort of influence over him.

HEDDA: Indeed?

MRS. ELVSTED: He gave up his old habits. Not because I asked him to, for I never
        dared do that. But of course he saw how repulsive they were to me; and
635   so he dropped them.

HEDDA: [Concealing an involuntary smile of scorn.] Then you have reclaimed him—
        as the saying goes—my little Thea.

MRS. ELVSTED: So he says himself, at any rate. And he, on his side, has made a real
        human being of me—taught me to think, and to understand so many
640   things.

HEDDA: Did he give you lessons too, then?

MRS. ELVSTED: No, not exactly lessons. But he talked to me—talked about such an
        infinity of things. And then came the lovely, happy time when I began to
        share in his work—when he allowed me to help him!

HEDDA: Oh he did, did he?

MRS. ELVSTED: Yes! He never wrote anything without my assistance.

HEDDA: You were two good comrades, in fact?

MRS. ELVSTED: [Eagerly.] Comrades! Yes, fancy, Hedda—that is the very word he
        used!—Oh, I ought to feel perfectly happy; and yet I cannot; for I don't
650   know how long it will last.

HEDDA: Are you no surer of him than that?

MRS. ELVSTED: [Gloomily.] A woman's shadow stands between Eilert Lovborg and
        me.

HEDDA: [Looks at her anxiously.] Who can that be?

MRS. ELVSTED: I don't know. Some one he knew in his—in his past. Some one he has
        never been able wholly to forget.

HEDDA: What has he told you—about this?

MRS. ELVSTED: He has only once—quite vaguely—alluded to it.

HEDDA: Well! And what did he say?

MRS. ELVSTED: He said that when they parted, she threatened to shoot him with a
        pistol.

HEDDA: [With cold composure.] Oh nonsense! No one does that sort of thing here.

MRS. ELVSTED: No. And that is why I think it must have been that red-haired singing-
        woman whom he once—

HEDDA: Yes, very likely.

MRS. ELVSTED: For I remember they used to say of her that she carried loaded
        firearms.

HEDDA: Oh—then of course it must have been she.

MRS. ELVSTED: [Wringing her hands.] And now just fancy, Hedda—I hear that this
670   singing-woman—that she is in town again! Oh, I don't know what to
        do—

HEDDA: [Glancing towards the inner room.] Hush! Here comes Tesman. [Rises and
        whispers.] Thea—all this must remain between you and me.

MRS. ELVSTED: [Springing up.] Oh yes—yes! For heaven's sake—!

675   GEORGE TESMAN, with a letter in his hand, comes from the right
        through the inner room.

TESMAN: There now—the epistle is finished.

HEDDA: That's right. And now Mrs. Elvsted is just going. Wait a moment—I'll go
        with you to the garden gate.

TESMAN: Do you think Berta could post the letter, Hedda dear?

HEDDA: [Takes it.] I will tell her to. BERTA enters from the hall.

BERTA: Judge Brack wishes to know if Mrs. Tesman will receive him.

HEDDA: Yes, ask Judge Brack to come in. And look here—put this letter in the post.

BERTA: [Taking the letter.] Yes, ma'am.

685   [She opens the door for JUDGE BRACK and goes out herself. Brack is a
        main of forty-five; thick set, but well-built and elastic in his movements.
        His face is roundish with an aristocratic profile. His hair is short, still
        almost black, and carefully dressed. His eyebrows thick. His moustaches
        are also thick, with short-cut ends. He wears a well-cut walking-suit, a
690   little too youthful for his age. He uses an eye-glass, which he now and
        then lets drop.

JUDGE BRACK: [With his hat in his hand, bowing.] May one venture to call so early in
        the day?

HEDDA: Of course one may.

TESMAN: [Presses his hand.] You are welcome at any time. [Introducing him.] Judge
        Brack—Miss Rysing—

HEDDA: Oh—!

BRACK: [Bowing.] Ah—delighted—

HEDDA: [Looks at him and laughs.] It's nice to have a look at you by daylight, Judge

BRACK: So you find me—altered?

HEDDA: A little younger, I think.

BRACK: Thank you so much.

TESMAN: But what do you think of Hedda—eh? Doesn't she look flourishing? She
        has actually—

HEDDA: Oh, do leave me alone. You haven't thanked Judge Brack for all the trouble
        he has taken—

BRACK: Oh, nonsense—it was a pleasure to me—

HEDDA: Yes, you are a friend indeed. But here stands Thea all impatience to be off—
        so "au revoir" Judge. I shall be back again presently.

710   [Mutual salutations. MRS. ELVSTED and HEDDA go out by the hall
        door.

BRACK: Well,—is your wife tolerably satisfied—

TESMAN: Yes, we can't thank you sufficiently. Of course she talks of a little re-
arrangement here and there; and one or two things are still wanting. We
715   shall have to buy some additional trifles.

BRACK: Indeed!

TESMAN: But we won't trouble you about these things. Hedda say she herself will
look after what is wanting.—Shan't we sit down? Eh?

BRACK: Thanks, for a moment. [Seats himself beside the table.] There is something I
720   wanted to speak to about, my dear Tesman.

TESMAN: Indeed? Ah, I understand! [Seating himself.] I suppose it's the serious part
of the frolic that is coming now. Eh?

BRACK: Oh, the money question is not so very pressing; though, for that matter, I
wish we had gone a little more economically to work.

TESMAN: But that would never have done, you know! Think of Hedda, my dear
fellow! You, who know her so well—! I couldn't possibly ask her to put
up with a shabby style of living!

BRACK: No, no—that is just the difficulty.

TESMAN: And then—fortunately—it can't be long before I receive my appointment.

BRACK: Well, you see—such things are often apt to hang fire for a long time.

TESMAN: Have you heard anything definite? Eh?

BRACK: Nothing exactly definite—. [Interrupting himself.] But by-the-bye —I have
one piece of news for you.

TESMAN: Well?

BRACK: Your old friend, Eilert Lovborg, has returned to town.

TESMAN: I know that already.

BRACK: Indeed! How did you learn it?

TESMAN: From that lady who went out with Hedda.

BRACK: Really? What was her name? I didn't quite catch it.

TESMAN: Mrs. Elvsted.

BRACK: Aha—Sheriff Elvsted's wife? Of course—he has been living up in their
regions.

TESMAN: And fancy—I'm delighted to hear that he is quite a reformed character.

BRACK: So they say.

TESMAN: And then he has published a new book—eh?

BRACK: Yes, indeed he has.

TESMAN: And I hear it has made some sensation!

BRACK: Quite an unusual sensation.

TESMAN: Fancy—isn't that good news! A man of such extraordinary talents—I felt
750   so grieved to think that he had gone irretrievably to ruin.

BRACK: That was what everybody thought.

TESMAN: But I cannot imagine what he will take to now! How in the world will he be
able to make his living? Eh?
[During the last words, HEDDA has entered by the hall door.]

HEDDA: [To BRACK, laughing with a touch of scorn.] Tesman is for ever worrying
about how people are to make their living.

TESMAN: Well you see, dear—we were talking about poor Eilert Lovborg.

HEDDA: [Glancing at him rapidly.] Oh, indeed? [Sets herself in the armchair beside
the stove and asks indifferently:] What is the matter with him?

TESMAN: Well—no doubt he has run through all his property long ago; and he can scarcely write a new book every year—eh? So I really can't see what is to become of him.

BRACK: Perhaps I can give you some information on that point.

TESMAN: Indeed!

BRACK: You must remember that his relations have a good deal of influence.

TESMAN: Oh, his relations, unfortunately, have entirely washed their hands o him.

BRACK: At one time they called him the hope of the family.

TESMAN: At one time, yes! But he has put an end to all that.

HEDDA: Who knows? [With a slight smile.] I hear they have reclaimed him up at
770   Sheriff Elvsted's—

BRACK: And then this book that he has published—

TESMAN: Well well, I hope to goodness they may find something for him to do. I have just written to him. I asked him to come and see us this evening, Hedda dear.

BRACK: But my dear fellow, you are booked for my bachelor's party this evening. You promised on the pier last night.

HEDDA: Had you forgotten, Tesman?

TESMAN: Yes, I had utterly forgotten.

BRACK: But it doesn't matter, for you may be sure he won't come.

TESMAN: What makes you think that? Eh?

BRACK: [With a little hesitation, rising and resting his hands on the back of his chair.] My dear Tesman—and you too, Mrs. Tesman—I think I ought not to keep you in the dark about something that—that—

TESMAN: That concerns Eilert—?

BRACK: Both you and him.

TESMAN: Well, my dear Judge, out with it.

BRACK: You must be prepared to find your appointment deferred longer than you desired or expected.

TESMAN: [Jumping up uneasily.] Is there some hitch about it? Eh?

BRACK: The nomination may perhaps be made conditional on the result of a competition—

TESMAN: Competition! Think of that, Hedda!

HEDDA: [Leans further back in the chair.] Aha—aha!

TESMAN: But who can my competitor be? Surely not—?

BRACK: Yes, precisely—Eilert Lovborg.

TESMAN: [Clasping his hands.] No, no—it's quite impossible! Eh?

BRACK: H'm—that is what it may come to, all the same.

TESMAN: Well but, Judge Brack—it would show the most incredible lack of consideration for me. [Gesticulates with his arms.] For—just think—I'm
800   a married man! We have married on the strength of these prospects, Hedda and I; and run deep into debt; and borrowed money from Aunt Julia too. Good heavens, they had as good as promised me the appointment. Eh?

BRACK: Well, well, well—no doubt you will get it in the end; only after a contest.

HEDDA: [Immovable in her arm-chair.] Fancy, Tesman, there will be a sort of sporting interest in that.

TESMAN: Why, my dearest Hedda, how can you be so indifferent about it?

HEDDA: [As before.] I am not at all indifferent. I am most eager to see who wins.

BRACK: In any case, Mrs. Tesman, it is best that you should know how matters stand.
810   I mean—before you set about the little purchases I hear you are threatening.

HEDDA: This can make no difference.

BRACK: Indeed! Then I have no more to say. Good-bye! [To TESMAN.] I shall look in on my way back from my afternoon walk, and take you home with
815   me.

TESMAN: Oh yes, yes—your news has quite upset me.

HEDDA: [Reclining, holds out her hand.] Good-bye, Judge; and be sure you call in the afternoon.

BRACK: Many thanks. Good-bye, good-bye!

TESMAN: [Accompanying him to the door.] Good-bye my dear Judge! You must really excuse me— [JUDGE BRACK goes out by the hall door.]

TESMAN: [Crosses the room.] Oh Hedda—one should never rush into adventures. Eh?

HEDDA: [Looks at him, smiling.] Do you do that?

TESMAN: Yes, dear—there is no denying—it was adventurous to go and marry and
825   set up house upon mere expectations.

HEDDA: Perhaps you are right there.

TESMAN: Well—at all events, we have our delightful home, Hedda! Fancy, the home we both dreamed of—the home we were in love with, I may almost say. Eh?

HEDDA: [Rising slowly and wearily.] It was part of our compact that we were to go into society—to keep open house.

TESMAN: Yes, if you only knew how I had been looking forward to it! Fancy—to see you as hostess—in a select circle! Eh? Well, well, well—for the present we shall have to get on without society, Hedda—only to invite Aunt
835   Julia now and then.—Oh, I intended you to lead such an utterly different life, dear—!

HEDDA: Of course I cannot have my man in livery just yet.

TESMAN: Oh, no, unfortunately. It would be out of the question for us to keep a footman, you know.

HEDDA: And the saddle-horse I was to have had—

TESMAN: [Aghast.] The saddle-horse!

HEDDA: —I suppose I must not think of that now.

TESMAN: Good heavens, no!—that's as clear as daylight!

HEDDA: [Goes up the room.] Well, I shall have one thing at least to kill time with in
845   the meanwhile.

TESMAN: [Beaming.] Oh thank heaven for that! What is it, Hedda. Eh?

HEDDA: [In the middle doorway, looks at him with covert scorn.] My pistols, George.

TESMAN: [In alarm.] Your pistols!

HEDDA: [With cold eyes.] General Gabler's pistols.
     [She goes out through the inner room, to the left.]

TESMAN: [Rushes up to the middle doorway and calls after her:] No, for heaven's sake, Hedda darling—don't touch those dangerous things! For my sake Hedda! Eh?

ACT SECOND

The room at the TESMANS' as in the first Act, except that the piano has been removed, and an elegant little writing-table with the book-shelves put in its place. A smaller table stands near the sofa on the left. Most of the bouquets have been taken away. MRS. ELVSTED'S bouquet is upon the large table in front.—It is afternoon.

HEDDA, dressed to receive callers, is alone in the room. She stands by the open glass door, loading a revolver. The fellow to it lies in an open pistol-case on the writing-table.

HEDDA: [Looks down the garden, and calls:] So you are here again, Judge!
BRACK: [Is heard calling from a distance.] As you see, Mrs. Tesman!
HEDDA: [Raises the pistol and points.] Now I'll shoot you, Judge Brack!
BRACK: [Calling unseen.] No, no, no! Don't stand aiming at me!
HEDDA: This is what comes of sneaking in by the back way.[7] [She fires.]
BRACK: [Nearer.] Are you out of your senses—!
HEDDA: Dear me—did I happen to hit you?
BRACK: [Still outside.] I wish you would let these pranks alone!
HEDDA: Come in then, Judge.
10   JUDGE BRACK, dressed as though for a men's party, enters by the glass door. He carries a light overcoat over his arm.
BRACK: What the deuce—haven't you tired of that sport, yet? What are you shooting at?
HEDDA: Oh, I am only firing in the air.
BRACK: [Gently takes the pistol out of her hand.] Allow me, madam! [Looks at it.] Ah—I know this pistol well! [Looks around.] Where is the case? Ah, here it is. [Lays the pistol in it, and shuts it.] Now we won't play at that game any more to-day.
HEDDA: Then what in heaven's name would you have me do with myself?
BRACK: Have you had no visitors?
HEDDA: [Closing the glass door.] Not one. I suppose all our set are still out of town.
BRACK: And is Tesman not at home either?
HEDDA: [At the writing-table, putting the pistol-case in a drawer which she shuts.] No. He rushed off to his aunt's directly after lunch; he didn't expect you
25   so early.
BRACK: H'm—how stupid of me not to have thought of that!
HEDDA: [Turning her head to look at him.] Why stupid?
BRACK: Because if I had thought of it I should have come a little—earlier.
HEDDA: [Crossing the room.] Then you would have found no one to receive you; for
30   I have been in my room changing my dress ever since lunch.
BRACK: And is there no sort of little chink that we could hold a parley through?
HEDDA: You have forgotten to arrange one.
BRACK: That was another piece of stupidity.
HEDDA: Well, we must just settle down here—and wait. Tesman is not likely to be
35   back for some time yet.
BRACK: Never mind; I shall not be impatient.

---

7 "Bagveje" means both "back ways" and "underhand courses."

HEDDA seats herself in the corner of the sofa. BRACK lays his overcoat over the back of the nearest chair, and sits down, but keeps his hat in his hand. A short silence. They look at each other.

HEDDA: Well?

BRACK: [In the same tone.] Well?

HEDDA: I spoke first.

BRACK: [Bending a little forward.] Come, let us have a cosy little chat, Mrs. Hedda.[8]

HEDDA: [Leaning further back in the sofa.] Does it not seem like a whole eternity since our last talk? Of course I don't count those few words yesterday evening and this morning.

BRACK: You mean since out last confidential talk? Our last "tete-a-tete"?

HEDDA: Well yes—since you put it so.

BRACK: Not a day passed but I have wished that you were home again.

HEDDA: And I have done nothing but wish the same thing.

BRACK: You? Really, Mrs. Hedda? And I thought you had been enjoying your tour so much!

HEDDA: Oh yes, you may be sure of that!

BRACK: But Tesman's letters spoke of nothing but happiness.

HEDDA: Oh, Tesman! You see, he thinks nothing is so delightful as grubbing in libraries and making copies of old parchments, or whatever you call them.

BRACK: [With a smile of malice.] Well, that is his vocation in life—or part of it at
60   any rate.

HEDDA: Yes, of course; and no doubt when it's your vocation—. But *I*! Oh, my dear Mr. Brack, how mortally bored I have been.

BRACK: [Sympathetically.] Do you really say so? In downright earnest?

HEDDA: Yes, you can surely understand it—! To go for six whole months without
65   meeting a soul that knew anything of our circle, or could talk about things we were interested in.

BRACK: Yes, yes—I too should feel that a deprivation.

HEDDA: And then, what I found most intolerable of all—

BRACK: Well?

HEDDA: —was being everlastingly in the company of—one and the same person—

BRACK: [With a nod of assent.] Morning, noon, and night, yes—at all possible times and seasons.

HEDDA: I said "everlastingly."

BRACK: Just so. But I should have thought, with our excellent Tesman, one could—

HEDDA: Tesman is—a specialist, my dear Judge.

BRACK: Undeniable.

HEDDA: And specialists are not at all amusing to travel with. Not in the long run at any rate.

BRACK: Not even—the specialist one happens to love?

HEDDA: Faugh—don't use that sickening word!

BRACK: [Taken aback.] What do you say, Mrs. Hedda?

---

8 As this form of address is contrary to English usage, and as the note of familiarity would be lacking in "Mrs. Tesman," Brack may, in stage representation, say "Miss Hedda," thus ignoring her marriage and reverting to the form of address no doubt customarry between them of old.

HEDDA: [Half laughing, half irritated.] You should just try it! To hear of nothing but the history of civilisation, morning, noon, and night—

BRACK: Everlastingly.

HEDDA: Yes yes yes! And then all this about the domestic industry of the middle ages—! That's the most disgusting part of it!

BRACK: [Looks searchingly at her.] But tell me—in that case, how am I to understand your—? H'm—

HEDDA: My accepting George Tesman, you mean?

BRACK: Well, let us put it so.

HEDDA: Good heavens, do you see anything so wonderful in that?

BRACK: Yes and no—Mrs. Hedda.

HEDDA: I had positively danced myself tired, my dear Judge. My day was done— [With a slight shudder.] Oh no—I won't say that; nor think it either!

BRACK: You have assuredly no reason to.

HEDDA: Oh, reasons— [Watching him closely.] And George Tesman—after all, you must admit that he is correctness itself.

BRACK: His correctness and respectability are beyond all question.

HEDDA: And I don't see anything absolutely ridiculous about him.—Do you?

BRACK: Ridiculous? N—no—I shouldn't exactly say so—

HEDDA: Well—and his powers of research, at all events, are untiring.—I see no reason why he should not one day come to the front, after all.

BRACK: [Looks at her hesitatingly.] I thought that you, like every one else, expected him to attain the highest distinction.

HEDDA: [With an expression of fatigue.] Yes, so I did.—And then, since he was bent, at all hazards, on being allowed to provide for me—I really don't know why I should not have accepted his offer?

BRACK: No—if you look at it in that light—

HEDDA: It was more than my other adorers were prepared to do for me, my dear
110   Judge.

BRACK: [Laughing.] Well, I can't answer for all the rest; but as for myself, you know quite well that I have always entertained a—a certain respect for the marriage tie—for marriage as an institution, Mrs. Hedda.

HEDDA: [Jestingly.] Oh, I assure you I have never cherished any hopes with respect
115   to you.

BRACK: All I require is a pleasant and intimate interior, where I can make myself useful in every way, and am free to come and go as—as a trusted friend—

HEDDA: Of the master of the house, do you mean?

BRACK: [Bowing.] Frankly—of the mistress first of all; but of course of the master too, in the second place. Such a triangular friendship—if I may call it so—is really a great convenience for all the parties, let me tell you.

HEDDA: Yes, I have many a time longed for some one to make a third on our travels. Oh—those railway-carriage "tete-a-tetes"—!

BRACK: Fortunately your wedding journey is over now.

HEDDA: [Shaking her head.] Not by a long—long way. I have only arrived at a station on the line.

BRACK: Well, then the passengers jump out and move about a little, Mrs. Hedda.

HEDDA: I never jump out.

BRACK: Really?

HEDDA: No—because there is always some one standing by to—

BRACK: [Laughing.] To look at your ankles, do you mean?

HEDDA: Precisely.

BRACK: Well but, dear me—

HEDDA: [With a gesture of repulsion.] I won't have it. I would rather keep my seat where I happen to be—and continue the "tete-a-tete".

BRACK: But suppose a third person were to jump in and join the couple.

HEDDA: Ah—that is quite another matter!

BRACK: A trusted, sympathetic friend—

HEDDA: —with a fund of conversation on all sorts of lively topics—

BRACK: —and not the least bit of a specialist!

HEDDA: [With an audible sigh.] Yes, that would be a relief indeed.

BRACK: [Hears the front door open, and glances in that direction.] The triangle is completed.

HEDDA: [Half aloud.] And on goes the train.

GEORGE TESMAN, in a grey walking-suit, with a soft felt hat, enters from the hall. He has a number of unbound books under his arm and in his pockets.

TESMAN: [Goes up to the table beside the corner settee.] Ouf—what a load for a warm day—all these books. [Lays them on the table.] I'm positively
150   perspiring, Hedda. Hallo—are you there already, my dear Judge? Eh? Berta didn't tell me.

BRACK: [Rising.] I came in through the garden.

HEDDA: What books have you got there?

TESMAN: [Stands looking them through.] Some new books on my special subjects—
155   quite indispensable to me.

HEDDA: Your special subjects?

BRACK: Yes, books on his special subjects, Mrs. Tesman.
        [BRACK and HEDDA exchange a confidential smile.]

HEDDA: Do you need still more books on your special subjects?

TESMAN: Yes, my dear Hedda, one can never have too many of them. Of course one must keep up with all that is written and published.

HEDDA: Yes, I suppose one must.

TESMAN: [Searching among his books.] And look here—I have got hold of Eilert Lovborg's new book too. [Offering it to her.] Perhaps you would like to
165   glance through it, Hedda? Eh?

HEDDA: No, thank you. Or rather—afterwards perhaps.

TESMAN: I looked into it a little on the way home.

BRACK: Well, what do you think of it—as a specialist?

TESMAN: I think it shows quite remarkable soundness of judgment. He never wrote
170   like that before. [Putting the books together.] Now I shall take all these into my study. I'm longing to cut the leaves—! And then I must change my clothes. [To BRACK] I suppose we needn't start just yet? Eh?

BRACK: Oh, dear no—there is not the slightest hurry.

TESMAN: Well then, I will take my time. [Is going with his books, but stops in the
175   doorway and turns.] By-the-bye, Hedda—Aunt Julia is not coming this evening.

HEDDA: Not coming? Is it that affair of the bonnet that keeps her away?

TESMAN: Oh, not at all. How could you think such a thing of Aunt Julia? Just fancy—! The fact is, Aunt Rina is very ill.

HEDDA: She always is.

TESMAN: Yes, but to-day she is much worse than usual, poor dear.

HEDDA: Oh, then it's only natural that her sister should remain with her. I must bear my disappointment.

TESMAN: And you can't imagine, dear, how delighted Aunt Julia seemed to be—
185   because you had come home looking so flourishing!

HEDDA: [Half aloud, rising.] Oh, those everlasting Aunts!

TESMAN: What?

HEDDA: [Going to the glass door.] Nothing.

TESMAN: Oh, all right. [He goes through the inner room, out to the right.]

BRACK: What bonnet were you talking about?

HEDDA: Oh, it was a little episode with Miss Tesman this morning. She had laid down her bonnet on the chair there—[Looks at him and smiles.]—and I pretended to think it was the servant's.

BRACK: [Shaking his head.] Now my dear Mrs. Hedda, how could you do such a
195   thing? To the excellent old lady, too!

HEDDA: [Nervously crossing the room.] Well, you see—these impulses come over me all of a sudden; and I cannot resist them. [Throws herself down in the easy-chair by the stove.] Oh, I don't know how to explain it.

BRACK: [Behind the easy-chair.] You are not really happy—that is at the bottom of
200   it.

HEDDA: [Looking straight before her.] I know of no reason why I should be—happy. Perhaps you can give me one?

BRACK: Well-amongst other things, because you have got exactly the home you had set your heart on.

HEDDA: [Looks up at him and laughs.] Do you too believe in that legend?

BRACK: Is there nothing in it, then?

HEDDA: Oh yes, there is something in it.

BRACK: Well?

HEDDA: There is this in it, that I made use of Tesman to see me home from evening
210   parties last summer—

BRACK: I, unfortunately, had to go quite a different way.

HEDDA: That's true. I know you were going a different way last summer.

BRACK: [Laughing.] Oh fie, Mrs. Hedda! Well, then—you and Tesman—?

HEDDA: Well, we happened to pass here one evening; Tesman, poor fellow, was
215   writhing in the agony of having to find conversation; so I took pity on the learned man—

BRACK: [Smiles doubtfully.] You took pity? H'm—

HEDDA: Yes, I really did. And so—to help him out of his torment—I happened to say, in pure thoughtlessness, that I should like to live in this villa.

BRACK: No more than that?

HEDDA: Not that evening.

BRACK: But afterwards?

HEDDA: Yes, my thoughtlessness had consequences, my dear Judge.

BRACK: Unfortunately that too often happens, Mrs. Hedda.

HEDDA: Thanks! So you see it was this enthusiasm for Secretary Falk's villa that first constituted a bond of sympathy between George Tesman and me. From that came our engagement and our marriage, and our wedding journey, and all the rest of it. Well, well, my dear Judge—as you make your bed so you must lie, I could almost say.

BRACK: This is exquisite! And you really cared not a rap about it all the time?

HEDDA: No, heaven knows I didn't.

BRACK: But now? Now that we have made it so homelike for you?

HEDDA: Uh—the rooms all seem to smell of lavender and dried rose-leaves.—But perhaps it's Aunt Julia that has brought that scent with her.

BRACK: [Laughing.] No, I think it must be a legacy from the late Mrs. Secretary Falk.

HEDDA: Yes, there is an odour of mortality about it. It reminds me of a bouquet—the day after the ball. [Clasps her hands behind her head, leans back in her chair and looks at him.] Oh, my dear Judge—you cannot imagine how
240   horribly I shall bore myself here.

BRACK: Why should not you, too, find some sort of vocation in life, Mrs. Hedda?

HEDDA: A vocation—that should attract me?

BRACK: If possible, of course.

HEDDA: Heaven knows what sort of a vocation that could be. I often wonder
245   whether— [Breaking off.] But that would never do either.

BRACK: Who can tell? Let me hear what it is.

HEDDA: Whether I might not get Tesman to go into politics, I mean.

BRACK: [Laughing.] Tesman? No really now, political life is not the thing for him— not at all in his line.

HEDDA: No, I daresay not.—But if I could get him into it all the same?

BRACK: Why—what satisfaction could you find in that? If he is not fitted for that sort of thing, why should you want to drive him into it?

HEDDA: Because I am bored, I tell you! [After a pause.] So you think it quite out of the question that Tesman should ever get into the ministry?

BRACK: H'm—you see, my dear Mrs. Hedda—to get into the ministry, he would have to be a tolerably rich man.

HEDDA: [Rising impatiently.] Yes, there we have it! It is this genteel poverty I have managed to drop into—! [Crosses the room.] That is what makes life so pitiable! So utterly ludicrous!—For that's what it is.

BRACK: Now *I* should say the fault lay elsewhere.

HEDDA: Where, then?

BRACK: You have never gone through any really stimulating experience.

HEDDA: Anything serious, you mean?

BRACK: Yes, you may call it so. But now you may perhaps have one in store.

HEDDA: [Tossing her head.] Oh, you're thinking of the annoyances about this wretched professorship! But that must be Tesman's own affair. I assure you I shall not waste a thought upon it.

BRACK: No, no, I daresay not. But suppose now that what people call—in elegant language—a solemn responsibility were to come upon you? [Smiling.] A
270   new responsibility, Mrs. Hedda?

HEDDA: [Angrily.] Be quiet! Nothing of that sort will ever happen!

BRACK: [Warily.] We will speak of this again a year hence—at the very outside.

HEDDA: [Curtly.] I have no turn for anything of the sort, Judge Brack. No
　　　　responsibilities for me!

BRACK: Are you so unlike the generality of women as to have no turn for duties
　　　　which—?

HEDDA: [Beside the glass door.] Oh, be quiet, I tell you!—I often think there is only
　　　　one thing in the world I have any turn for.

BRACK: [Drawing near to her.] And what is that, if I may ask?

HEDDA: [Stands looking out.] Boring myself to death. Now you know it. [Turns,
　　　　looks towards the inner room, and laughs.] Yes, as I thought! Here
　　　　comes the Professor.

BRACK: [Softly, in a tone of warning.] Come, come, come, Mrs. Hedda!

　　　　GEORGE TESMAN, dressed for the party, with his gloves and hat in his
285　　hand, enters from the right through the inner room.

TESMAN: Hedda, has no message come from Eilert Lovborg? Eh?

HEDDA: No.

TESMAN: Then you'll see he'll be here presently.

BRACK: Do you really think he will come?

TESMAN: Yes, I am almost sure of it. For what you were telling us this morning must
　　　　have been a mere floating rumour.

BRACK: You think so?

TESMAN: At any rate, Aunt Julia said she did not believe for a moment that he would
　　　　ever stand in my way again. Fancy that!

BRACK: Well then, that's all right.

TESMAN: [Placing his hat and gloves on a chair on the right.] Yes, but you must
　　　　really let me wait for him as long as possible.

BRACK: We have plenty of time yet. None of my guests will arrive before seven or
　　　　half-past.

TESMAN: Then meanwhile we can keep Hedda company, and see what happens. Eh?

HEDDA: [Placing BRACK'S hat and overcoat upon the corner settee.] And at the
　　　　worst Mr. Lovborg can remain here with me.

BRACK: [Offering to take his things.] Oh, allow me, Mrs. Tesman!—What do you
　　　　mean by "At the worst"?

HEDDA: If he won't go with you and Tesman.

TESMAN: [Looks dubiously at her.] But, Hedda dear—do you think it would quite do
　　　　for him to remain here with you? Eh? Remember, Aunt Julia can't come.

HEDDA: No, but Mrs. Elvsted is coming. We three can have a cup of tea together.

TESMAN: Oh yes, that will be all right.

BRACK: [Smiling.] And that would perhaps be the safest plan for him.

HEDDA: Why so?

BRACK: Well, you know, Mrs. Tesman, how you used to gird at my little bachelor
　　　　parties. You declared they were adapted only for men of the strictest
　　　　principles.

HEDDA: But no doubt Mr. Lovborg's principles are strict enough now. A converted
　　　　sinner— [BERTA appears at the hall door.]

BERTA: There's a gentleman asking if you are at home, ma'am—

HEDDA: Well, show him in.

TESMAN: [Softly.] I'm sure it is he! Fancy that!

320   EILERT LOVBORG enters from the hall. He is slim and lean; of the same age as TESMAN, but looks older and somewhat worn-out. His hair and beard are of a blackish brown, his face long and pale, but with patches of colour on the cheeks. He is dressed in a well-cut black visiting suit, quite new. He has dark gloves and a silk hat. He stops near the door,
325   and makes a rapid bow, seeming somewhat embarrassed.

TESMAN: [Goes up to him and shakes him warmly by the hand.] Well, my dear Eilert—so at last we meet again!

EILERT LOVBORG: [Speaks in a subdued voice.] Thanks for your letter, Tesman. [Approaching HEDDA.] Will you too shake hands with me, Mrs.
330   Tesman?

HEDDA: [Taking his hand.] I am glad to see you, Mr. Lovborg. [With a motion of her hand.] I don't know whether you two gentlemen—?

LOVBORG: [Bowing slightly.] Judge Brack, I think.

BRACK: [Doing likewise.] Oh yes,—in the old days—

TESMAN: [To LOVBORG, with his hands on his shoulders.] And now you must make yourself entirely at home, Eilert! Mustn't he, Hedda?—For I hear you are going to settle in town again? Eh?

LOVBORG: Yes, I am.

TESMAN: Quite right, quite right. Let me tell you, I have got hold of your new book;
340   but I haven't had time to read it yet.

LOVBORG: You may spare yourself the trouble.

TESMAN: Why so?

LOVBORG: Because there is very little in it.

TESMAN: Just fancy—how can you say so?

BRACK: But it has been very much praised, I hear.

LOVBORG: That was what I wanted; so I put nothing into the book but what every one would agree with.

BRACK: Very wise of you.

TESMAN: Well but, my dear Eilert—!

LOVBORG: For now I mean to win myself a position again—to make a fresh start.

TESMAN: [A little embarrassed.] Ah, that is what you wish to do? Eh?

LOVBORG: [Smiling, lays down his hat, and draws a packet wrapped in paper, from his coat pocket.] But when this one appears, George Tesman, you will have to read it. For this is the real book—the book I have put my true
355   self into.

TESMAN: Indeed? And what is it?

LOVBORG: It is the continuation.

TESMAN: The continuation? Of what?

LOVBORG: Of the book.

TESMAN: Of the new book?

LOVBORG: Of course.

TESMAN: Why, my dear Eilert—does it not come down to our own days?

LOVBORG: Yes, it does; and this one deals with the future.

TESMAN: With the future! But, good heavens, we know nothing of the future!

LOVBORG: No; but there is a thing or two to be said about it all the same. [Opens the packet.] Look here—

TESMAN: Why, that's not your handwriting.

LOVBORG: I dictated it. [Turning over the pages.] It falls into two sections. The first
          deals with the civilising forces of the future. And here is the second—
370   [running through the pages towards the end]—forecasting the probable
          line of development.
TESMAN: How odd now! I should never have thought of writing anything of that sort.
HEDDA: [At the glass door, drumming on the pane.] H'm—. I daresay not.
LOVBORG: [Replacing the manuscript in its paper and laying the packet on the table.]
375   I brought it, thinking I might read you a little of it this evening.
TESMAN: That was very good of you, Eilert. But this evening—? [Looking back at
          BRACK] I don't see how we can manage it—
LOVBORG: Well then, some other time. There is no hurry.
BRACK: I must tell you, Mr. Lovborg—there is a little gathering at my house this
380   evening—mainly in honour of Tesman, you know—
LOVBORG: [Looking for his hat.] Oh—then I won't detain you—
BRACK: No, but listen—will you not do me the favour of joining us?
LOVBORG: [Curtly and decidedly.] No, I can't—thank you very much.
BRACK: Oh, nonsense—do! We shall be quite a select little circle. And I assure you
385   we shall have a "lively time," as Mrs. Hed—as Mrs. Tesman says.
LOVBORG: I have no doubt of it. But nevertheless—
BRACK: And then you might bring your manuscript with you, and read it to Tesman
          at my house. I could give you a room to yourselves.
TESMAN: Yes, think of that, Eilert,—why shouldn't you? Eh?
HEDDA: [Interposing.] But, Tesman, if Mr. Lovborg would really rather not! I am
          sure Mr. Lovborg is much more inclined to remain here and have supper
          with me.
LOVBORG: [Looking at her.] With you, Mrs. Tesman?
HEDDA: And with Mrs. Elvsted.
LOVBORG: Ah— [Lightly.] I saw her for a moment this morning.
HEDDA: Did you? Well, she is coming this evening. So you see you are almost bound
          to remain, Mr. Lovborg, or she will have no one to see her home.
LOVBORG: That's true. Many thanks, Mrs. Tesman—in that case I will remain.
HEDDA: Then I have one or two orders to give the servant—
400   [She goes to the hall door and rings. BERTA enters. HEDDA talks to her
          in a whisper, and points towards the inner room. BERTA nods and goes
          out again.
TESMAN: [At the same time, to LOVBORG] Tell me, Eilert—is it this new subject—
          the future—that you are going to lecture about?
LOVBORG: Yes.
TESMAN: They told me at the bookseller's that you are going to deliver a course of
          lectures this autumn.
LOVBORG: That is my intention. I hope you won't take it ill, Tesman.
TESMAN: Oh no, not in the least! But—?
LOVBORG: I can quite understand that it must be very disagreeable to you.
TESMAN: [Cast down.] Oh, I can't expect you, out of consideration for me, to—
LOVBORG: But I shall wait till you have received your appointment.
TESMAN: Will you wait? Yes but—yes but—are you not going to compete with me?
          Eh?
LOVBORG: No; it is only the moral victory I care for.

TESMAN: Why, bless me—then Aunt Julia was right after all! Oh yes—I knew it! Hedda! Just fancy—Eilert Lovborg is not going to stand in our way!

HEDDA: [Curtly.] Our way? Pray leave me out of the question.

420   [She goes up towards the inner room, where BERTA is placing a tray with decanters and glasses on the table. HEDDA nods approval, and comes forward again. BERTA goes out.

TESMAN: [At the same time.] And you, Judge Brack—what do you say to this? Eh?

BRACK: Well, I say that a moral victory—h'm—may be all very fine—

TESMAN: Yes, certainly. But all the same—

HEDDA: [Looking at TESMAN with a cold smile.] You stand there looking as if you were thunderstruck—

TESMAN: Yes—so I am—I almost think—

BRACK: Don't you see, Mrs. Tesman, a thunderstorm has just passed over?

HEDDA: [Pointing towards the room.] Will you not take a glass of cold punch,
430   gentlemen?

BRACK: [Looking at his watch.] A stirrup-cup? Yes, it wouldn't come amiss.

TESMAN: A capital idea, Hedda! Just the thing! Now that the weight has been taken off my mind—

HEDDA: Will you not join them, Mr. Lovborg?

LOVBORG: [With a gesture of refusal.] No, thank you. Nothing for me.

BRACK: Why bless me—cold punch is surely not poison.

LOVBORG: Perhaps not for everyone.

HEDDA: I will deep Mr. Lovborg company in the meantime.

TESMAN: Yes, yes, Hedda dear, do.

440   [He and BRACK go into the inner room, seat themselves, drink punch, smoke cigarettes, and carry on a lively conversation during what follows. EILERT LOVBORG remains standing beside the stove. HEDDA goes to the writing-table.

HEDDA: [Raising her voice a little.] Do you care to look at some photographs, Mr.
445   Lovborg? You know Tesman and I made a tour in they Tyrol on our way home?
    [She takes up an album, and places it on the table beside the sofa, in the further corner of which she seats herself. EILERT LOVBORG approaches, stops, and looks at her. Then he takes a chair and seats
450   himself to her left.

HEDDA: [Opening the album.] Do you see this range of mountains, Mr. Lovborg? It's the Ortler group. Tesman has written the name underneath. Here it is: "The Ortler group near Meran."

LOVBORG: [Who has never taken his eyes off her, says softly and slowly:] Hedda—
455   Gabler!

HEDDA: [Glancing hastily at him.] Ah! Hush!

LOVBORG: [Repeats softly.] Hedda Gabler!

HEDDA: [Looking at the album.] That was my name in the old days—when we two knew each other.

LOVBORG: And I must teach myself never to say Hedda Gabler again—never, as long as I live.

HEDDA: [Still turning over the pages.] Yes, you must. And I think you ought to practise in time. The sooner the better, I should say.

LOVBORG: [In a tone of indignation.] Hedda Gabler married? And married to—
465   George Tesman!

HEDDA: Yes—so the world goes.

LOVBORG: Oh, Hedda, Hedda—how could you(9) throw yourself away!

HEDDA: [Looks sharply at him.] What? I can't allow this!

LOVBORG: What do you mean?

470   [TESMAN comes into the room and goes towards the sofa.]

HEDDA: [Hears him coming and says in an indifferent tone.] And this is a view from
        the Val d'Ampezzo, Mr. Lovborg Just look at these peaks! [Looks
        affectionately up at TESMAN.] What's the name of these curious peaks,
        dear?

TESMAN: Let me see. Oh, those are the Dolomites.

HEDDA: Yes, that's it!—Those are the Dolomites, Mr. Lovborg.

TESMAN: Hedda, dear,—I only wanted to ask whether I shouldn't bring you a little
        punch after all? For yourself at any rate—eh?

HEDDA: Yes, do, please; and perhaps a few biscuits.

TESMAN: No cigarettes?

HEDDA: No.

TESMAN: Very well.
        [He goes into the inner room and out to the right. BRACK sits in the
        inner room, and keeps an eye from time to time on HEDDA and
485   LOVBORG.

LOVBORG: [Softly, as before.] Answer me, Hedda—how could you go and do this?

HEDDA: [Apparently absorbed in the album.] If you continue to say "du" to me I
        won't talk to you.

LOVBORG: May I not say "du" even when we are alone?

HEDDA: No. You may think it; but you mustn't say it.

LOVBORG: Ah, I understand. It is an offence against George Tesman, whom
        you(10)—love.

HEDDA: [Glances at him and smiles.] Love? What an idea!

LOVBORG: You don't love him then!

HEDDA: But I won't hear of any sort of unfaithfulness! Remember that.

LOVBORG: Hedda—answer me one thing—

HEDDA: Hush! [TESMAN enters with a small tray from the inner room.]

TESMAN: Here you are! Isn't this tempting? [He puts the tray on the table.]

HEDDA: Why do you bring it yourself?

TESMAN: [Filling the glasses.] Because I think it's such fun to wait upon you, Hedda.

HEDDA: But you have poured out two glasses. Mr. Lovborg said he wouldn't have
        any—

TESMAN: No, but Mrs. Elvsted will soon be here, won't she?

HEDDA: Yes, by-the-bye—Mrs. Elvsted—

TESMAN: Had you forgotten her? Eh?

HEDDA: We were so absorbed in these photographs. [Shows him a picture.] Do you
        remember this little village?

TESMAN: Oh, it's that one just below the Brenner Pass. It was there we passed the
        night—

HEDDA: —and met that lively party of tourists.

---

(9) He uses the familiar "du".   (10)From this point onward Lovborg use the formal "De".

TESMAN: Yes, that was the place. Fancy—if we could only have had you wit us, Eilert! Eh?

[He returns to the inner room and sits beside BRACK.]

LOVBORG: Answer me one thing, Hedda—

HEDDA: Well?

LOVBORG: Was there no love in your friendship for me either? Not a spark—not a tinge of love in it?

HEDDA: I wonder if there was? To me it seems as though we were two good comrades—two thoroughly intimate friends. [Smilingly.] You especially
520   were frankness itself.

LOVBORG: It was you that made me so.

HEDDA: As I look back upon it all, I think there was really something beautiful, something fascinating—something daring—in—in that secret intimacy—that comradeship which no living creature so much as
525   dreamed of.

LOVBORG: Yes, yes, Hedda! Was there not?—When I used to come to your father's in the afternoon—and the General sat over at the window reading his papers—with his back towards us—

HEDDA: And we two on the corner sofa—

LOVBORG: Always with the same illustrated paper before us—

HEDDA: For want of an album, yes.

LOVBORG: Yes, Hedda, and when I made my confessions to you—told you about myself, things that at that time no one else knew! There I would sit and tell you of my escapades—my days and nights of devilment. Oh,
535   Hedda—what was the power in you that forced me to confess these things?

HEDDA: Do you think it was any power in me?

LOVBORG: How else can I explain it? And all those—those roundabout questions you used to put to me—

HEDDA: Which you understood so particularly well—

LOVBORG: How could you sit and question me like that? Question me quite frankly—

HEDDA: In roundabout terms, please observe.

LOVBORG: Yes, but frankly nevertheless. Cross-question me about—all that sort of
545   thing?

HEDDA: And how could you answer, Mr. Lovborg?

LOVBORG: Yes, that is just what I can't understand—in looking back upon it. But tell me now, Hedda—was there not love at the bottom of our friendship? On your side, did you not feel as though you might purge my stains away—
550   if I made you my confessor? Was it not so?

HEDDA: No, not quite.

LOVBORG: What was you motive, then?

HEDDA: Do think it quite incomprehensible that a young girl—when it can be done— without any one knowing—

LOVBORG: Well?

HEDDA: —should be glad to have a peep, now and then, into a world which—?

LOVBORG: Which—?

HEDDA: —which she is forbidden to know anything about?

LOVBORG: So that was it?

HEDDA: Partly. Partly—I almost think.

LOVBORG: Comradeship in the thirst for life. But why should not that, at any rate, have continued?

HEDDA: The fault was yours.

LOVBORG: It was you that broke with me.

HEDDA: Yes, when our friendship threatened to develop into something more serious. Shame upon you, Eilert Lovborg! How could you think of wronging your—your frank comrade.

LOVBORG: [Clenches his hands.] Oh, why did you not carry out your threat? Why did you not shoot me down?

HEDDA: Because I have such a dread of scandal.

LOVBORG: Yes, Hedda, you are a coward at heart.

HEDDA: A terrible coward. [Changing her tone.] But it was a lucky thing for you. And now you have found ample consolation at the Elvsteds'.

LOVBORG: I know what Thea has confided to you.

HEDDA: And perhaps you have confided to her something about us?

LOVBORG: Not a word. She is too stupid to understand anything of that sort.

HEDDA: Stupid?

LOVBORG: She is stupid about matters of that sort.

HEDDA: And I am cowardly. [Bends over towards him, without looking him in the
580   face, and says more softly:] But now I will confide something to you.

LOVBORG: [Eagerly.] Well?

HEDDA: The fact that I dared not shoot you down—

LOVBORG: Yes!

HEDDA: —that was not my arrant cowardice—that evening.

LOVBORG: [Looks at her a moment, understands, and whispers passionately.] Oh, Hedda! Hedda Gabler! Now I begin to see a hidden reason beneath our comradeship! You[11] and I—! After all, then, it was your craving for life—

HEDDA: [Softly, with a sharp glance.] Take care! Believe nothing of the sort!
590   [Twilight has begun to fall. The hall door is opened from without by BERTA.

HEDDA: [Closes the album with a bang and calls smilingly:] Ah, at last! My darling Thea,—come along!
        MRS. ELVSTED enters from the hall. She is in evening dress. The door
595   is closed behind her.

HEDDA: [On the sofa, stretches out her arms towards her.] My sweet Thea—you can't think how I have been longing for you!
        [MRS. ELVSTED, in passing, exchanges slight salutations with the gentlemen in the inner room, then goes up to the table and gives HEDDA
600   her hand. EILERT LOVBORG has risen. He and MRS. ELVSTED greet each other with a silent nod.

MRS. ELVSTED: Ought I to go in and talk to your husband for a moment?

HEDDA: Oh, not at all. Leave those two alone. They will soon be going.

MRS. ELVSTED: Are they going out?

HEDDA: Yes, to a supper-party.

11 In this speech he once more says "du". Hedda addresses him throughout as "De".

MRS. ELVSTED: [Quickly, to LOVBORG] Not you?

LOVBORG: No.

HEDDA: Mr. Lovborg remains with us.

MRS. ELVSTED: [Takes a chair and is about to seat herself at his side.] Oh, how nice it
610   is here!

HEDDA: No, thank you, my little Thea! Not there! You'll be good enough to come
        over here to me. I will sit between you.

MRS. ELVSTED: Yes, just as you please.

        [She goes round the table and seats herself on the sofa on HEDDA'S
615   right. LOVBORG re-seats himself on his chair.]

LOVBORG: [After a short pause, to HEDDA.] Is not she lovely to look at?

HEDDA: [Lightly stroking her hair.] Only to look at!

LOVBORG: Yes. For we two—she and I—we are two real comrades. We have
        absolute faith in each other; so we can sit and talk with perfect
620   frankness—

HEDDA: Not round about, Mr. Lovborg?

LOVBORG: Well—

MRS. ELVSTED: [Softly clinging close to HEDDA.] Oh, how happy I am, Hedda! For
        only think, he says I have inspired him too.

HEDDA: [Looks at her with a smile.] Ah! Does he say that, dear?

LOVBORG: And then she is so brave, Mrs. Tesman!

MRS. ELVSTED: Good heavens—am I brave?

LOVBORG: Exceedingly—where your comrade is concerned.

HEDDA: Exceedingly—where your comrade is concerned.

HEDDA: Ah, yes—courage! If one only had that!

LOVBORG: What then? What do you mean?

HEDDA: Then life would perhaps be liveable, after all. [With a sudden change of
        tone.] But now, my dearest Thea, you really must have a glass of cold
        punch.

MRS. ELVSTED: No, thanks—I never take anything of that kind.

HEDDA: Well then, you, Mr. Lovborg

LOVBORG: Nor I, thank you.

MRS. ELVSTED: No, he doesn't either.

HEDDA: [Looks fixedly at him.] But if I say you shall?

LOVBORG: It would be of no use.

HEDDA: [Laughing.] Then I, poor creature, have no sort of power over you?

LOVBORG: Not in that respect.

HEDDA: But seriously, I think you ought to—for your own sake.

MRS. ELVSTED: Why, Hedda—!

LOVBORG: How so?

HEDDA: Or rather on account of other people.

LOVBORG: Indeed?

HEDDA: Otherwise people might be apt to suspect that—in your heart of hearts—you
        did not feel quite secure—quite confident in yourself.

MRS. ELVSTED: [Softly.] Oh please, Hedda—!

LOVBORG: People may suspect what they like—for the present.

MRS. ELVSTED: [Joyfully.] Yes, let them!

HEDDA: I saw it plainly in Judge Brack's face a moment ago.

LOVBORG: What did you see?

HEDDA: His contemptuous smile, when you dared not go with them into the inner
          room.
LOVBORG: Dared not? Of course I preferred to stop here and talk to you.
MRS. ELVSTED: What could be more natural, Hedda?
HEDDA: But the Judge could not guess that. And I say, too, the way he smiled and
660   glanced at Tesman when you dared not accept his invitation to this
          wretched little supper-party of his.
LOVBORG: Dared not! Do you say I dared not?
HEDDA: "I" don't say so. But that was how Judge Brack understood it.
LOVBORG: Well, let him.
HEDDA: Then you are not going with them?
LOVBORG: I will stay here with you and Thea.
MRS. ELVSTED: Yes, Hedda—how can you doubt that?
HEDDA: [Smiles and nods approvingly to LOVBORG] Firm as a rock! Faithful to
          your principles, now and for ever! Ah, that is how a man should be!
670   [Turns to MRS. ELVSTED and caresses her.] Well now, what did I tell
          you, when you came to us this morning in such a state of distraction—
LOVBORG: [Surprised] Distraction!
MRS. ELVSTED: [Terrified.] Hedda—oh Hedda—!
HEDDA: You can see for yourself! You haven't the slightest reason to be in such
675   mortal terror— [Interrupting herself.] There! Now we can all three enjoy
          ourselves!
LOVBORG: [Who has given a start.] Ah—what is all this, Mrs. Tesman?
MRS. ELVSTED: Oh my God, Hedda! What are you saying? What are you doing?
HEDDA: Don't get excited! That horrid Judge Brack is sitting watching you.
LOVBORG: So she was in mortal terror! On my account!
MRS. ELVSTED: [Softly and piteously.] Oh, Hedda—now you have ruined everything!
LOVBORG: [Looks fixedly at her for a moment. His face is distorted.] So that was my
          comrade's frank confidence in me?
MRS. ELVSTED: [Imploringly.] Oh, my dearest friend—only let me tell you—
LOVBORG: [Takes one of the glasses of punch, raises it to his lips, and says in a low,
          husky voice.] Your health, Thea!
          [He empties the glass, puts it down, and takes the second.
MRS. ELVSTED: [Softly.] Oh, Hedda, Hedda—how could you do this?
HEDDA: "I" do it? "I"? Are you crazy?
LOVBORG: Here's to your health too, Mrs. Tesman. Thanks for the truth. Hurrah for
          the truth!
          [He empties the glass and is about to re-fill it.
HEDDA: [Lays her hand on his arm.] Come, come—no more for the present.
          Remember you are going out to supper.
MRS. ELVSTED: No, no, no!
HEDDA: Hush! They are sitting watching you.
LOVBORG: [Putting down the glass.] Now, Thea—tell me the truth—
MRS. ELVSTED: Yes.
LOVBORG: Did your husband know that you had come after me?
MRS. ELVSTED: [Wringing her hands.] Oh, Hedda—do you hear what his is asking?

LOVBORG: Was it arranged between you and him that you were to come to town and look after me? Perhaps it was the Sheriff himself that urged you to come? Aha, my dear—no doubt he wanted my help in his office! Or was it at the card-table that he missed me?

MRS. ELVSTED: [Softly, in agony.] Oh, Lovborg, Lovborg—!

LOVBORG: [Seizes a glass and is on the point of filling it.] Here's a glass for the old Sheriff too!

HEDDA: [Preventing him.] No more just now. Remember, you have to read your manuscript to Tesman.

LOVBORG: [Calmly, putting down the glass.] It was stupid of me all this. Thea—to take it in this way, I mean. Don't be angry with me, my dear, dear comrade. You shall see—both you and the others—that if I was fallen once—now I have risen again! Thanks to you, Thea.

MRS. ELVSTED: [Radiant with joy.] Oh, heaven be praised—!

715   [BRACK has in the meantime looked at his watch. He and TESMAN rise and come into the drawing-room.

BRACK: [Takes his hat and overcoat.] Well, Mrs. Tesman, our time has come.

HEDDA: I suppose it has.

LOVBORG: [Rising.] Mine too, Judge Brack.

MRS. ELVSTED: [Softly and imploringly.] Oh, Lovborg, don't do it!

HEDDA: [Pinching her arm.] They can hear you!

MRS. ELVSTED: [With a suppressed shriek.] Ow!

LOVBORG: [To BRACK] You were good enough to invite me.

JUDGE BRACK: Well, are you coming after all?

LOVBORG: Yes, many thanks.

BRACK: I'm delighted—

LOVBORG: [To TESMAN, putting the parcel of MS. in his pocket.] I should like to show you one or two things before I send it to the printers.

TESMAN: Fancy—that will be delightful. But, Hedda dear, how is Mrs. Elvsted to get
730   home? Eh?

HEDDA: Oh, that can be managed somehow.

LOVBORG: [Looking towards the ladies.] Mrs. Elvsted? Of course, I'll come again and fetch her. [Approaching.] At ten or thereabouts, Mrs. Tesman? Will that do?

HEDDA: Certainly. That will do capitally.

TESMAN: Well, then, that's all right. But you must not expect me so early, Hedda.

HEDDA: Oh, you may stop as long—as long as ever you please.

MRS. ELVSTED: [Trying to conceal her anxiety.] Well then, Mr. Lovborg—I shall remain here until you come.

LOVBORG: [With his hat in his hand.] Pray do, Mrs. Elvsted.

BRACK: And now off goes the excursion train, gentlemen! I hope we shall have a lively time, as a certain fair lady puts it.

HEDDA: Ah, if only the fair lady could be present unseen—!

BRACK: Why unseen?

HEDDA: In order to hear a little of your liveliness at first hand, Judge Brack.

BRACK: [Laughing.] I should not advise the fair lady to try it.

TESMAN: [Also laughing.] Come, you're a nice one Hedda! Fancy that!

BRACK: Well, good-bye, good-bye, ladies.

LOVBORG: [Bowing.] About ten o'clock, then,

750   [BRACK, LOVBORG, and TESMAN go out by the hall door. At the same time, BERTA enters from the inner room with a lighted lamp, which she places on the drawing-room table; she goes out by the way she came.

MRS. ELVSTED: [Who has risen and is wandering restlessly about the room.] Hedda—
755   Hedda—what will come of all this?

HEDDA: At ten o'clock—he will be here. I can see him already—with vine-leaves in his hair—flushed and fearless—

MRS. ELVSTED: Oh, I hope he may.

HEDDA: And then, you see—then he will have regained control over himself. Then
760   he will be a free man for all his days.

MRS. ELVSTED: Oh God!—if he would only come as you see him now!

HEDDA: He will come as I see him—so, and not otherwise! [Rises and approaches THEA.] You may doubt him as long as you please; "I" believe in him. And now we will try—

MRS. ELVSTED: You have some hidden motive in this, Hedda!

HEDDA: Yes, I have. I want for once in my life to have power to mould a human destiny.

MRS. ELVSTED: Have you not the power?

HEDDA: I have not—and have never had it.

MRS. ELVSTED: Not your husband's?

HEDDA: Do you think that is worth the trouble? Oh, if you could only understand how poor I am. And fate has made you so rich! [Clasps her passionately in her arms.] I think I must burn your hair off after all.

MRS. ELVSTED: Let me go! Let me go! I am afraid of you, Hedda!

BERTA: [In the middle doorway.] Tea is laid in the dining-room, ma'am.

HEDDA: Very well. We are coming

MRS. ELVSTED: No, no, no! I would rather go home alone! At once!

HEDDA: Nonsense! First you shall have a cup of tea, you little stupid. And then—at ten o'clock—Eilert Lovborg will be here—with vine-leaves in his hair.
780   [She drags MRS. ELVSTED almost by force to the middle doorway.

ACT THIRD

The room at the TESMANS'. The curtains are drawn over the middle doorway, and also over the glass door. The lamp half turned down, and with a shade over it, is burning on the table. In the stove, the door of which stands open, there has been a fire, which is now nearly burnt out.

MRS. ELVSTED, wrapped in a large shawl, and with her feet upon a foot-rest, sits close to the stove, sunk back in the arm-chair. HEDDA, fully dressed, lies sleeping upon the sofa, with a sofa-blanket over her.

MRS. ELVSTED: [After a pause, suddenly sits up in her chair, and listens eagerly. Then she sinks back again wearily, moaning to herself.] Not yet!—Oh God— oh God—not yet!

BERTA slips cautiously in by the hall door. She has a letter in her hand.

MRS. ELVSTED: [Turns and whispers eagerly.] Well—has any one come?

BERTA: [Softly.] Yes, a girl has just brought this letter.

MRS. ELVSTED: [Quickly, holding out her hand.] A letter! Give it to me!

BERTA: No, it's for Dr. Tesman, ma'am.

MRS. ELVSTED: Oh, indeed.

BERTA: It was Miss Tesman's servant that brought it. I'll lay it here on the table.

MRS. ELVSTED: Yes, do.

BERTA: [Laying down the letter.] I think I had better put out the lamp. It's smoking.

MRS. ELVSTED: Yes, put it out. It must soon be daylight now.

BERTA: [Putting out the lamp.] It is daylight already, ma'am.

MRS. ELVSTED: Yes, broad day! And no one come back yet—!

BERTA: Lord bless you, ma'am—I guessed how it would be.

MRS. ELVSTED: You guessed?

BERTA: Yes, when I saw that a certain person had come back to town—and that he
went off with them. For we've heard enough about that gentleman before
20   now.

MRS. ELVSTED: Don't speak so loud. You will waken Mrs. Tesman.

BERTA: [Looks towards the sofa and sighs.] No, no—let her sleep, poor thing. Shan't
I put some wood on the fire?

MRS. ELVSTED: Thanks, not for me.

BERTA: Oh, very well. [She goes softly out by the hall door.]

HEDDA: [Is wakened by the shutting of the door, and looks up.] What's that—?

MRS. ELVSTED: It was only the servant.

HEDDA: [Looking about her.] Oh, we're here—! Yes, now I remember. [Sits erect
upon the sofa, stretches herself, and rubs her eyes.] What o'clock is it,
30   Thea?

MRS. ELVSTED: [Looks at her watch.] It's past seven.

HEDDA: When did Tesman come home?

MRS. ELVSTED: He has not come.

HEDDA: Not come home yet?

MRS. ELVSTED: [Rising.] No one has come.

HEDDA: Think of our watching and waiting here till four in the morning—

MRS. ELVSTED: [Wringing her hands.] And how I watched and waited for him!

HEDDA: [Yawns, and says with her hand before her mouth.] Well well—we might
have spared ourselves the trouble.

MRS. ELVSTED: Did you get a little sleep?

HEDDA: Oh yes; I believe I have slept pretty well. Have you not?

MRS. ELVSTED: Not for a moment. I couldn't, Hedda!—not to save my life.

HEDDA: [Rises and goes towards her.] There there there! There's nothing to be so
alarmed about. I understand quite well what has happened.

MRS. ELVSTED: Well, what do you think? Won't you tell me?

HEDDA: Why, of course it has been a very late affair at Judge Brack's—

MRS. ELVSTED: Yes, yes—that is clear enough. But all the same—

HEDDA: And then, you see, Tesman hasn't cared to come home and ring us up in the
middle of the night. [Laughing.] Perhaps he wasn't inclined to show
50   himself either—immediately after a jollification.

MRS. ELVSTED: But in that case—where can he have gone?

HEDDA: Of course he has gone to his Aunts' and slept there. They have his old room
ready for him.

MRS. ELVSTED: No, he can't be with them for a letter has just come for him from
55   Miss Tesman. There it lies.

HEDDA: Indeed? [Looks at the address.] Why yes, it's addressed in Aunt Julia's
        hand. Well then, he has remained at Judge Brack's. And as for Eilert
        Lovborg—he is sitting, with vine leaves in his hair, reading his
        manuscript.

MRS. ELVSTED: Oh, Hedda, you are just saying things you don't believe a bit.

HEDDA: You really are a little blockhead, Thea.

MRS. ELVSTED: Oh yes, I suppose I am.

HEDDA: And how mortally tired you look.

MRS. ELVSTED: Yes, I am mortally tired.

HEDDA: Well then, you must do as I tell you. You must go into my room and lie
        down for a little while.

MRS. ELVSTED: Oh no, no—I shouldn't be able to sleep.

HEDDA: I am sure you would.

MRS. ELVSTED: Well, but your husband is certain to come soon now; and then I want

70   to know at once—

HEDDA: I shall take care to let you know when he comes.

MRS. ELVSTED: Do you promise me, Hedda?

HEDDA: Yes, rely upon me. Just you go in and have a sleep in the meantime.

MRS. ELVSTED: Thanks; then I'll try. [She goes off to the inner room.]

75   [HEDDA goes up to the glass door and draws back the curtains. The
        broad daylight streams into the room. Then she takes a little hand-glass
        from the writing-table, looks at herself in it, and arranges her hair. Next
        she goes to the hall door and presses the bell-button.
        BERTA presently appears at the hall door.

BERTA: Did you want anything, ma'am?

HEDDA: Yes; you must put some more wood in the stove. I am shivering.

BERTA: Bless me—I'll make up the fire at once. [She rakes the embers together and
        lays a piece of wood upon them; then stops and listens.] That was a ring
        at the front door, ma'am.

HEDDA: Then go to the door. I will look after the fire.

BERTA: It'll soon burn up. [She goes out by the hall door.]
        [HEDDA kneels on the foot-rest and lays some more pieces of wood in
        the stove. After a short pause, GEORGE TESMAN enters from the hall.
        He steals on tiptoe towards the middle doorway and is about to slip

90   through the curtains.]

HEDDA: [At the stove, without looking up.] Good morning.

TESMAN: [Turns.] Hedda! [Approaching her.] Good heavens—are you up so early?
        Eh?

HEDDA: Yes, I am up very early this morning.

TESMAN: And I never doubted you were still sound asleep! Fancy that, Hedda!

HEDDA: Don't speak so loud. Mrs. Elvsted is resting in my room.

TESMAN: Has Mrs. Elvsted been here all night?

HEDDA: Yes, since no one came to fetch her.

TESMAN: Ah, to be sure.

HEDDA: [Closes the door of the stove and rises.] Well, did you enjoy yourselves at
        Judge Brack's?

TESMAN: Have you been anxious about me? Eh?

HEDDA: No, I should never think of being anxious. But I asked if you had enjoyed
        yourself.

TESMAN: Oh yes,—for once in a way. Especially the beginning of the evening; for then Eilert read me part of his book. We arrived more than an hour too early—fancy that! And Brack had all sorts of arrangements to make—so Eilert read to me.

HEDDA: [Seating herself by the table on the right.] Well? Tell me then—

TESMAN: [Sitting on a footstool near the stove.] Oh, Hedda, you can't conceive what a book that is going to be! I believe it is one of the most remarkable things that have ever been written. Fancy that!

HEDDA: Yes yes; I don't care about that—

TESMAN: I must make a confession to you, Hedda. When he had finished reading—a
115   horrid feeling came over me.

HEDDA: A horrid feeling?

TESMAN: I felt jealous of Eilert for having had it in him to write such a book. Only think, Hedda!

HEDDA: Yes, yes, I am thinking!

TESMAN: And then how pitiful to think that he—with all his gifts—should be irreclaimable, after all.

HEDDA: I suppose you mean that he has more courage than the rest?

TESMAN: No, not at all—I mean that he is incapable of taking his pleasure in moderation.

HEDDA: And what came of it all—in the end?

TESMAN: Well, to tell the truth, I think it might best be described as an orgie, Hedda.

HEDDA: Had he vine-leaves in his hair?

TESMAN: Vine-leaves? No, I saw nothing of the sort. But he made a long, rambling speech in honour of the woman who had inspired him in his work—that
130   was the phrase he used.

HEDDA: Did he name her?

TESMAN: No, he didn't; but I can't help thinking he meant Mrs. Elvsted. You may be sure he did.

HEDDA: Well—where did you part from him?

TESMAN: On the way to town. We broke up—the last of us at any rate—all together; and Brack came with us to get a breath of fresh air. And then, you see, we agreed to take Eilert home; for he had had far more than was good for him.

HEDDA: I daresay.

TESMAN: But now comes the strange part of it, Hedda; or, I should rather say, the melancholy part of it. I declare I am almost ashamed—on Eilert's account—to tell you—

HEDDA: Oh, go on—!

TESMAN: Well, as we were getting near town, you see, I happened to drop a little
145   behind the others. Only for a minute or two—fancy that!

HEDDA: Yes yes yes, but—?

TESMAN: And then, as I hurried after them—what do you think I found by the wayside? Eh?

HEDDA: Oh, how should I know!

TESMAN: You mustn't speak of it to a soul, Hedda! Do you hear! Promise me, for Eilert's sake. [Draws a parcel, wrapped in paper, from his coat pocket.] Fancy, dear—I found this.

HEDDA: Is not that the parcel he had with him yesterday?

TESMAN: Yes, it is the whole of his precious, irreplaceable manuscript! And he had
155   gone and lost it, and knew nothing about it. Only fancy, Hedda! So
           deplorably —
HEDDA: But why did you not give him back the parcel at once?
TESMAN: I didn't dare to — in the state he was then in —
HEDDA: Did you not tell any of the others that you had found it?
TESMAN: Oh, far from it! You can surely understand that, for Eilert's sake, I
           wouldn't do that.
HEDDA: So no one knows that Eilert Lovborg's manuscript is in your possession?
TESMAN: No. And no one must know it.
HEDDA: Then what did you say to him afterwards?
TESMAN: I didn't talk to him again at all; for when we got in among the streets, he
           and two or three of the others gave us the slip and disappeared. Fancy
           that!
HEDDA: Indeed! They must have taken him home then.
TESMAN: Yes, so it would appear. And Brack, too, left us.
HEDDA: And what have you been doing with yourself since?
TESMAN: Well, I and some of the others went home with one of the party, a jolly
           fellow, and took our morning coffee with him; or perhaps I should rather
           call it our night coffee — eh? But now, when I have rested a little, and
           given Eilert, poor fellow, time to have his sleep out, I must take this back
175   to him.
HEDDA: [Holds out her hand for the packet.] No — don't give it to him! Not in such a
           hurry, I mean. Let me read it first.
TESMAN: No, my dearest Hedda, I mustn't, I really mustn't.
HEDDA: You must not?
TESMAN: No — for you can imagine what a state of despair he will be in when he
           wakens and misses the manuscript. He has no copy of it, you must know!
           He told me so.
HEDDA: [Looking searchingly at him.] Can such a thing not be reproduced? Written
           over again?
TESMAN: No, I don't think that would be possible. For the inspiration, you see —
HEDDA: Yes, yes — I suppose it depends on that — [Lightly.] But, by-the-bye — here is
           a letter for you.
TESMAN: Fancy — !
HEDDA: [Handing it to him.] It came early this morning.
TESMAN: It's from Aunt Julia! What can it be? [He lays the packet on the other
           footstool, opens the letter, runs his eye through it, and jumps up.] Oh,
           Hedda — she says that poor Aunt Rina is dying!
HEDDA: Well, we were prepared for that.
TESMAN: And that if I want to see her again, I must make haste. I'll run in to them at
195   once.
HEDDA: [Suppressing a smile.] Will you run?
TESMAN: Oh, my dearest Hedda — if you could only make up your mind to come with
           me! Just think!
HEDDA: [Rises and says wearily, repelling the idea.] No, no don't ask me. I will not
200   look upon sickness and death. I loathe all sorts of ugliness.

TESMAN: Well, well, then—! [Bustling around.] My hat—? My overcoat—? Oh, in the hall—. I do hope I mayn't come too late, Hedda! Eh?

HEDDA: Oh, if you run— [BERTA appears at the hall door.

BERTA: Judge Brack is at the door, and wishes to know if he may come in.

TESMAN: At this time! No, I can't possibly see him.

HEDDA: But I can. [To BERTA.] Ask Judge Brack to come in. [BERTA goes out.]

HEDDA: [Quickly, whispering.] The parcel, Tesman!
[She snatches it up from the stool.]

TESMAN: Yes, give it to me!

HEDDA: No, no, I will keep it till you come back.
[She goes to the writing-table and places it in the bookcase. TESMAN stands in a flurry of haste, and cannot get his gloves on.
JUDGE BRACK enters from the hall.

HEDDA: [Nodding to him.] You are an early bird, I must say.

BRACK: Yes, don't you think so! [To TESMAN.] Are you on the move, too?

TESMAN: Yes, I must rush of to my aunts'. Fancy—the invalid one is lying at death's door, poor creature.

BRACK: Dear me, is she indeed? Then on no account let me detain you. At such a critical moment—

TESMAN: Yes, I must really rush— Good-bye! Good-bye!
[He hastens out by the hall door.

HEDDA: [Approaching.] You seem to have made a particularly lively night of it at your rooms, Judge Brack.

BRACK: I assure you I have not had my clothes off, Mrs. Hedda.

HEDDA: Not you, either?

BRACK: No, as you may see. But what has Tesman been telling you of the night's adventures?

HEDDA: Oh, some tiresome story. Only that they went and had coffee somewhere or other.

BRACK: I have heard about that coffee-party already. Eilert Lovborg was not with them, I fancy?

HEDDA: No, they had taken him home before that.

BRACK: Tesman too?

HEDDA: No, but some of the others, he said.

BRACK: [Smiling.] George Tesman is really an ingenuous creature, Mrs. Hedda.

HEDDA: Yes, heaven knows he is. Then is there something behind all this?

BRACK: Yes, perhaps there may be.

HEDDA: Well then, sit down, my dear Judge, and tell your story in comfort.
[She seats herself to the left of the table. BRACK sits near her, at the
240   long side of the table.

HEDDA: Now then?

BRACK: I had special reasons for keeping track of my guests—last night.

HEDDA: Of Eilert Lovborg among the rest, perhaps?

BRACK: Frankly, yes.

HEDDA: Now you make me really curious—

BRACK: Do you know where he and one or two of the others finished the night, Mrs. Hedda?

HEDDA: If it is not quite unmentionable, tell me.

BRACK: Oh no, it's not at all unmentionable. Well, they put in an appearance at a
250   particularly animated soiree.
HEDDA: Of the lively kind?
BRACK: Of the very liveliest—
HEDDA: Tell me more of this, Judge Brack—
BRACK: Lovborg, as well as the others, had been invited in advance. I knew all about
255   it. But he had declined the invitation; for now, as you know, he has
             become a new man.
HEDDA: Up at the Elvsteds', yes. But he went after all, then?
BRACK: Well, you see, Mrs. Hedda—unhappily the spirit moved him at my rooms
             last evening—
HEDDA: Yes, I hear he found inspiration.
BRACK: Pretty violent inspiration. Well, I fancy that altered his purpose; for we
             menfolk are unfortunately not always so firm in our principles as we
             ought to be.
HEDDA: Oh, I am sure you are an exception, Judge Brack. But as to Lovborg—?
BRACK: To make a long story short—he landed at last in Mademoiselle Diana's
             rooms.
HEDDA: Mademoiselle Diana's?
BRACK: It was Mademoiselle Diana that was giving the soiree, to a select circle of
             her admirers and her lady friends.
HEDDA: Is she a red-haired woman?
BRACK: Precisely.
HEDDA: A sort of a—singer?
BRACK: Oh yes—in her leisure moments. And moreover a mighty huntress—of
             men—Mrs. Hedda. You have no doubt heard of her. Eilert Lovborg was
275   one of her most enthusiastic protectors—in the days of his glory.
HEDDA: And how did all this end?
BRACK: Far from amicably, it appears. After a most tender meeting, they seem to
             have come to blows—
HEDDA: Lovborg and she?
BRACK: Yes. He accused her or her friends of having robbed him. He declared that
             his pocket-book had disappeared—and other things as well. In short, he
             seems to have made a furious disturbance.
HEDDA: And what came of it all?
BRACK: It came to a general scrimmage, in which the ladies as well as the gentlemen
285   took part. Fortunately the police at last appeared on the scene.
HEDDA: The police too?
BRACK: Yes. I fancy it will prove a costly frolic for Eilert Lovborg, crazy being that
             he is.
HEDDA: How so?
BRACK: He seems to have made a violent resistance—to have hit one of the
             constables on the head and torn the coat off his back. So they had to
             march him off to the police-station with the rest.
HEDDA: How have you learnt all this?
BRACK: From the police themselves.
HEDDA: [Gazing straight before her.] So that is what happened. Then he had no vine-
             leaves in his hair.
BRACK: Vine-leaves, Mrs. Hedda?

HEDDA: [Changing her tone.] But tell me now, Judge—what is your real reason for tracking out Eilert Lovborg's movements so carefully?

BRACK: In the first place, it could not be entirely indifferent to me if it should appear in the police-court that he came straight from my house.

HEDDA: Will the matter come into court then?

BRACK: Of course. However, I should scarcely have troubled so much about that. But I thought that, as a friend of the family, it was my duty to supply you
305   and Tesman with a full account of his nocturnal exploits.

HEDDA: Why so, Judge Brack?

BRACK: Why, because I have a shrewd suspicion that he intends to use you as a sort of blind.

HEDDA: Oh, how can you think such a thing!

BRACK: Good heavens, Mrs. Hedda—we have eyes in our head. Mark my words! This Mrs. Elvsted will be in no hurry to leave town again.

HEDDA: Well, even if there should be anything between them, I suppose there are plenty of other places where they could meet.

BRACK: Not a single home. Henceforth, as before, every respectable house will be
315   closed against Eilert Lovborg.

HEDDA: And so ought mine to be, you mean?

BRACK: Yes. I confess it would be more than painful to me if this personage were to be made free of your house. How superfluous, how intrusive, he would be, if he were to force his way into—

HEDDA: —into the triangle?

BRACK: Precisely. It would simply mean that I should find myself homeless.

HEDDA: [Looks at him with a smile.] So you want to be the one cock in the basket^{12}—that is your aim.

BRACK: [Nods slowly and lowers his voice.] Yes, that is my aim. And for that I will
325   fight—with every weapon I can command.

HEDDA: [Her smile vanishing.] I see you are a dangerous person—when it comes to the point.

BRACK: Do you think so?

HEDDA: I am beginning to think so. And I am exceedingly glad to think—that you
330   have no sort of hold over me.

BRACK: [Laughing equivocally.] Well well, Mrs. Hedda—perhaps you are right there. If I had, who knows what I might be capable of?

HEDDA: Come come now, Judge Brack! That sounds almost like a threat.

BRACK: [Rising.] Oh, not at all! The triangle, you know, ought, if possible, to be
335   spontaneously constructed.

HEDDA: There I agree with you.

BRACK: Well, now I have said all I had to say; and I had better be getting back to town. Good-bye, Mrs. Hedda. [He goes towards the glass door.]

HEDDA: [Rising.] Are you going through the garden?

BRACK: Yes, it's a short cut for me.

HEDDA: And then it is a back way, too.

BRACK: Quite so. I have no objection to back ways. They may be piquant enough at times.

HEDDA: When there is ball practice going on, you mean?

12 "Enest hane i kurven"—a proverbial saying.

BRACK: [In the doorway, laughing to her.] Oh, people don't shoot their tame poultry, I fancy.

HEDDA: [Also laughing.] Oh no, when there is only one cock in the basket—
[They exchange laughing nods of farewell. He goes. She closes the door behind him.]

350   [HEDDA, who has become quite serious, stands for a moment looking out. Presently she goes and peeps through the curtain over the middle doorway. Then she goes to the writing-table, takes LOVBORG'S packet out of the bookcase, and is on the point of looking through its contents. BERTA is heard speaking loudly in the hall. HEDDA turns and listens.

355   Then she hastily locks up the packet in the drawer, and lays the key on the inkstand.]
EILERT LOVBORG, with his greatcoat on and his hat in his hand, tears open the hall door. He looks somewhat confused and irritated.

LOVBORG: [Looking towards the hall.] and I tell you I must and will come in! There!

360   [He closes the door, turns, sees HEDDA, at once regains his self-control, and bows.]

HEDDA: [At the writing-table.] Well, Mr. Lovborg, this is rather a late hour to call for Thea.

LOVBORG: You mean rather an early hour to call on you. Pray pardon me.

HEDDA: How do you know that she is still here?

LOVBORG: They told me at her lodgings that she had been out all night.

HEDDA: [Going to the oval table.] Did you notice anything about the people of the house when they said that?

LOVBORG: [Looks inquiringly at her.] Notice anything about them?

HEDDA: I mean, did they seem to think it odd?

LOVBORG: [Suddenly understanding.] Oh yes, of course! I am dragging her down with me! However, I didn't notice anything.—I suppose Tesman is not up yet.

HEDDA: No—I think not—

LOVBORG: When did he come home?

HEDDA: Very late.

LOVBORG: Did he tell you anything?

HEDDA: Yes, I gathered that you had had an exceedingly jolly evening at Judge Brack's.

LOVBORG: Nothing more?

HEDDA: I don't think so. However, I was so dreadfully sleepy—
MRS. ELVSTED enters through the curtains of the middle doorway.

MRS. ELVSTED: [Going towards him.] Ah, Lovborg! At last—!

LOVBORG: Yes, at last. And too late!

MRS. ELVSTED: [Looks anxiously at him.] What is too late?

LOVBORG: Everything is too late now. It is all over with me.

MRS. ELVSTED: Oh no, no—don't say that!

LOVBORG: You will say the same when you hear—

MRS. ELVSTED: I won't hear anything!

HEDDA: Perhaps you would prefer to talk to her alone? If so, I will leave you.

LOVBORG: No, stay—you too. I beg you to stay.

MRS. ELVSTED: Yes, but I won't hear anything, I tell you.

LOVBORG: It is not last night's adventures that I want to talk about.

MRS. ELVSTED: What is it then—?

LOVBORG: I want to say that now our ways must part.

MRS. ELVSTED: Part!

HEDDA: [Involuntarily.] I knew it!

LOVBORG: You can be of no more service to me, Thea.

MRS. ELVSTED: How can you stand there and say that! No more service to you! Am I
400   not to help you now, as before? Are we not to go on working together?

LOVBORG: Henceforward I shall do no work.

MRS. ELVSTED: [Despairingly.] Then what am I to do with my life?

LOVBORG: You must try to live your life as if you had never know me.

MRS. ELVSTED: But you know I cannot do that!

LOVBORG: Try if you cannot, Thea. You must go home again—

MRS. ELVSTED: [In vehement protest.] Never in this world! Where you are, there will
          I be also! I will not let myself be driven away like this! I will remain
          here! I will be with you when the book appears.

HEDDA: [Half aloud, in suspense.] Ah yes—the book!

LOVBORG: [Looks at her.] My book and Thea's; for that is what it is.

MRS. ELVSTED: Yes, I feel that it is. And that is why I have a right to be with you
          when it appears! I will see with my own eyes how respect and honour
          pour in upon you afresh. And the happiness—the happiness—oh, I must
          share it with you!

LOVBORG: Thea—our book will never appear.

HEDDA: Ah!

MRS. ELVSTED: Never appear!

LOVBORG: Can never appear.

MRS. ELVSTED: [In agonised foreboding.] Lovborg—what have you done with the
420   manuscript?

HEDDA: [Looks anxiously at him.] Yes, the manuscript—?

MRS. ELVSTED: Where is it?

LOVBORG: The manuscript—. Well then—I have torn the manuscript into a thousand
          pieces.

MRS. ELVSTED: [Shrieks.] Oh no, no—!

HEDDA: [Involuntarily.] But that's not—

LOVBORG: [Looks at her.] Not true, you think?

HEDDA: [Collecting herself.] Oh well, of course—since you say so. But it sounded so
          improbable—

LOVBORG: It is true, all the same.

MRS. ELVSTED: [Wringing her hands.] Oh God—oh God, Hedda—torn his own work
          to pieces!

LOVBORG: I have torn my own life to pieces. So why should I not tear my life-work
          too—?

MRS. ELVSTED: And you did this last night?

LOVBORG: Yes, I tell you! Tore it into a thousand pieces—and scattered them on the
          fiord—far out. There there is cool sea-water at any rate—let them drift
          upon it—drift with the current and the wind. And then presently they
          will sink—deeper and deeper—as I shall, Thea.

MRS. ELVSTED: Do you know, Lovborg, that what you have done with the book—I
          shall think of it to my dying day as though you had killed a little child.

LOVBORG: Yes, you are right. It is a sort of child-murder.

MRS. ELVSTED: How could you, then—! Did not the child belong to me too?

HEDDA: [Almost inaudibly.] Ah, the child—

MRS. ELVSTED: [Breathing heavily.] It is all over then. Well well, now I will go, Hedda.

HEDDA: But you are not going away from town?

MRS. ELVSTED: Oh, I don't know what I shall do. I see nothing but darkness before me. [She goes out by the hall door.]

HEDDA: [Stands waiting for a moment.] So you are not going to see her home, Mr. Lovborg?

LOVBORG: I? Through the streets? Would you have people see her walking with me?

HEDDA: Of course I don't know what else may have happened last night. But is it so utterly irretrievable?

LOVBORG: It will not end with last night—I know that perfectly well. And the thing is that now I have no taste for that sort of life either. I won't begin it anew. She has broken my courage and my power of braving life out.

HEDDA: [Looking straight before her.] So that pretty little fool has had her fingers in a man's destiny. [Looks at him.] But all the same, how could you treat
460   her so heartlessly.

LOVBORG: Oh, don't say that I was heartless!

HEDDA: To go and destroy what has filled her whole soul for months and years! You do not call that heartless!

LOVBORG: To you I can tell the truth, Hedda.

HEDDA: The truth?

LOVBORG: First promise me—give me your word—that what I now confide in you Thea shall never know.

HEDDA: I give you my word.

LOVBORG: Good. Then let me tell you that what I said just now was untrue.

HEDDA: About the manuscript?

LOVBORG: Yes. I have not torn it to pieces—nor thrown it into the fiord.

HEDDA: No, no—. But—where is it then?

LOVBORG: I have destroyed it none the less—utterly destroyed it, Hedda!

HEDDA: I don't understand.

LOVBORG: Thea said that what I had done seemed to her like a child-murder.

HEDDA: Yes, so she said.

LOVBORG: But to kill his child—that is not the worst thing a father can do to it.

HEDDA: Not the worst?

LOVBORG: Suppose now, Hedda, that a man—in the small hours of the morning—
480   came home to his child's mother after a night of riot and debauchery, and said: "Listen—I have been here and there—in this place and in that. And I have taken our child with—to this place and to that. And I have lost the child—utterly lost it. The devil knows into what hands it may have fallen—who may have had their clutches on it."

HEDDA: Well—but when all is said and done, you know—this was only a book—

LOVBORG: Thea's pure soul was in that book.

HEDDA: Yes, so I understand.

LOVBORG: And you can understand, too, that for her and me together no future is possible.

HEDDA: What path do you mean to take then?

LOVBORG: None. I will only try to make an end of it all—the sooner the better.

HEDDA: [A step nearer him.] Eilert Lovborg—listen to me.—Will you not try to—to do it beautifully?

LOVBORG: Beautifully? [Smiling.] With vine-leaves in my hair, as you used to dream in the old days—?
495

HEDDA: No, no. I have lost my faith in the vine-leaves. But beautifully nevertheless! For once in a way!—Good-bye! You must go now—and do not come here any more.

LOVBORG: Good-bye, Mrs. Tesman. And give George Tesman my love.
500   [He is on the point of going.]

HEDDA: No, wait! I must give you a memento to take with you.
        [She goes to the writing-table and opens the drawer and the pistol-case; then returns to LOVBORG with one of the pistols.

LOVBORG: [Looks at her.] This? Is this the memento?

HEDDA: [Nodding slowly.] Do you recognise it? It was aimed at you once.

LOVBORG: You should have used it then.

HEDDA: Take it—and do you use it now.

LOVBORG: [Puts the pistol in his breast pocket.] Thanks!

HEDDA: And beautifully, Eilert Lovborg Promise me that!

LOVBORG: Good-bye, Hedda Gabler. [He goes out by the hall door.]
        [HEDDA listens for a moment at the door. Then she goes up to the writing-table, takes out the packet of manuscript, peeps under the cover, draws a few of the sheets half out, and looks at them. Next she goes over and seats herself in the arm-chair beside the stove, with the packet in her
515   lap. Presently she opens the stove door, and then the packet.]

HEDDA: [Throws one of the quires into the fire and whispers to herself.] Now I am burning your child, Thea!—Burning it, curly-locks! [Throwing one or two more quires into the stove.] Your child and Eilert Lovborg's. [Throws the rest in.] I am burning—I am burning your child.

ACT FOURTH

The same rooms at the TESMANS'. It is evening. The drawing-room is in darkness. The back room is light by the hanging lamp over the table. The curtains over the glass door are drawn close.

HEDDA, dressed in black, walks to and fro in the dark room. Then she goes into the back room and disappears for a moment to the left. She is heard to strike a few chords on the piano. Presently she comes in sight again, and returns to the drawing-room.

BERTA enters from the right, through the inner room, with a lighted lamp, which she places on the table in front of the corner settee in the drawing-room. Her eyes are red with weeping, and she has black ribbons in her cap. She goes quietly and circumspectly out to the right. HEDDA goes up to the glass door, lifts the curtain a little aside, and looks out into the darkness.

Shortly afterwards, MISS TESMAN, in mourning, with a bonnet and veil on, comes in from the hall. HEDDA goes towards her and holds out her hand.

MISS TESMAN: Yes, Hedda, here I am, in mourning and forlorn; for now my poor
        sister has at last found peace.
HEDDA: I have heard the news already, as you see. Tesman sent me a card.
MISS TESMAN: Yes, he promised me he would. But nevertheless I thought that to
5   Hedda—here in the house of life—I ought myself to bring the tidings of
        death.
HEDDA: That was very kind of you.
MISS TESMAN: Ah, Rina ought not to have left us just now. This is not the time for
        Hedda's house to be a house of mourning.
HEDDA: [Changing the subject.] She died quite peacefully, did she not, Miss
        Tesman?
MISS TESMAN: Oh, her end was so calm, so beautiful. And then she had the
        unspeakable happiness of seeing George once more—and bidding him
        good-bye.—Has he not come home yet?
HEDDA: No. He wrote that he might be detained. But won't you sit down?
MISS TESMAN: No thank you, my dear, dear Hedda. I should like to, but I have so
        much to do. I must prepare my dear one for her rest as well as I can. She
        shall go to her grave looking her best.
HEDDA: Can I not help you in any way?
MISS TESMAN: Oh, you must not think of it! Hedda Tesman must have no hand in
        such mournful work. Nor let her thought dwell on it either—not at this
        time.
HEDDA: One is not always mistress of one's thoughts—
MISS TESMAN: [Continuing.] Ah yes, it is the way of the world. At home we shall be
25   sewing a shroud; and here there will soon be sewing too, I suppose —but
        of another sort, thank God!
        [GEORGE TESMAN enters by the hall door.]
HEDDA: Ah, you have come at last!
TESMAN: You here, Aunt Julia? With Hedda? Fancy that!
MISS TESMAN: I was just going, my dear boy. Well, have you done all you promised?
TESMAN: No; I'm really afraid I have forgotten half of it. I must come to you again
        to-morrow. To-day my brain is all in a whirl. I can't keep my thoughts
        together.
MISS TESMAN: Why, my dear George, you mustn't take it in this way.
TESMAN: Mustn't—? How do you mean?
MISS TESMAN: Even in your sorrow you must rejoice, as I do—rejoice that she is at
        rest.
TESMAN: Oh yes, yes—you are thinking of Aunt Rina.
HEDDA: You will feel lonely now, Miss Tesman.
MISS TESMAN: Just at first, yes. But that will not last very long, I hope. I daresay I
        shall soon find an occupant for Rina's little room.
TESMAN: Indeed? Who do you think will take it? Eh?
MISS TESMAN: Oh, there's always some poor invalid or other in want of nursing,
        unfortunately.
HEDDA: Would you really take such a burden upon you again?
MISS TESMAN: A burden! Heaven forgive you, child—it has been no burden to me.
HEDDA: But suppose you had a total stranger on your hands—
MISS TESMAN: Oh, one soon makes friends with sick folk; and it's such an absolute
        necessity for me to have some one to live for. Well, heaven be praised,
50   there may soon be something in this house, too, to keep an old aunt busy.

HEDDA: Oh, don't trouble about anything here.

TESMAN: Yes, just fancy what a nice time we three might have together, if—?

HEDDA: If—?

TESMAN: [Uneasily.] Oh nothing. It will all come right. Let us hope so—eh?

MISS TESMAN: Well well, I daresay you two want to talk to each other. [Smiling.] And perhaps Hedda may have something to tell you too, George. Goodbye! I must go home to Rina. [Turning at the door.] How strange it is to think that now Rina is with me and with my poor brother as well!

TESMAN: Yes, fancy that, Aunt Julia! Eh?

60   [MISS TESMAN goes out by the hall door.]

HEDDA: [Follows TESMAN coldly and searchingly with her eyes.] I almost believe your Aunt Rina's death affects you more than it does your Aunt Julia.

TESMAN: Oh, it's not that alone. It's Eilert I am so terribly uneasy about.

HEDDA: [Quickly.] Is there anything new about him?

TESMAN: I looked in at his rooms this afternoon, intending to tell him the manuscript was in safe keeping.

HEDDA: Well, did you find him?

TESMAN: No. He wasn't at home. But afterwards I met Mrs. Elvsted, and she told me that he had been here early this morning.

HEDDA: Yes, directly after you had gone.

TESMAN: And he said that he had torn his manuscript to pieces—eh?

HEDDA: Yes, so he declared.

TESMAN: Why, good heavens, he must have been completely out of his mind! And I suppose you thought it best not to give it back to him, Hedda?

HEDDA: No, he did not get it.

TESMAN: But of course you told him that we had it?

HEDDA: No. [Quickly.] Did you tell Mrs. Elvsted?

TESMAN: No; I thought I had better not. But you ought to have told him. Fancy, if, in desperation, he should go and do himself some injury! Let me have the manuscript, Hedda! I will take it to him at once. Where is it?

80

HEDDA: [Cold and immovable, leaning on the arm-chair.] I have not got it.

TESMAN: Have not got it? What in the world do you mean?

HEDDA: I have burnt it—every line of it.

TESMAN: [With a violent movement of terror.] Burnt! Burnt Eilert's manuscript!

HEDDA: Don't scream so. The servant might hear you.

TESMAN: Burnt! Why, good God—! No, no, no! It's impossible!

HEDDA: It is so, nevertheless.

TESMAN: Do you know what you have done, Hedda? It's unlawful appropriation of lost property. Fancy that! Just ask Judge Brack, and he'll tell you what it is.

90

HEDDA: I advise you not to speak of it—either to Judge Brack or to anyone else.

TESMAN: But how could you do anything so unheard-of? What put it into your head? What possessed you? Answer me that—eh?

HEDDA: [Suppressing an almost imperceptible smile.] I did it for your sake, George.

TESMAN: For my sake!

HEDDA: This morning, when you told me about what he had read to you—

TESMAN: Yes yes—what then?

HEDDA: You acknowledged that you envied him his work.

TESMAN: Oh, of course I didn't mean that literally.

HEDDA: No matter—I could not bear the idea that any one should throw you into the shade.

TESMAN: [In an outburst of mingled doubt and joy.] Hedda! Oh, is this true? But—but—I never knew you show your love like that before. Fancy that!

HEDDA: Well, I may as well tell you that—just at this time— [Impatiently breaking
105   off.] No, no; you can ask Aunt Julia. She well tell you, fast enough.

TESMAN: Oh, I almost think I understand you, Hedda! [Clasps his hands together.] Great heavens! do you really mean it! Eh?

HEDDA: Don't shout so. The servant might hear.

TESMAN: [Laughing in irrepressible glee.] The servant! Why, how absurd you are,
110   Hedda. It's only my old Berta! Why, I'll tell Berta myself.

HEDDA: [Clenching her hands together in desperation.] Oh, it is killing me,—it is killing me, all this!

TESMAN: What is, Hedda? Eh?

HEDDA: [Coldly, controlling herself.] All this—absurdity—George.

TESMAN: Absurdity! Do you see anything absurd in my being overjoyed at the news! But after all—perhaps I had better not say anything to Berta.

HEDDA: Oh—why not that too?

TESMAN: No, no, not yet! But I must certainly tell Aunt Julia. And then that you have begun to call me George too! Fancy that! Oh, Aunt Julia will be so
120   happy—so happy!

HEDDA: When she hears that I have burnt Eilert Lovborg's manuscript—for your sake?

TESMAN: No, by-the-bye—that affair of the manuscript—of course nobody must know about that. But that you love me so much,[13] Hedda—Aunt Julia must really share my joy in that! I wonder, now, whether this sort of thing is usual in young wives? Eh?

HEDDA: I think you had better ask Aunt Julia that question too.

TESMAN: I will indeed, some time or other. [Looks uneasy and downcast again.] And yet the manuscript—the manuscript! Good God! it is terrible to think
130   what will become of poor Eilert now.

MRS. ELVSTED, dressed as in the first Act, with hat and cloak, enters by the hall door.

MRS. ELVSTED: [Greets them hurriedly, and says in evident agitation.] Oh, dear Hedda, forgive my coming again.

HEDDA: What is the matter with you, Thea?

TESMAN: Something about Eilert Lovborg again—eh?

MRS. ELVSTED: Yes! I am dreadfully afraid some misfortune has happened to him.

HEDDA: [Seized her arm.] Ah,—do you think so?

TESMAN: Why, good Lord—what makes you think that, Mrs. Elvsted?

MRS. ELVSTED: I heard them talking of him at my boarding-house—just as I came in. Oh, the most incredible rumours are afloat about him to-day.

TESMAN: Yes, fancy, so I heard too! And I can bear witness that he went straight home to bed last night. Fancy that!

HEDDA: Well, what did they say at the boarding-house?

MRS. ELVSTED: Oh, I couldn't make out anything clearly. Either they knew nothing definite, or else—. They stopped talking when the saw me; and I did not dare to ask.

13 Literally, "That you burn for me."

TESMAN: [Moving about uneasily.] We must hope—we must hope that you
    misunderstood them, Mrs. Elvsted.

MRS. ELVSTED: No, no; I am sure it was of him they were talking. And I heard
    something about the hospital or—

TESMAN: The hospital?

HEDDA: No—surely that cannot be!

MRS. ELVSTED: Oh, I was in such mortal terror! I went to his lodgings and asked for
155   him there.

HEDDA: You could make up your mind to that, Thea!

MRS. ELVSTED: What else could I do? I really could bear the suspense no longer.

TESMAN: But you didn't find him either—eh?

MRS. ELVSTED: No. And the people knew nothing about him. He hadn't been home
160   since yesterday afternoon, they said.

TESMAN: Yesterday! Fancy, how could they say that?

MRS. ELVSTED: Oh, I am sure something terrible must have happened to him.

TESMAN: Hedda dear—how would it be if I were to go and make inquiries—?

HEDDA: No, no—don't you mix yourself up in this affair.

165   JUDGE BRACK, with his hat in his hand, enters by the hall door, which
    BERTA opens, and closes behind him. He looks grave and bows in
    silence.

TESMAN: Oh, is that you, my dear Judge? Eh?

BRACK: Yes. It was imperative I should see you this evening.

TESMAN: I can see you have heard the news about Aunt Rina?

BRACK: Yes, that among other things.

TESMAN: Isn't it sad—eh?

BRACK: Well, my dear Tesman, that depends on how you look at it.

TESMAN: [Looks doubtfully at him.] Has anything else happened?

BRACK: Yes.

HEDDA: [In suspense.] Anything sad, Judge Brack?

BRACK: That, too, depends on how you look at it, Mrs. Tesman.

MRS. ELVSTED: [Unable to restrain her anxiety.] Oh! it is something about Eilert
    Lovborg!

BRACK: [With a glance at her.] What makes you think that, Madam? Perhaps you
    have already heard something—?

MRS. ELVSTED: [In confusion.] No, nothing at all, but—

TESMAN: Oh, for heaven's sake, tell us!

BRACK: [Shrugging his shoulders.] Well, I regret to say Eilert Lovborg has been
185   taken to the hospital. He is lying at the point of death.

MRS. ELVSTED: [Shrieks.] Oh God! oh God—!

TESMAN: To the hospital! And at the point of death!

HEDDA: [Involuntarily.] So soon then—

MRS. ELVSTED: [Wailing.] And we parted in anger, Hedda!

HEDDA: [Whispers.] Thea—Thea—be careful!

MRS. ELVSTED: [Not heeding her.] I must go to him! I must see him alive!

BRACK: It is useless, Madam. No one will be admitted.

MRS. ELVSTED: Oh, at least tell me what has happened to him? What is it?

TESMAN: You don't mean to say that he has himself— Eh?

HEDDA: Yes, I am sure he has.

BRACK: [Keeping his eyes fixed upon her.] Unfortunately you have guessed quite correctly, Mrs. Tesman.

MRS. ELVSTED: Oh, how horrible!

TESMAN: Himself, then! Fancy that!

HEDDA: Shot himself!

BRACK: Rightly guessed again, Mrs. Tesman.

MRS. ELVSTED: [With an effort at self-control.] When did it happen, Mr. Brack?

BRACK: This afternoon—between three and four.

TESMAN: But, good Lord, where did he do it? Eh?

BRACK: [With some hesitation.] Where? Well—I suppose at his lodgings.

MRS. ELVSTED: No, that cannot be; for I was there between six and seven.

BRACK: Well then, somewhere else. I don't know exactly. I only know that he was found—. He had shot himself—in the breast.

MRS. ELVSTED: Oh, how terrible! That he should die like that!

HEDDA: [To BRACK] Was it in the breast?

BRACK: Yes—as I told you.

HEDDA: Not in the temple?

BRACK: In the breast, Mrs. Tesman.

HEDDA: Well, well—the breast is a good place, too.

BRACK: How do you mean, Mrs. Tesman?

HEDDA: [Evasively.] Oh, nothing—nothing.

TESMAN: And the wound is dangerous, you say—eh?

BRACK: Absolutely mortal. The end has probably come by this time.

MRS. ELVSTED: Yes, yes, I feel it. The end! The end! Oh, Hedda—!

TESMAN: But tell me, how have you learnt all this?

BRACK: [Curtly.] Through one of the police. A man I had some business with.

HEDDA: [In a clear voice.] At last a deed worth doing!

TESMAN: [Terrified.] Good heavens, Hedda! what are you saying?

HEDDA: I say there is beauty in this.

BRACK: H'm, Mrs. Tesman—

MRS. ELVSTED: Oh, Hedda, how can you talk of beauty in such an act!

HEDDA: Eilert Lovborg has himself made up his account with life. He has had the courage to do—the one right thing.

MRS. ELVSTED: No, you must never think that was how it happened! It must have
230   been in delirium that he did it.

TESMAN: In despair!

HEDDA: That he did not. I am certain of that.

MRS. ELVSTED: Yes, yes! In delirium! Just as when he tore up our manuscript.

BRACK: [Starting.] The manuscript? Has he torn that up?

MRS. ELVSTED: Yes, last night.

TESMAN: [Whispers softly.] Oh, Hedda, we shall never get over this.

BRACK: H'm, very extraordinary.

TESMAN: [Moving about the room.] To think of Eilert going out of the world in this way! And not leaving behind him the book that would have immortalised
240   his name—

MRS. ELVSTED: Oh, if only it could be put together again!

TESMAN: Yes, if it only could! I don't know what I would not give—

MRS. ELVSTED: Perhaps it can, Mr. Tesman.

TESMAN: What do you mean?

MRS. ELVSTED: [Searches in the pocket of her dress.] Look here. I have kept all the
        loose notes he used to dictate from.

HEDDA: [A step forward.] Ah—!

TESMAN: You have kept them, Mrs. Elvsted! Eh?

MRS. ELVSTED: Yes, I have them here. I put them in my pocket when I left home.
250   Here they still are—

TESMAN: Oh, do let me see them!

MRS. ELVSTED: [Hands him a bundle of papers.] But they are in such disorder—all
        mixed up.

TESMAN: Fancy, if we could make something out of them, after all! Perhaps if we
255   two put our heads together—

MRS. ELVSTED: Oh yes, at least let us try—

TESMAN: We will manage it! We must! I will dedicate my life to this task.

HEDDA: You, George? Your life?

TESMAN: Yes, or rather all the time I can spare. My own collections must wait in the
260   meantime. Hedda—you understand, eh? I owe this to Eilert's memory.

HEDDA: Perhaps.

TESMAN: And so, my dear Mrs. Elvsted, we will give our whole minds to it. There is
        no use in brooding over what can't be undone—eh? We must try to
        control our grief as much as possible, and—

MRS. ELVSTED: Yes, yes, Mr. Tesman, I will do the best I can.

TESMAN: Well then, come here. I can't rest until we have looked through the notes.
        Where shall we sit? Here? No, in there, in the back room. Excuse me, my
        dear Judge. Come with me, Mrs. Elvsted.

MRS. ELVSTED: Oh, if only it were possible!
270   [TESMAN and MRS. ELVSTED go into the back room. She takes off
        her hat and cloak. They both sit at the table under the hanging lamp, and
        are soon deep in an eager examination of the papers. HEDDA crosses to
        the stove and sits in the arm-chair. Presently BRACK goes up to her.]

HEDDA: [In a low voice.] Oh, what a sense of freedom it gives one, this act of Eilert
275   Lovborg's.

BRACK: Freedom, Mrs. Hedda? Well, of course, it is a release for him—

HEDDA: I mean for me. It gives me a sense of freedom to know that a deed of
        deliberate courage is still possible in this world,—a deed of spontaneous
        beauty.

BRACK: [Smiling.] H'm—my dear Mrs. Hedda—

HEDDA: Oh, I know what you are going to say. For you are a kind of specialist too,
        like—you know!

BRACK: [Looking hard at her.] Eilert Lovborg was more to you than perhaps you are
        willing to admit to yourself. Am I wrong?

HEDDA: I don't answer such questions. I only know that Eilert Lovborg has had the
        courage to live his life after his own fashion. And then—the last great
        act, with its beauty! Ah! that he should have the will and the strength to
        turn away from the banquet of life—so early.

BRACK: I am sorry, Mrs. Hedda,—but I fear I must dispel an amiable illusion.

HEDDA: Illusion?

BRACK: Which could not have lasted long in any case.

HEDDA: What do you mean?

BRACK: Eilert Lovborg did not shoot himself—voluntarily.

HEDDA: Not voluntarily?

BRACK: No. The thing did not happen exactly as I told it.

HEDDA: [In suspense.] Have you concealed something? What is it?

BRACK: For poor Mrs. Elvsted's sake I idealised the facts a little.

HEDDA: What are the facts?

BRACK: First, that he is already dead.

HEDDA: At the hospital?

BRACK: Yes—without regaining consciousness.

HEDDA: What more have you concealed?

BRACK: This—the event did not happen at his lodgings.

HEDDA: Oh, that can make no difference.

BRACK: Perhaps it may. For I must tell you—Eilert Lovborg was found shot in—in Mademoiselle Diana's boudoir.

HEDDA: [Makes a motion as if to rise, but sinks back again.] That is impossible, Judge Brack! He cannot have been there again to-day.

BRACK: He was there this afternoon. He went there, he said, to demand the return of
310   something which they had taken from him. Talked wildly about a lost child—

HEDDA: Ah—so that is why—

BRACK: I thought probably he meant his manuscript; but now I hear he destroyed that himself. So I suppose it must have been his pocket-book.

HEDDA: Yes, no doubt. And there—there he was found?

BRACK: Yes, there. With a pistol in his breast-pocket, discharged. The ball had lodged in a vital part.

HEDDA: In the breast—yes?

BRACK: No—in the bowels.

HEDDA: [Looks up at him with an expression of loathing.] That too! Oh, what curse is it that makes everything I touch turn ludicrous and mean?

BRACK: There is one point more, Mrs. Hedda—another disagreeable feature in the affair.

HEDDA: And what is that?

BRACK: The pistol he carried—

HEDDA: [Breathless.] Well? What of it?

BRACK: He must have stolen it.

HEDDA: [Leaps up.] Stolen it! That is not true! He did not steal it!

BRACK: No other explanation is possible. He must have stolen it—. Hush!
330   TESMAN and MRS. ELVSTED have risen from the table in the back-room, and come into the drawing-room.

TESMAN: [With the papers in both his hands.] Hedda, dear, it is almost impossible to see under that lamp. Think of that!

HEDDA: Yes, I am thinking.

TESMAN: Would you mind our sitting at your writing-table—eh?

HEDDA: If you like. [Quickly.] No, wait! Let me clear it first!

TESMAN: Oh, you needn't trouble, Hedda. There is plenty of room.

HEDDA: No no, let me clear it, I say! I will take these things in and put them on the piano. There!

340   [She has drawn out an object, covered with sheet music, from under the bookcase, places several other pieces of music upon it, and carries the whole into the inner room, to the left. TESMAN lays the scraps of paper on the writing-table, and moves the lamp there from the corner table. He and Mrs. Elvsted sit down and proceed with their work. HEDDA returns.]

HEDDA: [Behind Mrs. Elvsted's chair, gently ruffling her hair.] Well, my sweet Thea,—how goes it with Eilert Lovborg's monument?

MRS. ELVSTED: [Looks dispiritedly up at her.] Oh, it will be terribly hard to put in order.

TESMAN: We must manage it. I am determined. And arranging other people's papers
350   is just the work for me.
    [HEDDA goes over to the stove, and seats herself on one of the footstools. BRACK stands over her, leaning on the arm-chair.]

HEDDA: [Whispers.] What did you say about the pistol?

BRACK: [Softly.] That he must have stolen it.

HEDDA: Why stolen it?

BRACK: Because every other explanation ought to be impossible, Mrs. Hedda.

HEDDA: Indeed?

BRACK: [Glances at her.] Of course Eilert Lovborg was here this morning. Was he not?

HEDDA: Yes.

BRACK: Were you alone with him?

HEDDA: Part of the time.

BRACK: Did you not leave the room whilst he was here?

HEDDA: No.

BRACK: Try to recollect. Were you not out of the room a moment?

HEDDA: Yes, perhaps just a moment—out in the hall.

BRACK: And where was you pistol-case during that time?

HEDDA: I had it locked up in—

BRACK: Well, Mrs. Hedda?

HEDDA: The case stood there on the writing-table.

BRACK: Have you looked since, to see whether both the pistols are there?

HEDDA: No.

BRACK: Well, you need not. I saw the pistol found in Lovborg's pocket, and I knew it at once as the one I had seen yesterday—and before, too.

HEDDA: Have you it with you?

BRACK: No; the police have it.

HEDDA: What will the police do with it?

BRACK: Search till they find the owner.

HEDDA: Do you think they will succeed?

BRACK: [Bends over her and whispers.] No, Hedda Gabler—not so long as I say nothing.

HEDDA: [Looks frightened at him.] And if you do not say nothing,—what then?

BRACK: [Shrugs his shoulders.] There is always the possibility that the pistol was stolen.

HEDDA: [Firmly.] Death rather than that.

BRACK: [Smiling.] People say such things—but they don't do them.

HEDDA: [Without replying.] And supposing the pistol was not stolen, and the owner is discovered? What then?

BRACK: Well, Hedda—then comes the scandal!

HEDDA: The scandal!

BRACK: Yes, the scandal—of which you are so mortally afraid. You will, of course, be brought before the court—both you and Mademoiselle Diana. She will have to explain how the thing happened—whether it was an accidental shot or murder. Did the pistol go off as he was trying to take it

395   out of his pocket, to threaten her with? Or did she tear the pistol out of his hand, shoot him, and push it back into his pocket? That would be quite like her; for she is an able-bodied young person, this same Mademoiselle Diana.

HEDDA: But "I" have nothing to do with all this repulsive business.

BRACK: No. But you will have to answer the question: Why did you give Eilert the pistol? And what conclusions will people draw from the fact that you did give it to him?

HEDDA: [Lets her head sink.] That is true. I did not think of that.

BRACK: Well, fortunately, there is no danger, so long as I say nothing.

HEDDA: [Looks up at him.] So I am in your power, Judge Brack. You have me at your beck and call, from this time forward.

BRACK: [Whispers softly.] Dearest Hedda—believe me—I shall not abuse my advantage.

HEDDA: I am in your power none the less. Subject to your will and your demands. A

410   slave, a slave then! [Rises impetuously.] No, I cannot endure the thought of that! Never!

BRACK: [Looks half-mockingly at her.] People generally get used to the inevitable.

HEDDA: [Returns his look.] Yes, perhaps. [She crosses to the writing-table. Suppressing an involuntary smile, she imitates TESMAN'S intonations.]

415   Well? Are you getting on, George? Eh?

TESMAN: Heaven knows, dear. In any case it will be the work of months.

HEDDA: [As before.] Fancy that! [Passes her hands softly through Mrs. Elvsted's hair.] Doesn't it seem strange to you, Thea? Here are you sitting with Tesman—just as you used to sit with Eilert Lovborg?

MRS. ELVSTED: Ah, if I could only inspire your husband in the same way!

HEDDA: Oh, that will come too—in time.

TESMAN: Yes, do you know, Hedda—I really think I begin to feel something of the sort. But won't you go and sit with Brack again?

HEDDA: Is there nothing I can do to help you two?

TESMAN: No, nothing in the world. [Turning his head.] I trust to you to keep Hedda company, my dear Brack.

BRACK: [With a glance at HEDDA.] With the very greatest of pleasure.

HEDDA: Thanks. But I am tired this evening. I will go in and lie down a little on the sofa.

TESMAN: Yes, do dear—eh?

[HEDDA goes into the back room and draws the curtains. A short pause. Suddenly she is heard playing a wild dance on the piano.]

MRS. ELVSTED: [Starts from her chair.] Oh—what is that?

TESMAN: [Runs to the doorway.] Why, my dearest Hedda—don't play dance-music

435   to-night! Just think of Aunt Rina! And of Eilert too!

HEDDA: [Puts her head out between the curtains.] And of Aunt Julia. And of all the rest of them.—After this, I will be quiet. [Closes the curtains again.]

TESMAN: [At the writing-table.] It's not good for her to see us at this distressing
work. I'll tell you what, Mrs. Elvsted,—you shall take the empty room at
440   Aunt Julia's, and then I will come over in the evenings, and we can sit
and work there—eh?

HEDDA: [In the inner room.] I hear what you are saying, Tesman. But how am "I" to
get through the evenings out here?

TESMAN: [Turning over the papers.] Oh, I daresay Judge Brack will be so kind as to
445   look in now and then, even though I am out.

BRACK: [In the arm-chair, calls out gaily.] Every blessed evening, with all the
pleasure in life, Mrs. Tesman! We shall get on capitally together, we
two!

HEDDA: [Speaking loud and clear.] Yes, don't you flatter yourself we will, Judge
450   Brack? Now that you are the one cock in the basket—
[A shot is heard within. TESMAN, MRS. ELVSTED, and BRACK leap to
their feet.]

TESMAN: Oh, now she is playing with those pistols again.
[He throws back the curtains and runs in, followed by MRS. ELVSTED.
455   HEDDA lies stretched on the sofa, lifeless. Confusion and cries. BERTA
enters in alarm from the right.]

TESMAN: [Shrieks to BRACK.] Shot herself! Shot herself in the temple! Fancy that!

BRACK: [Half-fainting in the arm-chair.] Good God!—people don't do such things.

THE END

Anton Chekhov
The Cherry Orchard

A COMEDY IN FOUR ACTS

Characters

LUBOV ANDREYEVNA RANEVSKY (MME. RANEVSKY), *a landowner*
ANYA, *her daughter, aged seventeen*
VARYA (BARBARA), *her adopted daughter, aged twenty-seven*
LEONID ANDREYEVITCH GAEV, MME. *Ranevsky's brother*
ERMOLAI ALEXEYEVITCH LOPAKHIN, *a merchant*
PETER SERGEYEVITCH TROFIMOV, *a student*
BORIS BORISOVITCH SIMEONOV-PISCHIN, *a landowner*
CHARLOTTA IVANOVNA, *a governess*
SIMEON PANTELEYEVITCH EPIKHODOV, *a clerk*
DUNYASHA (AVDOTYA FEDOROVNA), *a maidservant*
FIERS, *an old footman, aged eighty-seven*
YASHA, *a young footman*
A TRAMP
A STATION-MASTER
POST-OFFICE CLERK
GUESTS
A SERVANT

The action takes place on Mme. RANEVSKY'S estate

ACT ONE

[A room which is still called the nursery. One of the doors leads into ANYA'S room. It is close on sunrise. It is May. The cherry-trees are in flower but it is chilly in the garden. There is an early frost. The windows of the room are shut. DUNYASHA comes in with a candle, and LOPAKHIN with a book in his hand.]

LOPAKHIN: The train's arrived, thank God. What's the time?
DUNYASHA: It will soon be two. [Blows out candle] It is light already.
LOPAKHIN: How much was the train late? Two hours at least. [Yawns and stretches
      himself] I have made a rotten mess of it! I came here on purpose to meet
5   them at the station, and then overslept myself . . . in my chair. It's a
      pity. I wish you'd wakened me.
DUNYASHA: I thought you'd gone away. [Listening] I think I hear them coming.

185

LOPAKHIN: [Listens] No. . . . They've got to collect their luggage and so on. . . .
[Pause] Lubov Andreyevna has been living abroad for five years; I don't
10   know what she'll be like now. . . . She's a good sort—an easy, simple
person. I remember when I was a boy of fifteen, my father, who is
dead—he used to keep a shop in the village here—hit me on the face
with his fist, and my nose bled. . . . We had gone into the yard together
for something or other, and he was a little drunk. Lubov Andreyevna, as
15   I remember her now, was still young, and very thin, and she took me to
the washstand here in this very room, the nursery. She said, "Don't cry,
little man, it'll be all right in time for your wedding." [Pause] "Little
man". . . . My father was a peasant, it's true, but here I am in a white
waistcoat and yellow shoes . . . a pearl out of an oyster. I'm rich now,
20   with lots of money, but just think about it and examine me, and you'll
find I'm still a peasant down to the marrow of my bones. [Turns over the
pages of his book] Here I've been reading this book, but I understood
nothing. I read and fell asleep. [Pause.]
DUNYASHA: The dogs didn't sleep all night; they know that they're coming.
LOPAKHIN: What's up with you, Dunyasha . . . ?
DUNYASHA: My hands are shaking. I shall faint.
LOPAKHIN: You're too sensitive, Dunyasha. You dress just like a lady, and you do
your hair like one too. You oughtn't. You should know your place.
EPIKHODOV: [Enters with a bouquet. He wears a short jacket and brilliantly polished
30   boots which squeak audibly. He drops the bouquet as he enters, then
picks it up] The gardener sent these; says they're to go into the dining-
room. [Gives the bouquet to DUNYASHA.]
LOPAKHIN: And you'll bring me some kvass.
DUNYASHA: Very well. [Exit.]
EPIKHODOV: There's a frost this morning—three degrees, and the cherry-trees are all
in flower. I can't approve of our climate. [Sighs] I can't. Our climate is
indisposed to favour us even this once. And, Ermolai Alexeyevitch,
allow me to say to you, in addition, that I bought myself some boots two
days ago, and I beg to assure you that they squeak in a perfectly
40   unbearable manner. What shall I put on them?
LOPAKHIN: Go away. You bore me.
EPIKHODOV: Some misfortune happens to me every day. But I don't complain; I'm
used to it, and I can smile. [DUNYASHA comes in and brings
LOPAKHIN some kvass] I shall go. [Knocks over a chair] There. . . .
45   [Triumphantly] There, you see, if I may use the word, what
circumstances I am in, so to speak. It is even simply marvellous. [Exit.]
DUNYASHA: I may confess to you, Ermolai Alexeyevitch, that Epikhodov has
proposed to me.
LOPAKHIN: Ah!
DUNYASHA: I don't know what to do about it. He's a nice young man, but every now
and again, when he begins talking, you can't understand a word he's
saying. I think I like him. He's madly in love with me. He's an unlucky
man; every day something happens. We tease him about it. They call him
"Two-and-twenty troubles."

LOPAKHIN: [Listens] There they come, I think.

DUNYASHA: They're coming! What's the matter with me? I'm cold all over.

LOPAKHIN: There they are, right enough. Let's go and meet them. Will she know me? We haven't seen each other for five years.

DUNYASHA: [Excited] I shall faint in a minute. . . . Oh, I'm fainting!

60   [Two carriages are heard driving up to the house. LOPAKHIN and DUNYASHA quickly go out. The stage is empty. A noise begins in the next room. FIERS, leaning on a stick, walks quickly across the stage; he has just been to meet LUBOV ANDREYEVNA. He wears an old-fashioned livery and a tall hat. He is saying something to himself, but

65   not a word of it can be made out. The noise behind the stage gets louder and louder. A voice is heard: "Let's go in there." Enter LUBOV ANDREYEVNA, ANYA, and CHARLOTTA IVANOVNA with a little dog on a chain, and all dressed in travelling clothes, VARYA in a long coat and with a kerchief on her head. GAEV, SIMEONOV-PISCHIN,

70   LOPAKHIN, DUNYASHA with a parcel and an umbrella, and a servant with luggage—all cross the room.]

ANYA: Let's come through here. Do you remember what this room is, mother?

LUBOV: [Joyfully, through her tears] The nursery!

VARYA: How cold it is! My hands are quite numb. [To LUBOV ANDREYEVNA]

75   Your rooms, the white one and the violet one, are just as they used to be, mother.

LUBOV: My dear nursery, oh, you beautiful room. . . . I used to sleep here when I was a baby. [Weeps] And here I am like a little girl again. [Kisses her brother, VARYA, then her brother again] And Varya is just as she used

80   to be, just like a nun. And I knew Dunyasha. [Kisses her.]

GAEV: The train was two hours late. There now; how's that for punctuality?

CHARLOTTA: [To PISCHIN] My dog eats nuts too.

PISCHIN: [Astonished] To think of that, now!

        [All go out except ANYA and DUNYASHA.]

DUNYASHA: We did have to wait for you!

        [Takes off ANYA'S cloak and hat.]

ANYA: I didn't get any sleep for four nights on the journey. . . . I'm awfully cold.

DUNYASHA: You went away during Lent, when it was snowing and frosty, but now? Darling! [Laughs and kisses her] We did have to wait for you, my joy,

90   my pet. . . . I must tell you at once, I can't bear to wait a minute.

ANYA: [Tired] Something else now . . .?

DUNYASHA: The clerk, Epikhodov, proposed to me after Easter.

ANYA: Always the same. . . . [Puts her hair straight] I've lost all my hairpins. . . . [She is very tired, and even staggers as she walks.]

DUNYASHA: I don't know what to think about it. He loves me, he loves me so much!

ANYA: [Looks into her room; in a gentle voice] My room, my windows, as if I'd never gone away. I'm at home! To-morrow morning I'll get up and have a run in the garden. . . .Oh, if I could only get to sleep! I didn't sleep the whole journey, I was so bothered.

DUNYASHA: Peter Sergeyevitch came two days ago.

ANYA: [Joyfully] Peter!

DUNYASHA: He sleeps in the bath-house, he lives there. He said he was afraid he'd be
            in the way. [Looks at her pocket-watch] I ought to wake him, but
            Barbara Mihailovna told me not to. "Don't wake him," she said.
105   [Enter VARYA, a bunch of keys on her belt.]
VARYA: Dunyasha, some coffee, quick. Mother wants some.
DUNYASHA: This minute. [Exit.]
VARYA: Well, you've come, glory be to God. Home again. [Caressing her] My
            darling is back again! My pretty one is back again!
ANYA: I did have an awful time, I tell you.
VARYA: I can just imagine it!
ANYA: I went away in Holy Week; it was very cold then. Charlotta talked the whole
            way and would go on performing her tricks. Why did you tie Charlotta
            on to me?
VARYA: You couldn't go alone, darling, at seventeen!
ANYA: We went to Paris; it's cold there and snowing. I talk French perfectly
            horribly. My mother lives on the fifth floor. I go to her, and find her
            there with various Frenchmen, women, an old abbe with a book, and
            everything in tobacco smoke and with no comfort at all. I suddenly
120   became very sorry for mother—so sorry that I took her head in my arms
            and hugged her and wouldn't let her go. Then mother started hugging me
            and crying. . . .
VARYA: [Weeping] Don't say any more, don't say any more. . . .
ANYA: She's already sold her villa near Mentone; she's nothing left, nothing. And I
125   haven't a copeck left either; we only just managed to get here. And
            mother won't understand! We had dinner at a station; she asked for all
            the expensive things, and tipped the waiters one rouble each. And
            Charlotta too. Yasha wants his share too—it's too bad. Mother's got a
            footman now, Yasha; we've brought him here.
VARYA: I saw the wretch.
ANYA: How's business? Has the interest been paid?
VARYA: Not much chance of that.
ANYA: Oh God, oh God . . .
VARYA: The place will be sold in August.
ANYA: O God. . . .
LOPAKHIN: [Looks in at the door and moos] Moo! . . . [Exit.]
VARYA: [Through her tears] I'd like to. . . . [Shakes her fist.]
ANYA: [Embraces VARYA, softly] Varya, has he proposed to you? [VARYA shakes
            head] But he loves you. . . . Why don't you make up your minds? Why
140   do you keep on waiting?
VARYA: I think that it will all come to nothing. He's a busy man. I'm not his
            affair . . . he pays no attention to me. Bless the man, I don't want to
            see him. . . . But everybody talks about our marriage, everybody
            congratulates me, and there's nothing in it at all, it's all like a dream.
145   [In another tone] You've got a brooch like a bee.
ANYA: [Sadly] Mother bought it. [Goes into her room, and talks lightly, like a child]
            In Paris I went up in a balloon!

VARYA: My darling's come back, my pretty one's come back! [DUNYASHA has
         already returned with the coffee-pot and is making the coffee, VARYA
150   stands near the door] I go about all day, looking after the house, and I
         think all the time, if only you could marry a rich man, then I'd be happy
         and would go away somewhere by myself, then to Kiev . . . to Moscow,
         and so on, from one holy place to another. I'd tramp and tramp. That
         would be splendid!

ANYA: The birds are singing in the garden. What time is it now?

VARYA: It must be getting on for three. Time you went to sleep, darling. [Goes into
         ANYA'S room] Splendid!
         [Enter YASHA with a plaid shawl and a travelling bag.]

YASHA: [Crossing the stage: Politely] May I go this way?

DUNYASHA: I hardly knew you, Yasha. You have changed abroad.

YASHA: Hm . . . and who are you?

DUNYASHA: When you went away I was only so high. [Showing with her hand] I'm
         Dunyasha, the daughter of Theodore Kozoyedov. You don't remember!

YASHA: Oh, you little cucumber!
165   [Looks round and embraces her. She screams and drops a saucer.
         YASHA goes out quickly.]

VARYA: [In the doorway: In an angry voice] What's that?

DUNYASHA: [Through her tears] I've broken a saucer.

VARYA: It may bring luck.

ANYA: [Coming out of her room] We must tell mother that Peter's here.

VARYA: I told them not to wake him.

ANYA: [Thoughtfully] Father died six years ago, and a month later my brother Grisha
         was drowned in the river—such a dear little boy of seven! Mother
         couldn't bear it; she went away, away, without looking round. . . .
175   [Shudders] How I understand her; if only she knew! [Pause] And Peter
         Trofimov was Grisha's tutor, he might tell her. . . .
         [Enter FIERS in a short jacket and white waistcoat.]

FIERS: [Goes to the coffee-pot, nervously] The mistress is going to have some food
         here. . . . [Puts on white gloves] Is the coffee ready? [To DUNYASHA,
180   severely] You! Where's the cream?

DUNYASHA: Oh, dear me . . .! [Rapid exit.]

FIERS: [Fussing round the coffee-pot] Oh, you bungler. . . . [Murmurs to himself]
         Back from Paris . . . the master went to Paris once . . . in a
         carriage. . . . [Laughs.]

VARYA: What are you talking about, Fiers?

FIERS: I beg your pardon? [Joyfully] The mistress is home again. I've lived to see
         her! Don't care if I die now. . . . [Weeps with joy.]
         [Enter LUBOV ANDREYEVNA, GAEV, LOPAKHIN, and
         SIMEONOV-PISCHIN, the latter in a long jacket of thin cloth and loose
190   trousers. GAEV, coming in, moves his arms and body about as if he is
         playing billiards.]

LUBOV: Let me remember now. Red into the corner! Twice into the centre!

GAEV: Right into the pocket! Once upon a time you and I used both to sleep in this
         room, and now I'm fifty-one; it does seem strange.

LOPAKHIN: Yes, time does go.

GAEV: Who does?

LOPAKHIN: I said that time does go.

GAEV: It smells of patchouli here.

ANYA: I'm going to bed. Good-night, mother. [Kisses her.]

LUBOV: My lovely little one. [Kisses her hand] Glad to be at home? I can't get over it.

ANYA: Good-night, uncle.

GAEV: [Kisses her face and hands] God be with you. How you do resemble your mother! [To his sister] You were just like her at her age, Luba.

205   [ANYA gives her hand to LOPAKHIN and PISCHIN and goes out, shutting the door behind her.]

LUBOV: She's awfully tired.

PISCHIN: It's a very long journey.

VARYA: [To LOPAKHIN and PISCHIN] Well, sirs, it's getting on for three, quite

210   time you went.

LUBOV: [Laughs] You're just the same as ever, Varya. [Draws her close and kisses her] I'll have some coffee now, then we'll all go. [FIERS lays a cushion under her feet] Thank you, dear. I'm used to coffee. I drink it day and night. Thank you, dear old man. [Kisses FIERS.]

VARYA: I'll go and see if they've brought in all the luggage. [Exit.]

LUBOV: Is it really I who am sitting here? [Laughs] I want to jump about and wave my arms. [Covers her face with her hands] But suppose I'm dreaming! God knows I love my own country, I love it deeply; I couldn't look out of the railway carriage, I cried so much. [Through her tears] Still, I must

220   have my coffee. Thank you, Fiers. Thank you, dear old man. I'm so glad you're still with us.

FIERS: The day before yesterday.

GAEV: He doesn't hear well.

LOPAKHIN: I've got to go off to Kharkov by the five o'clock train. I'm awfully sorry!

225   I should like to have a look at you, to gossip a little. You're as fine-looking as ever.

PISCHIN: [Breathes heavily] Even finer-looking . . . dressed in Paris fashions . . . confound it all.

LOPAKHIN: Your brother, Leonid Andreyevitch, says I'm a snob, a usurer, but that is

230   absolutely nothing to me. Let him talk. Only I do wish you would believe in me as you once did, that your wonderful, touching eyes would look at me as they did before. Merciful God! My father was the serf of your grandfather and your own father, but you—you more than anybody else—did so much for me once upon a time that I've forgotten

235   everything and love you as if you belonged to my family . . . and even more.

LUBOV: I can't sit still, I'm not in a state to do it. [Jumps up and walks about in great excitement] I'll never survive this happiness. . . . You can laugh at me; I'm a silly woman. . . . My dear little cupboard. [Kisses cupboard] My

240   little table.

GAEV: Nurse has died in your absence.

LUBOV: [Sits and drinks coffee] Yes, bless her soul. I heard by letter.

GAEV: And Anastasius has died too. Peter Kosoy has left me and now lives in town with the Commissioner of Police. [Takes a box of sugar-candy out of his
245   pocket and sucks a piece.]

PISCHIN: My daughter, Dashenka, sends her love.

LOPAKHIN: I want to say something very pleasant, very delightful, to you. [Looks at his watch] I'm going away at once, I haven't much time . . . but I'll tell you all about it in two or three words. As you already know, your cherry
250   orchard is to be sold to pay your debts, and the sale is fixed for August 22; but you needn't be alarmed, dear madam, you may sleep in peace; there's a way out. Here's my plan. Please attend carefully! Your estate is only thirteen miles from the town, the railway runs by, and if the cherry orchard and the land by the river are broken up into building lots and are
255   then leased off for villas you'll get at least twenty-five thousand roubles a year profit out of it.

GAEV: How utterly absurd!

LUBOV: I don't understand you at all, Ermolai Alexeyevitch.

LOPAKHIN: You will get twenty-five roubles a year for each dessiatin from the
260   leaseholders at the very least, and if you advertise now I'm willing to bet that you won't have a vacant plot left by the autumn; they'll all go. In a word, you're saved. I congratulate you. Only, of course, you'll have to put things straight, and clean up. . . . For instance, you'll have to pull down all the old buildings, this house, which isn't any use to anybody
265   now, and cut down the old cherry orchard. . . .

LUBOV: Cut it down? My dear man, you must excuse me, but you don't understand anything at all. If there's anything interesting or remarkable in the whole province, it's this cherry orchard of ours.

LOPAKHIN: The only remarkable thing about the orchard is that it's very large. It only
270   bears fruit every other year, and even then you don't know what to do with them; nobody buys any.

GAEV: This orchard is mentioned in the "Encyclopaedic Dictionary."

LOPAKHIN: [Looks at his watch] If we can't think of anything and don't make up our minds to anything, then on August 22, both the cherry orchard and the
275   whole estate will be up for auction. Make up your mind! I swear there's no other way out, I'll swear it again.

FIERS: In the old days, forty or fifty years back, they dried the cherries, soaked them and pickled them, and made jam of them, and it used to happen that . . .

GAEV: Be quiet, Fiers.

FIERS: And then we'd send the dried cherries off in carts to Moscow and Kharkov. And money! And the dried cherries were soft, juicy, sweet, and nicely scented. . . . They knew the way. . . .

LUBOV: What was the way?

FIERS: They've forgotten. Nobody remembers.

PISCHIN: [To LUBOV ANDREYEVNA] What about Paris? Eh? Did you eat frogs?

LUBOV: I ate crocodiles.

PISCHIN: To think of that, now.

LOPAKHIN: Up to now in the villages there were only the gentry and the labourers, and now the people who live in villas have arrived. All towns now, even small ones, are surrounded by villas. And it's safe to say that in twenty years' time the villa resident will be all over the place. At present he sits on his balcony and drinks tea, but it may well come to pass that he'll begin to cultivate his patch of land, and then your cherry orchard will be happy, rich, splendid. . . .

GAEV: [Angry] What rot!

[Enter VARYA and YASHA.]

VARYA: There are two telegrams for you, little mother. [Picks out a key and noisily unlocks an antique cupboard] Here they are.

LUBOV: They're from Paris. . . . [Tears them up without reading them] I've done with Paris.

GAEV: And do you know, Luba, how old this case is? A week ago I took out the bottom drawer; I looked and saw figures burnt out in it. That case was made exactly a hundred years ago. What do you think of that? What? We could celebrate its jubilee. It hasn't a soul of its own, but still, say what you will, it's a fine bookcase.

PISCHIN: [Astonished] A hundred years. . . . Think of that!

GAEV: Yes . . . it's a real thing. [Handling it] My dear and honoured case! I congratulate you on your existence, which has already for more than a hundred years been directed towards the bright ideals of good and justice; your silent call to productive labour has not grown less in the hundred years [Weeping] during which you have upheld virtue and faith in a better future to the generations of our race, educating us up to ideals of goodness and to the knowledge of a common consciousness. [Pause.]

LOPAKHIN: Yes. . . .

LUBOV: You're just the same as ever, Leon.

GAEV: [A little confused] Off the white on the right, into the corner pocket. Red ball goes into the middle pocket!

LOPAKHIN: [Looks at his watch] It's time I went.

YASHA: [Giving LUBOV ANDREYEVNA her medicine] Will you take your pills now?

PISCHIN: You oughtn't to take medicines, dear madam; they do you neither harm nor good. . . . Give them here, dear madam. [Takes the pills, turns them out into the palm of his hand, blows on them, puts them into his mouth, and drinks some kvass] There!

LUBOV: [Frightened] You're off your head!

PISCHIN: I've taken all the pills.

LOPAKHIN: Gormandizer! [All laugh.]

FIERS: They were here in Easter week and ate half a pailful of cucumbers. . . . [Mumbles.]

LUBOV: What's he driving at?

VARYA: He's been mumbling away for three years. We're used to that.

YASHA: Senile decay.

[CHARLOTTA IVANOVNA crosses the stage, dressed in white: she is very thin and tightly laced; has a lorgnette at her waist.]

LOPAKHIN: Excuse me, Charlotta Ivanovna, I haven't said "How do you do" to you yet. [Tries to kiss her hand.]

CHARLOTTA: [Takes her hand away] If you let people kiss your hand, then they'll want your elbow, then your shoulder, and then . . .

LOPAKHIN: My luck's out to-day! [All laugh] Show us a trick, Charlotta Ivanovna!

LUBOV ANDREYEVNA: Charlotta, do us a trick.

CHARLOTTA: It's not necessary. I want to go to bed. [Exit.]

LOPAKHIN: We shall see each other in three weeks. [Kisses LUBOV ANDREYEVNA'S hand] Now, good-bye. It's time to go. [To GAEV] See you again. [Kisses PISCHIN] Au revoir. [Gives his hand to
145   VARYA, then to FIERS and to YASHA] I don't want to go away. [To LUBOV ANDREYEVNA]. If you think about the villas and make up your mind, then just let me know, and I'll raise a loan of 50,000 roubles at once. Think about it seriously.

VARYA: [Angrily] Do go, now!

LOPAKHIN: I'm going, I'm going. . . . [Exit.]

GAEV: Snob. Still, I beg pardon. . . . Varya's going to marry him, he's Varya's young man.

VARYA: Don't talk too much, uncle.

LUBOV: Why not, Varya? I should be very glad. He's a good man.

PISCHIN: To speak the honest truth . . . he's a worthy man. . . . And my Dashenka . . . also says that . . . she says lots of things. [Snores, but wakes up again at once] But still, dear madam, if you could lend me . . . 240 roubles . . . to pay the interest on my mortgage to-morrow . . .

VARYA: [Frightened] We haven't got it, we haven't got it!

LUBOV: It's quite true. I've nothing at all.

PISCHIN: I'll find it all right [Laughs] I never lose hope. I used to think, "Everything's lost now. I'm a dead man," when, lo and behold, a railway was built over my land . . . and they paid me for it. And something else will happen to-day or to-morrow. Dashenka may win 20,000 roubles
165   . . . she's got a lottery ticket.

LUBOV: The coffee's all gone, we can go to bed.

FIERS: [Brushing GAEV'S trousers; in an insistent tone] You've put on the wrong trousers again. What am I to do with you?

VARYA: [Quietly] Anya's asleep. [Opens window quietly] The sun has risen already;
170   it isn't cold. Look, little mother: what lovely trees! And the air! The starlings are singing!

GAEV: [Opens the other window] The whole garden's white. You haven't forgotten, Luba? There's that long avenue going straight, straight, like a stretched strap; it shines on moonlight nights. Do you remember? You haven't
175   forgotten?

LUBOV: [Looks out into the garden] Oh, my childhood, days of my innocence! In this nursery I used to sleep; I used to look out from here into the orchard. Happiness used to wake with me every morning, and then it was just as it is now; nothing has changed. [Laughs from joy] It's all, all white! Oh,
180   my orchard! After the dark autumns and the cold winters, you're young again, full of happiness, the angels of heaven haven't left you. . . . If only I could take my heavy burden off my breast and shoulders, if I could forget my past!

GAEV: Yes, and they'll sell this orchard to pay off debts. How strange it seems!

LUBOV: Look, there's my dead mother going in the orchard . . . dressed in white! [Laughs from joy] That's she.

GAEV: Where?

VARYA: God bless you, little mother.

LUBOV: There's nobody there; I thought I saw somebody. On the right, at the turning
190   by the summer-house, a white little tree bent down, looking just like a woman. [Enter TROFIMOV in a worn student uniform and spectacles] What a marvellous garden! White masses of flowers, the blue sky. . . .

TROFIMOV: Lubov Andreyevna! [She looks round at him] I only want to show myself, and I'll go away. [Kisses her hand warmly] I was told to wait till
195   the morning, but I didn't have the patience.

[LUBOV ANDREYEVNA looks surprised.]

VARYA: [Crying] It's Peter Trofimov.

TROFIMOV: Peter Trofimov, once the tutor of your Grisha. . . . Have I changed so much?

200   [LUBOV ANDREYEVNA embraces him and cries softly.]

GAEV: [Confused] That's enough, that's enough, Luba.

VARYA: [Weeps] But I told you, Peter, to wait till to-morrow.

LUBOV: My Grisha . . . my boy . . . Grisha . . . my son.

VARYA: What are we to do, little mother? It's the will of God.

TROFIMOV: [Softly, through his tears] It's all right, it's all right.

LUBOV: [Still weeping] My boy's dead; he was drowned. Why? Why, my friend? [Softly] Anya's asleep in there. I am speaking so loudly, making such a noise. . . . Well, Peter? What's made you look so bad? Why have you grown so old?

TROFIMOV: In the train an old woman called me a decayed gentleman.

LUBOV: You were quite a boy then, a nice little student, and now your hair is not at all thick and you wear spectacles. Are you really still a student? [Goes to the door.]

TROFIMOV: I suppose I shall always be a student.

LUBOV: [Kisses her brother, then VARYA] Well, let's go to bed. . . . And you've grown older, Leonid.

PISCHIN: [Follows her] Yes, we've got to go to bed. . . . Oh, my gout! I'll stay the night here. If only, Lubov Andreyevna, my dear, you could get me 240 roubles to-morrow morning—

GAEV: Still the same story.

PISCHIN: Two hundred and forty roubles . . . to pay the interest on the mortgage.

LUBOV: I haven't any money, dear man.

PISCHIN: I'll give it back . . . it's a small sum. . . .

LUBOV: Well, then, Leonid will give it to you. . . . Let him have it, Leonid.

GAEV: By all means; hold out your hand.

LUBOV: Why not? He wants it; he'll give it back.

[LUBOV ANDREYEVNA, TROFIMOV, PISCHIN, and FIERS go out. GAEV, VARYA, and YASHA remain.]

GAEV: My sister hasn't lost the habit of throwing money about. [To YASHA] Stand
240   off, do; you smell of poultry.

YASHA: [Grins] You are just the same as ever, Leonid Andreyevitch.

GAEV: Really? [To VARYA] What's he saying?

VARYA: [To YASHA] Your mother's come from the village; she's been sitting in the servants' room since yesterday, and wants to see you. . . .

YASHA: Bless the woman!

VARYA: Shameless man.

YASHA: A lot of use there is in her coming. She might have come tomorrow just as well. [Exit.]

VARYA: Mother hasn't altered a scrap, she's just as she always was. She'd give away
250   everything, if the idea only entered her head.

GAEV: Yes. . . . [Pause] If there's any illness for which people offer many remedies, you may be sure that particular illness is incurable, I think. I work my brains to their hardest. I've several remedies, very many, and that really means I've none at all. It would be nice to inherit a fortune
255   from somebody, it would be nice to marry our Anya to a rich man, it would be nice to go to Yaroslav and try my luck with my aunt the Countess. My aunt is very, very rich.

VARYA: [Weeps] If only God helped us.

GAEV: Don't cry. My aunt's very rich, but she doesn't like us. My sister, in the first
260   place, married an advocate, not a noble. . . . [ANYA appears in the doorway] She not only married a man who was not a noble, but she behaved herself in a way which cannot be described as proper. She's nice and kind and charming, and I'm very fond of her, but say what you will in her favour and you still have to admit that she's wicked; you can
265   feel it in her slightest movements.

VARYA: [Whispers] Anya's in the doorway.

GAEV: Really? [Pause] It's curious, something's got into my right eye . . . I can't see properly out of it. And on Thursday, when I was at the District Court . . .
270   [Enter ANYA.]

VARYA: Why aren't you in bed, Anya?

ANYA: Can't sleep. It's no good.

GAEV: My darling! [Kisses ANYA'S face and hands] My child. . . . [Crying] You're not my niece, you're my angel, you're my all. . . . Believe in
275   me, believe . . .

ANYA: I do believe in you, uncle. Everybody loves you and respects you . . . but, uncle dear, you ought to say nothing, no more than that. What were you saying just now about my mother, your own sister? Why did you say those things?

GAEV: Yes, yes. [Covers his face with her hand] Yes, really, it was awful. Save me, my God! And only just now I made a speech before a bookcase . . . it's so silly! And only when I'd finished I knew how silly it was.

VARYA: Yes, uncle dear, you really ought to say less. Keep quiet, that's all.

ANYA: You'd be so much happier in yourself if you only kept quiet.

GAEV: All right, I'll be quiet. [Kisses their hands] I'll be quiet. But let's talk business. On Thursday I was in the District Court, and a lot of us met there together, and we began to talk of this, that, and the other, and now I think I can arrange a loan to pay the interest into the bank.

VARYA: If only God would help us!

GAEV: I'll go on Tuesday. I'll talk with them about it again. [To VARYA] Don't
howl. [To ANYA] Your mother will have a talk to Lopakhin; he, of
course, won't refuse . . . And when you've rested you'll go to Yaroslav
to the Countess, your grandmother. So you see, we'll have three irons in
the fire, and we'll be safe. We'll pay up the interest. I'm certain. [Puts
295   some sugar-candy into his mouth] I swear on my honour, on anything
you will, that the estate will not be sold! [Excitedly] I swear on my
happiness! Here's my hand. You may call me a dishonourable wretch if I
let it go to auction! I swear by all I am!
ANYA: [She is calm again and happy] How good and clever you are, uncle.
300   [Embraces him] I'm happy now! I'm happy! All's well!
[Enter FIERS.]
FIERS: [Reproachfully] Leonid Andreyevitch, don't you fear God? When are you
going to bed?
GAEV: Soon, soon. You go away, Fiers. I'll undress myself. Well, children, bye-
305   bye . . . ! I'll give you the details to-morrow, but let's go to bed now.
[Kisses ANYA and VARYA] I'm a man of the eighties. . . . People
don't praise those years much, but I can still say that I've suffered for my
beliefs. The peasants don't love me for nothing, I assure you. We've got
to learn to know the peasants! We ought to learn how. . . .
ANYA: You're doing it again, uncle!
VARYA: Be quiet, uncle!
FIERS: [Angrily] Leonid Andreyevitch!
GAEV: I'm coming, I'm coming. . . . Go to bed now. Off two cushions into the
middle! I turn over a new leaf. . . . [Exit. FIERS goes out after him.]
ANYA: I'm quieter now. I don't want to go to Yaroslav, I don't like grandmother; but
I'm calm now; thanks to uncle. [Sits down.]
VARYA: It's time to go to sleep. I'll go. There's been an unpleasantness here while
you were away. In the old servants' part of the house, as you know, only
the old people live—little old Efim and Polya and Evstigney, and Karp
320   as well. They started letting some tramps or other spend the night
there—I said nothing. Then I heard that they were saying that I had
ordered them to be fed on peas and nothing else; from meanness, you
see. . . . And it was all Evstigney's doing. . . . Very well, I thought, if
that's what the matter is, just you wait. So I call Evstigney. . . .
325   [Yawns] He comes. "What's this," I say, "Evstigney, you old fool." . . .
[Looks at ANYA] Anya dear! [Pause] She's dropped off. . . . [Takes
ANYA'S arm] Let's go to bye-bye. . . . Come along! . . . [Leads her]
My darling's gone to sleep! Come on. . . . [They go. In the distance, the
other side of the orchard, a shepherd plays his pipe. TROFIMOV crosses
330   the stage and stops on seeing VARYA and ANYA] Sh! She's asleep,
asleep. Come on, dear.
ANYA: [Quietly, half-asleep] I'm so tired . . . all the bells . . . uncle, dear! Mother
and uncle!
VARYA: Come on, dear, come on! [They go into ANYA'S room.]
TROFIMOV: [Moved] My sun! My spring!

CURTAIN

A CT   T WO

[In a field. An old, crooked shrine, which has been long abandoned; near it a well and large stones, which apparently are old tombstones, and an old garden seat. The road is seen to GAEV'S estate. On one side rise dark poplars, behind them begins the cherry orchard. In the distance is a row of telegraph poles, and far, far away on the horizon are the indistinct signs of a large town, which can only be seen on the finest and clearest days. It is close on sunset. CHARLOTTA, YASHA, and DUNYASHA are sitting on the seat; EPIKHODOV stands by and plays on a guitar; all seem thoughtful. CHARLOTTA wears a man's old peaked cap; she has unslung a rifle from her shoulders and is putting to rights the buckle on the strap.]

CHARLOTTA: [Thoughtfully] I haven't a real passport. I don't know how old I am, and I think I'm young. When I was a little girl my father and mother used to go round fairs and give very good performances and I used to do the "salto mortale" and various little things. And when papa and mamma
5   died a German lady took me to her and began to teach me. I liked it. I grew up and became a governess. And where I came from and who I am, I don't know. . . . Who my parents were—perhaps they weren't married—I don't know. [Takes a cucumber out of her pocket and eats] I don't know anything. [Pause] I do want to talk, but I haven't anybody to
10   talk to . . . I haven't anybody at all.
EPIKHODOV: [Plays on the guitar and sings]
        "What is this noisy earth to me,
        What matter friends and foes?"
        I do like playing on the mandoline!
DUNYASHA: That's a guitar, not a mandoline. [Looks at herself in a little mirror and powders herself.]
EPIKHODOV: For the enamoured madman, this is a mandoline. [Sings]
        "Oh that the heart was warmed,
        By all the flames of love returned!"
20   [YASHA sings too.]
CHARLOTTA: These people sing terribly. . . . Foo! Like jackals.
DUNYASHA: [To YASHA] Still, it must be nice to live abroad.
YASHA: Yes, certainly. I cannot differ from you there. [Yawns and lights a cigar.]
EPIKHODOV: That is perfectly natural. Abroad everything is in full complexity.
YASHA: That goes without saying.
EPIKHODOV: I'm an educated man, I read various remarkable books, but I cannot understand the direction I myself want to go—whether to live or to shoot myself, as it were. So, in case, I always carry a revolver about with me. Here it is. [Shows a revolver.]
CHARLOTTA: I've done. Now I'll go. [Slings the rifle] You, Epikhodov, are a very clever man and very terrible; women must be madly in love with you. Brrr! [Going] These wise ones are all so stupid. I've nobody to talk to. I'm always alone, alone; I've nobody at all . . . and I don't know who I am or why I live. [Exit slowly.]

EPIKHODOV: As a matter of fact, independently of everything else, I must express my
feeling, among other things, that fate has been as pitiless in her dealings
with me as a storm is to a small ship. Suppose, let us grant, I am wrong;
then why did I wake up this morning, to give an example, and behold an
enormous spider on my chest, like that. [Shows with both hands] And if I
do drink some kvass, why is it that there is bound to be something of the
most indelicate nature in it, such as a beetle? [Pause] Have you read
Buckle? [Pause] I should like to trouble you, Avdotya Fedorovna, for
two words.
DUNYASHA: Say on.
EPIKHODOV: I should prefer to be alone with you. [Sighs.]
DUNYASHA: [Shy] Very well, only first bring me my little cloak. . . . It's by the
cupboard. It's a little damp here.
EPIKHODOV: Very well . . . I'll bring it. . . . Now I know what to do with my
revolver. [Takes guitar and exits, strumming.]
YASHA: Two-and-twenty troubles! A silly man, between you and me and the
gatepost. [Yawns.]
DUNYASHA: I hope to goodness he won't shoot himself. [Pause] I'm so nervous, I'm
worried. I went into service when I was quite a little girl, and now I'm
not used to common life, and my hands are white, white as a lady's. I'm
so tender and so delicate now; respectable and afraid of everything. . . .
I'm so frightened. And I don't know what will happen to my nerves if
you deceive me, Yasha.
YASHA: [Kisses her] Little cucumber! Of course, every girl must respect herself;
there's nothing I dislike more than a badly behaved girl.
DUNYASHA: I'm awfully in love with you; you're educated, you can talk about
everything. [Pause.]
YASHA: [Yawns] Yes. I think this: if a girl loves anybody, then that means she's
immoral. [Pause] It's nice to smoke a cigar out in the open air. . . .
[Listens] Somebody's coming. It's the mistress, and people with her.
[DUNYASHA embraces him suddenly] Go to the house, as if you'd
been bathing in the river; go by this path, or they'll meet you and will
think I've been meeting you. I can't stand that sort of thing.
DUNYASHA: [Coughs quietly] My head's aching because of your cigar.
[Exit. YASHA remains, sitting by the shrine. Enter LUBOV
ANDREYEVNA, GAEV, and LOPAKHIN.]
LOPAKHIN: You must make up your mind definitely—there's no time to waste. The
question is perfectly plain. Are you willing to let the land for villas or
no? Just one word, yes or no? Just one word!
LUBOV: Who's smoking horrible cigars here? [Sits.]
GAEV: They built that railway; that's made this place very handy. [Sits] Went to
town and had lunch . . . red in the middle! I'd like to go in now and
have just one game.
LUBOV: You'll have time.
LOPAKHIN: Just one word! [Imploringly] Give me an answer!
GAEV: [Yawns] Really!

LUBOV: [Looks in her purse] I had a lot of money yesterday, but there's very little to-day. My poor Varya feeds everybody on milk soup to save money, in the kitchen the old people only get peas, and I spend recklessly. [Drops the purse, scattering gold coins] There, they are all over the place.

YASHA: Permit me to pick them up. [Collects the coins.]

LUBOV: Please do, Yasha. And why did I go and have lunch there? . . . A horrid restaurant with band and tablecloths smelling of soap. . . . Why do you drink so much, Leon? Why do you eat so much? Why do you talk so much? You talked again too much to-day in the restaurant, and it wasn't
90   at all to the point—about the seventies and about decadents. And to whom? Talking to the waiters about decadents!

LOPAKHIN: Yes.

GAEV: [Waves his hand] I can't be cured, that's obvious. . . . [Irritably to YASHA] What's the matter? Why do you keep twisting about in front of me?

YASHA: [Laughs] I can't listen to your voice without laughing.

GAEV: [To his sister] Either he or I . . .

LUBOV: Go away, Yasha; get out of this. . . .

YASHA: [Gives purse to LUBOV ANDREYEVNA] I'll go at once. [Hardly able to keep from laughing] This minute. . . . [Exit.]

LOPAKHIN: That rich man Deriganov is preparing to buy your estate. They say he'll come to the sale himself.

LUBOV: Where did you hear that?

LOPAKHIN: They say so in town.

GAEV: Our Yaroslav aunt has promised to send something, but I don't know when or
105   how much.

LOPAKHIN: How much will she send? A hundred thousand roubles? Or two, perhaps?

LUBOV: I'd be glad of ten or fifteen thousand.

LOPAKHIN: You must excuse my saying so, but I've never met such frivolous people as you before, or anybody so unbusinesslike and peculiar. Here I am
110   telling you in plain language that your estate will be sold, and you don't seem to understand.

LUBOV: What are we to do? Tell us, what?

LOPAKHIN: I tell you every day. I say the same thing every day. Both the cherry orchard and the land must be leased off for villas and at once,
115   immediately—the auction is staring you in the face: Understand! Once you do definitely make up your minds to the villas, then you'll have as much money as you want and you'll be saved.

LUBOV: Villas and villa residents—it's so vulgar, excuse me.

GAEV: I entirely agree with you.

LOPAKHIN: I must cry or yell or faint. I can't stand it! You're too much for me! [To GAEV] You old woman!

GAEV: Really!

LOPAKHIN: Old woman! [Going out.]

LUBOV: [Frightened] No, don't go away, do stop; be a dear. Please. Perhaps we'll
125   find some way out!

LOPAKHIN: What's the good of trying to think!

LUBOV: Please don't go away. It's nicer when you're here. . . . [Pause] I keep on waiting for something to happen, as if the house is going to collapse over our heads.

GAEV: [Thinking deeply] Double in the corner . . . across the middle. . . .

LUBOV: We have been too sinful. . . .

LOPAKHIN: What sins have you committed?

GAEV: [Puts candy into his mouth] They say that I've eaten all my substance in
sugar-candies. [Laughs.]

LUBOV: Oh, my sins. . . . I've always scattered money about without holding
myself in, like a madwoman, and I married a man who made nothing but
debts. My husband died of champagne—he drank terribly—and to my
misfortune, I fell in love with another man and went off with him, and
just at that time—it was my first punishment, a blow that hit me right on
140   the head—here, in the river . . . my boy was drowned, and I went away,
quite away, never to return, never to see this river again . . . I shut my
eyes and ran without thinking, but "he" ran after me . . . without pity,
without respect. I bought a villa near Mentone because "he" fell ill there,
and for three years I knew no rest either by day or night; the sick man
145   wore me out, and my soul dried up. And last year, when they had sold
the villa to pay my debts, I went away to Paris, and there he robbed me
of all I had and threw me over and went off with another woman. I tried
to poison myself. . . . It was so silly, so shameful. . . . And suddenly I
longed to be back in Russia, my own land, with my little girl. . . .
150   [Wipes her tears] Lord, Lord be merciful to me, forgive me my sins!
Punish me no more! [Takes a telegram out of her pocket] I had this
to-day from Paris. . . . He begs my forgiveness, he implores me to
return. . . . [Tears it up] Don't I hear music? [Listens.]

GAEV: That is our celebrated Jewish band. You remember—four violins, a flute, and
155   a double-bass.

LUBOV: So it still exists? It would be nice if they came along some evening.

LOPAKHIN: [Listens] I can't hear. . . . [Sings quietly] "For money will the Germans
make a Frenchman of a Russian." [Laughs] I saw such an awfully funny
thing at the theatre last night.

LUBOV: I'm quite sure there wasn't anything at all funny. You oughtn't to go and see
plays, you ought to go and look at yourself. What a grey life you lead,
what a lot you talk unnecessarily.

LOPAKHIN: It's true. To speak the straight truth, we live a silly life. [Pause] My father
was a peasant, an idiot, he understood nothing, he didn't teach me, he
165   was always drunk, and always used a stick on me. In point of fact, I'm a
fool and an idiot too. I've never learned anything, my handwriting is bad,
I write so that I'm quite ashamed before people, like a pig!

LUBOV: You ought to get married, my friend.

LOPAKHIN: Yes . . . that's true.

LUBOV: Why not to our Varya? She's a nice girl.

LOPAKHIN: Yes.

LUBOV: She's quite homely in her ways, works all day, and, what matters most, she's
in love with you. And you've liked her for a long time.

LOPAKHIN: Well? I don't mind . . . she's a nice girl. [Pause.]

GAEV: I'm offered a place in a bank. Six thousand roubles a year. . . . Did you
hear?

LUBOV: What's the matter with you! Stay where you are. . . .
[Enter FIERS with an overcoat.]

FIERS: [To GAEV] Please, sir, put this on, it's damp.

GAEV: [Putting it on] You're a nuisance, old man.

FIERS: It's all very well. . . . You went away this morning without telling me. [Examining GAEV.]

LUBOV: How old you've grown, Fiers!

FIERS: I beg your pardon?

LOPAKHIN: She says you've grown very old!

FIERS: I've been alive a long time. They were already getting ready to marry me before your father was born. . . . [Laughs] And when the Emancipation came I was already first valet. Only I didn't agree with the Emancipation and remained with my people. . . . [Pause] I remember everybody was
190   happy, but they didn't know why.

LOPAKHIN: It was very good for them in the old days. At any rate, they used to beat them.

FIERS: [Not hearing] Rather. The peasants kept their distance from the masters and the masters kept their distance from the peasants, but now everything's
195   all anyhow and you can't understand anything.

GAEV: Be quiet, Fiers. I've got to go to town tomorrow. I've been promised an introduction to a General who may lend me money on a bill.

LOPAKHIN: Nothing will come of it. And you won't pay your interest, don't you worry.

LUBOV: He's talking rubbish. There's no General at all. [Enter TROFIMOV, ANYA, and VARYA.]

GAEV: Here they are.

ANYA: Mother's sitting down here.

LUBOV: [Tenderly] Come, come, my dears. . . . [Embracing ANYA and VARYA]
205   If you two only knew how much I love you. Sit down next to me, like that. [All sit down.]

LOPAKHIN: Our eternal student is always with the ladies.

TROFIMOV: That's not your business.

LOPAKHIN: He'll soon be fifty, and he's still a student.

TROFIMOV: Leave off your silly jokes!

LOPAKHIN: Getting angry, eh, silly?

TROFIMOV: Shut up, can't you.

LOPAKHIN: [Laughs] I wonder what you think of me?

TROFIMOV: I think, Ermolai Alexeyevitch, that you're a rich man, and you'll soon be
215   a millionaire. Just as the wild beast which eats everything it finds is needed for changes to take place in matter, so you are needed too. [All laugh.]

VARYA: Better tell us something about the planets, Peter.

LUBOV ANDREYEVNA: No, let's go on with yesterday's talk!

TROFIMOV: About what?

GAEV: About the proud man.

TROFIMOV: Yesterday we talked for a long time but we didn't come to anything in the end. There's something mystical about the proud man, in your sense. Perhaps you are right from your point of view, but if you take the matter
225   simply, without complicating it, then what pride can there be, what sense can there be in it, if a man is imperfectly made, physiologically speaking, if in the vast majority of cases he is coarse and stupid and deeply unhappy? We must stop admiring one another. We must work, nothing more.

GAEV: You'll die, all the same.

TROFIMOV: Who knows? And what does it mean—you'll die? Perhaps a man has a hundred senses, and when he dies only the five known to us are destroyed and the remaining ninety-five are left alive.

LUBOV: How clever of you, Peter!

LOPAKHIN: [Ironically] Oh, awfully!

TROFIMOV: The human race progresses, perfecting its powers. Everything that is unattainable now will some day be near at hand and comprehensible, but we must work, we must help with all our strength those who seek to know what fate will bring. Meanwhile in Russia only a very few of us work. The vast majority of those intellectuals whom I know seek for
240 nothing, do nothing, and are at present incapable of hard work. They call themselves intellectuals, but they use "thou" and "thee" to their servants, they treat the peasants like animals, they learn badly, they read nothing seriously, they do absolutely nothing, about science they only talk, about art they understand little. They are all serious, they all have severe faces,
245 they all talk about important things. They philosophize, and at the same time, the vast majority of us, ninety-nine out of a hundred, live like savages, fighting and cursing at the slightest opportunity, eating filthily, sleeping in the dirt, in stuffiness, with fleas, stinks, smells, moral filth, and so on. . . And it's obvious that all our nice talk is only carried on to
250 distract ourselves and others. Tell me, where are those creches we hear so much of? and where are those reading-rooms? People only write novels about them; they don't really exist. Only dirt, vulgarity, and Asiatic plagues really exist. . . . I'm afraid, and I don't at all like serious faces; I don't like serious conversations. Let's be quiet sooner.

LOPAKHIN: You know, I get up at five every morning, I work from morning till evening, I am always dealing with money—my own and other people's—and I see what people are like. You've only got to begin to do anything to find out how few honest, honourable people there are. Sometimes, when I can't sleep, I think: "Oh Lord, you've given us huge
260 forests, infinite fields, and endless horizons, and we, living here, ought really to be giants."

LUBOV: You want giants, do you? . . . They're only good in stories, and even there they frighten one. [EPIKHODOV enters at the back of the stage playing his guitar. Thoughtfully:] Epikhodov's there.

ANYA: [Thoughtfully] Epikhodov's there.

GAEV: The sun's set, ladies and gentlemen.

TROFIMOV: Yes.

GAEV: [Not loudly, as if declaiming] O Nature, thou art wonderful, thou shinest with eternal radiance! Oh, beautiful and indifferent one, thou whom we call
270 mother, thou containest in thyself existence and death, thou livest and destroyest. . . .

VARYA: [Entreatingly] Uncle, dear!

ANYA: Uncle, you're doing it again!

TROFIMOV: You'd better double the red into the middle.

GAEV: I'll be quiet, I'll be quiet.

[They all sit thoughtfully. It is quiet. Only the mumbling of FIERS is heard. Suddenly a distant sound is heard as if from the sky, the sound of a breaking string, which dies away sadly.]

LUBOV: What's that?

LOPAKHIN: I don't know. It may be a bucket fallen down a well somewhere. But it's some way off.

GAEV: Or perhaps it's some bird . . . like a heron.

TROFIMOV: Or an owl.

LUBOV: [Shudders] It's unpleasant, somehow. [A pause.]

FIERS: Before the misfortune the same thing happened. An owl screamed and the samovar hummed without stopping.

GAEV: Before what misfortune?

FIERS: Before the Emancipation. [A pause.]

LUBOV: You know, my friends, let's go in; it's evening now. [To ANYA] You've
290   tears in your eyes. . . . What is it, little girl? [Embraces her.]

ANYA: It's nothing, mother.

TROFIMOV: Some one's coming.

    [Enter a TRAMP in an old white peaked cap and overcoat. He is a little drunk.]

TRAMP: Excuse me, may I go this way straight through to the station?

GAEV: You may. Go along this path.

TRAMP: I thank you from the bottom of my heart. [Hiccups] Lovely weather. . . .
        [Declaims] My brother, my suffering brother. . . . Come out on the
        Volga, you whose groans . . . [To VARYA] Mademoiselle, please give
300   a hungry Russian thirty copecks. . . .
        [VARYA screams, frightened.]

LOPAKHIN: [Angrily] There's manners everybody's got to keep!

LUBOV: [With a start] Take this . . . here you are. . . . [Feels in her purse] There's no silver. . . . It doesn't matter, here's gold.

TRAMP: I am deeply grateful to you! [Exit. Laughter.]

VARYA: [Frightened] I'm going, I'm going. . . . Oh, little mother, at home there's nothing for the servants to eat, and you gave him gold.

LUBOV: What is to be done with such a fool as I am! At home I'll give you everything I've got. Ermolai Alexeyevitch, lend me some more! . . .

LOPAKHIN: Very well.

LUBOV: Let's go, it's time. And Varya, we've settled your affair; I congratulate you.

VARYA: [Crying] You shouldn't joke about this, mother.

LOPAKHIN: Oh, feel me, get thee to a nunnery.

GAEV: My hands are all trembling; I haven't played billiards for a long time.

LOPAKHIN: Oh, feel me, nymph, remember me in thine orisons.

LUBOV: Come along; it'll soon be supper-time.

VARYA: He did frighten me. My heart is beating hard.

LOPAKHIN: Let me remind you, ladies and gentlemen, on August 22 the cherry orchard will be sold. Think of that! . . . Think of that! . . .

320   [All go out except TROFIMOV and ANYA.]

ANYA: [Laughs] Thanks to the tramp who frightened Barbara, we're alone now.

TROFIMOV: Varya's afraid we may fall in love with each other and won't get away
        from us for days on end. Her narrow mind won't allow her to understand
        that we are above love. To escape all the petty and deceptive things
325   which prevent our being happy and free, that is the aim and meaning of
        our lives. Forward! We go irresistibly on to that bright star which burns
        there, in the distance! Don't lag behind, friends!

ANYA: [Clapping her hands] How beautifully you talk! [Pause] It is glorious here to-day!

TROFIMOV: Yes, the weather is wonderful.

ANYA: What have you done to me, Peter? I don't love the cherry orchard as I used to. I loved it so tenderly, I thought there was no better place in the world than our orchard.

TROFIMOV: All Russia is our orchard. The land is great and beautiful, there are many
335   marvellous places in it. [Pause] Think, Anya, your grandfather, your great-grandfather, and all your ancestors were serf-owners, they owned living souls; and now, doesn't something human look at you from every cherry in the orchard, every leaf and every stalk? Don't you hear voices . . .? Oh, it's awful, your orchard is terrible; and when in the
340   evening or at night you walk through the orchard, then the old bark on the trees sheds a dim light and the old cherry-trees seem to be dreaming of all that was a hundred, two hundred years ago, and are oppressed by their heavy visions. Still, at any rate, we've left those two hundred years behind us. So far we've gained nothing at all—we don't yet know what
345   the past is to be to us—we only philosophize, we complain that we are dull, or we drink vodka. For it's so clear that in order to begin to live in the present we must first redeem the past, and that can only be done by suffering, by strenuous, uninterrupted labour. Understand that, Anya.

ANYA: The house in which we live has long ceased to be our house; I shall go away.
350   I give you my word.

TROFIMOV: If you have the housekeeping keys, throw them down the well and go away. Be as free as the wind.

ANYA: [Enthusiastically] How nicely you said that!

TROFIMOV: Believe me, Anya, believe me! I'm not thirty yet, I'm young, I'm still a
355   student, but I have undergone a great deal! I'm as hungry as the winter, I'm ill, I'm shaken. I'm as poor as a beggar, and where haven't I been— fate has tossed me everywhere! But my soul is always my own; every minute of the day and the night it is filled with unspeakable presentiments. I know that happiness is coming, Anya, I see it
360   already. . . .

ANYA: [Thoughtful] The moon is rising.

[EPIKHODOV is heard playing the same sad song on his guitar. The moon rises. Somewhere by the poplars VARYA is looking for ANYA and calling, "Anya, where are you?"]

TROFIMOV: Yes, the moon has risen. [Pause] There is happiness, there it comes; it comes nearer and nearer; I hear its steps already. And if we do not see it we shall not know it, but what does that matter? Others will see it!

THE VOICE OF VARYA: Anya! Where are you?

TROFIMOV: That's Varya again! [Angry] Disgraceful!

ANYA: Never mind. Let's go to the river. It's nice there.

TROFIMOV: Let's go. [They go out.]

THE VOICE OF VARYA: Anya! Anya!

CURTAIN

ACT THREE

[A reception-room cut off from a drawing-room by an arch. Chandelier lighted. A Jewish band, the one mentioned in Act II, is heard playing in another room. Evening. In the drawing-room the grand rond is being danced. Voice of SIMEONOV PISCHIN "Promenade a une paire!" Dancers come into the reception-room; the first pair are PISCHIN and CHARLOTTA IVANOVNA; the second, TROFIMOV and LUBOV ANDREYEVNA; the third, ANYA and the POST OFFICE CLERK; the fourth, VARYA and the STATION-MASTER, and so on. VARYA is crying gently and wipes away her tears as she dances. DUNYASHA is in the last pair. They go off into the drawing-room, PISCHIN shouting, "Grand rond, balancez:" and "Les cavaliers a genou et remerciez vos dames!" FIERS, in a dress-coat, carries a tray with seltzer-water across. Enter PISCHIN and TROFIMOV from the drawing-room.]

PISCHIN: I'm full-blooded and have already had two strokes; it's hard for me to dance, but, as they say, if you're in Rome, you must do as Rome does. I've got the strength of a horse. My dead father, who liked a joke, peace to his bones, used to say, talking of our ancestors, that the ancient stock
5   of the Simeonov-Pischins was descended from that identical horse that Caligula made a senator. . . . [Sits] But the trouble is, I've no money! A hungry dog only believes in meat. [Snores and wakes up again immediately] So I . . . only believe in money. . . .
TROFIMOV: Yes. There is something equine about your figure.
PISCHIN: Well . . . a horse is a fine animal . . . you can sell a horse.
        [Billiard playing can be heard in the next room. VARYA appears under the arch.]
TROFIMOV: [Teasing] Madame Lopakhin! Madame Lopakhin!
VARYA: [Angry] Decayed gentleman!
TROFIMOV: Yes, I am a decayed gentleman, and I'm proud of it!
VARYA: [Bitterly] We've hired the musicians, but how are they to be paid? [Exit.]
TROFIMOV: [To PISCHIN] If the energy which you, in the course of your life, have spent in looking for money to pay interest had been used for something else, then, I believe, after all, you'd be able to turn everything upside
20   down.
PISCHIN: Nietzsche . . . a philosopher . . . a very great, a most celebrated man . . . a man of enormous brain, says in his books that you can forge banknotes.
TROFIMOV: And have you read Nietzsche?
PISCHIN: Well . . . Dashenka told me. Now I'm in such a position, I wouldn't mind forging them . . . I've got to pay 310 roubles the day after to-morrow . . . I've got 130 already. . . . [Feels his pockets, nervously] I've lost the money! The money's gone! [Crying] Where's the money? [Joyfully] Here it is behind the lining . . . I even began to perspire.
30   [Enter LUBOV ANDREYEVNA and CHARLOTTA IVANOVNA.]
LUBOV: [Humming a Caucasian dance] Why is Leonid away so long? What's he doing in town? [To DUNYASHA] Dunyasha, give the musicians some tea.
TROFIMOV: Business is off, I suppose.

LUBOV: And the musicians needn't have come, and we needn't have got up this
        ball. . . . Well, never mind. . . . [Sits and sings softly.]
CHARLOTTA: [Gives a pack of cards to PISCHIN] Here's a pack of cards, think of
        any one card you like.
PISCHIN: I've thought of one.
CHARLOTTA: Now shuffle. All right, now. Give them here, oh my dear Mr. Pischin.
        "Ein, zwei, drei"! Now look and you'll find it in your coat-tail pocket.
PISCHIN: [Takes a card out of his coat-tail pocket] Eight of spades, quite right!
        [Surprised] Think of that now!
CHARLOTTA: [Holds the pack of cards on the palm of her hand. To TROFIMOV]
45   Now tell me quickly. What's the top card?
TROFIMOV: Well, the queen of spades.
CHARLOTTA: Right! [To PISCHIN] Well now? What card's on top?
PISCHIN: Ace of hearts.
CHARLOTTA: Right! [Claps her hands, the pack of cards vanishes] How lovely the
50   weather is to-day. [A mysterious woman's voice answers her, as if from
        under the floor, "Oh yes, it's lovely weather, madam."] You are so
        beautiful, you are my ideal. [Voice, "You, madam, please me very much
        too."]
STATION-MASTER: [Applauds] Madame ventriloquist, bravo!
PISCHIN: [Surprised] Think of that, now! Delightful, Charlotte Ivanovna . . . I'm
        simply in love. . . .
CHARLOTTA: In love? [Shrugging her shoulders] Can you love? "Guter Mensch aber
        schlechter Musikant".
TROFIMOV: [Slaps PISCHIN on the shoulder] Oh, you horse!
CHARLOTTA: Attention please, here's another trick. [Takes a shawl from a chair]
        Here's a very nice plaid shawl, I'm going to sell it. . . . [Shakes it]
        Won't anybody buy it?
PISCHIN: [Astonished] Think of that now!
CHARLOTTA: "Ein, zwei, drei".
65   [She quickly lifts up the shawl, which is hanging down. ANYA is
        standing behind it; she bows and runs to her mother, hugs her and runs
        back to the drawing-room amid general applause.]
LUBOV: [Applauds] Bravo, bravo!
CHARLOTTA: Once again! "Ein, zwei, drei"!
70   [Lifts the shawl. VARYA stands behind it and bows.]
PISCHIN: [Astonished] Think of that, now.
CHARLOTTA: The end!
        [Throws the shawl at PISCHIN, curtseys and runs into the drawing-
        room.]
PISCHIN: [Runs after her] Little wretch. . . . What? Would you? [Exit.]
LUBOV: Leonid hasn't come yet. I don't understand what he's doing so long in town!
        Everything must be over by now. The estate must be sold; or, if the sale
        never came off, then why does he stay so long?
VARYA: [Tries to soothe her] Uncle has bought it. I'm certain of it.
TROFIMOV: [Sarcastically] Oh, yes!

VARYA: Grandmother sent him her authority for him to buy it in her name and transfer the debt to her. She's doing it for Anya. And I'm certain that God will help us and uncle will buy it.

LUBOV: Grandmother sent fifteen thousand roubles from Yaroslav to buy the
85   property in her name—she won't trust us—and that wasn't even enough to pay the interest. [Covers her face with her hands] My fate will be settled to-day, my fate. . . .

TROFIMOV: [Teasing VARYA] Madame Lopakhin!

VARYA: [Angry] Eternal student! He's already been expelled twice from the
90   university.

LUBOV: Why are you getting angry, Varya? He's teasing you about Lopakhin, well what of it? You can marry Lopakhin if you want to, he's a good, interesting man. . . . You needn't if you don't want to; nobody wants to force you against your will, my darling.

VARYA: I do look at the matter seriously, little mother, to be quite frank. He's a good man, and I like him.

LUBOV: Then marry him. I don't understand what you're waiting for.

VARYA: I can't propose to him myself, little mother. People have been talking about him to me for two years now, but he either says nothing, or jokes about
100   it. I understand. He's getting rich, he's busy, he can't bother about me. If I had some money, even a little, even only a hundred roubles, I'd throw up everything and go away. I'd go into a convent.

TROFIMOV: How nice!

VARYA: [To TROFIMOV] A student ought to have sense! [Gently, in tears] How
105   ugly you are now, Peter, how old you've grown! [To LUBOV ANDREYEVNA, no longer crying] But I can't go on without working, little mother. I want to be doing something every minute. [Enter YASHA.]

YASHA: [Nearly laughing] Epikhodov's broken a billiard cue! [Exit.]

VARYA: Why is Epikhodov here? Who said he could play billiards? I don't understand these people. [Exit.]

LUBOV: Don't tease her, Peter, you see that she's quite unhappy without that.

TROFIMOV: She takes too much on herself, she keeps on interfering in other people's business. The whole summer she's given no peace to me or to Anya,
115   she's afraid we'll have a romance all to ourselves. What has it to do with her? As if I'd ever given her grounds to believe I'd stoop to such vulgarity! We are above love.

LUBOV: Then I suppose I must be beneath love. [In agitation] Why isn't Leonid here? If I only knew whether the estate is sold or not! The disaster seems
120   to me so improbable that I don't know what to think, I'm all at sea . . . I may scream . . . or do something silly. Save me, Peter. Say something, say something.

TROFIMOV: Isn't it all the same whether the estate is sold to-day or isn't? It's been all up with it for a long time; there's no turning back, the path's grown over.
125   Be calm, dear, you shouldn't deceive yourself, for once in your life at any rate you must look the truth straight in the face.

LUBOV: What truth? You see where truth is, and where untruth is, but I seem to have
    lost my sight and see nothing. You boldly settle all important questions,
    but tell me, dear, isn't it because you're young, because you haven't had
130   time to suffer till you settled a single one of your questions? You boldly
    look forward, isn't it because you cannot foresee or expect anything
    terrible, because so far life has been hidden from your young eyes? You
    are bolder, more honest, deeper than we are, but think only, be just a
    little magnanimous, and have mercy on me. I was born here, my father
135   and mother lived here, my grandfather too, I love this house. I couldn't
    understand my life without that cherry orchard, and if it really must be
    sold, sell me with it! [Embraces TROFIMOV, kisses his forehead]. My
    son was drowned here. . . . [Weeps] Have pity on me, good, kind man.
TROFIMOV: You know I sympathize with all my soul.
LUBOV: Yes, but it ought to be said differently, differently. . . . [Takes another
    handkerchief, a telegram falls on the floor] I'm so sick at heart to-day,
    you can't imagine. Here it's so noisy, my soul shakes at every sound. I
    shake all over, and I can't go away by myself, I'm afraid of the silence.
    Don't judge me harshly, Peter . . . I loved you, as if you belonged to my
145   family. I'd gladly let Anya marry you, I swear it, only dear, you ought to
    work, finish your studies. You don't do anything, only fate throws you
    about from place to place, it's so odd. . . . Isn't it true? Yes? And you
    ought to do something to your beard to make it grow better [Laughs]
    You are funny!
TROFIMOV: [Picking up telegram] I don't want to be a Beau Brummel.
LUBOV: This telegram's from Paris. I get one every day. Yesterday and to-day. That
    wild man is ill again, he's bad again. . . . He begs for forgiveness, and
    implores me to come, and I really ought to go to Paris to be near him.
    You look severe, Peter, but what can I do, my dear, what can I do; he's
155   ill, he's alone, unhappy, and who's to look after him, who's to keep him
    away from his errors, to give him his medicine punctually? And why
    should I conceal it and say nothing about it; I love him, that's plain, I
    love him, I love him. . . . That love is a stone round my neck; I'm
    going with it to the bottom, but I love that stone and can't live without it.
160   [Squeezes TROFIMOV'S hand] Don't think badly of me, Peter, don't
    say anything to me, don't say . . .
TROFIMOV: [Weeping] For God's sake forgive my speaking candidly, but that man
    has robbed you!
LUBOV: No, no, no, you oughtn't to say that! [Stops her ears.]
TROFIMOV: But he's a wretch, you alone don't know it! He's a petty thief, a
    nobody. . . .
LUBOV: [Angry, but restrained] You're twenty-six or twenty-seven, and still a
    schoolboy of the second class!
TROFIMOV: Why not!
LUBOV: You ought to be a man, at your age you ought to be able to understand those
    who love. And you ought to be in love yourself, you must fall in love!
    [Angry] Yes, yes! You aren't pure, you're just a freak, a queer fellow, a
    funny growth . . .
TROFIMOV: [In horror] What is she saying!

LUBOV: "I'm above love!" You're not above love, you're just what our Fiers calls a
    bungler. Not to have a mistress at your age!

TROFIMOV: [In horror] This is awful! What is she saying? [Goes quickly up into the
    drawing-room, clutching his head] It's awful . . . I can't stand it, I'll go
    away. [Exit, but returns at once] All is over between us! [Exit.]

LUBOV: [Shouts after him] Peter, wait! Silly man, I was joking! Peter! [Somebody is
    heard going out and falling downstairs noisily. ANYA and VARYA
    scream; laughter is heard immediately] What's that?
    [ANYA comes running in, laughing.]

ANYA: Peter's fallen downstairs! [Runs out again.]

LUBOV: This Peter's a marvel.
    [The STATION-MASTER stands in the middle of the drawing-room and
    recites "The Magdalen" by Tolstoy. He is listened to, but he has only
    delivered a few lines when a waltz is heard from the front room, and the
    recitation is stopped. Everybody dances. TROFIMOV, ANYA, VARYA,
190   and LUBOV ANDREYEVNA come in from the front room.]

LUBOV: Well, Peter . . . you pure soul . . . I beg your pardon . . . let's dance.
    [She dances with PETER. ANYA and VARYA dance. FIERS enters and
    stands his stick by a side door. YASHA has also come in and looks on at
    the dance.]

YASHA: Well, grandfather?

FIERS: I'm not well. At our balls some time back, generals and barons and admirals
    used to dance, and now we send for post-office clerks and the Station-
    master, and even they come as a favour. I'm very weak. The dead
    master, the grandfather, used to give everybody sealing-wax when
200   anything was wrong. I've taken sealing-wax every day for twenty years,
    and more; perhaps that's why I still live.

YASHA: I'm tired of you, grandfather. [Yawns] If you'd only hurry up and kick the
    bucket.

FIERS: Oh you . . . bungler! [Mutters.]

205   [TROFIMOV and LUBOV ANDREYEVNA dance in the reception-
    room, then into the sitting-room.]

LUBOV: "Merci". I'll sit down. [Sits] I'm tired.
    [Enter ANYA.]

ANYA: [Excited] Somebody in the kitchen was saying just now that the cherry
210   orchard was sold to-day.

LUBOV: Sold to whom?

ANYA: He didn't say to whom. He's gone now. [Dances out into the reception-room
    with TROFIMOV.]

YASHA: Some old man was chattering about it a long time ago. A stranger!

FIERS: And Leonid Andreyevitch isn't here yet, he hasn't come. He's wearing a
    light, "demi-saison" overcoat. He'll catch cold. Oh these young fellows.

LUBOV: I'll die of this. Go and find out, Yasha, to whom it's sold.

YASHA: Oh, but he's been gone a long time, the old man. [Laughs.]

LUBOV: [Slightly vexed] Why do you laugh? What are you glad about?

YASHA: Epikhodov's too funny. He's a silly man. Two-and-twenty troubles.

LUBOV: Fiers, if the estate is sold, where will you go?

FIERS: I'll go wherever you order me to go.

LUBOV: Why do you look like that? Are you ill? I think you ought to go to bed. . . .

FIERS: Yes . . . [With a smile] I'll go to bed, and who'll hand things round and give
225   orders without me? I've the whole house on my shoulders.
YASHA: [To LUBOV ANDREYEVNA] Lubov Andreyevna! I want to ask a favour
           of you, if you'll be so kind! If you go to Paris again, then please take me
           with you. It's absolutely impossible for me to stop here. [Looking round;
           in an undertone] What's the good of talking about it, you see for yourself
230   that this is an uneducated country, with an immoral population, and it's
           so dull. The food in the kitchen is beastly, and here's this Fiers walking
           about mumbling various inappropriate things. Take me with you, be so
           kind!
           [Enter PISCHIN.]
PISCHIN: I come to ask for the pleasure of a little waltz, dear lady. . . . [LUBOV
           ANDREYEVNA goes to him] But all the same, you wonderful woman, I
           must have 180 little roubles from you . . . I must. . . . [They dance]
           180 little roubles. . . . [They go through into the drawing-room.]
YASHA: [Sings softly]
240   "Oh, will you understand
           My soul's deep restlessness?"
           [In the drawing-room a figure in a grey top-hat and in baggy check trousers
           is waving its hands and jumping about; there are cries of "Bravo,
           Charlotta Ivanovna!"]
DUNYASHA: [Stops to powder her face] The young mistress tells me to dance—there
           are a lot of gentlemen, but few ladies—and my head goes round when I
           dance, and my heart beats, Fiers Nicolaevitch; the Post-office clerk told
           me something just now which made me catch my breath. [The music
           grows faint.]
FIERS: What did he say to you?
DUNYASHA: He says, "You're like a little flower."
YASHA: [Yawns] Impolite. . . . [Exit.]
DUNYASHA: Like a little flower. I'm such a delicate girl; I simply love words of
           tenderness.
FIERS: You'll lose your head.
           [Enter EPIKHODOV.]
EPIKHODOV: You, Avdotya Fedorovna, want to see me no more than if I was some
           insect. [Sighs] Oh, life!
DUNYASHA: What do you want?
EPIKHODOV: Undoubtedly, perhaps, you may be right. [Sighs] But, certainly, if you
           regard the matter from the aspect, then you, if I may say so, and you
           must excuse my candidness, have absolutely reduced me to a state of
           mind. I know my fate, every day something unfortunate happens to me,
           and I've grown used to it a long time ago, I even look at my fate with a
265   smile. You gave me your word, and though I . . .
DUNYASHA: Please, we'll talk later on, but leave me alone now. I'm meditating now.
           [Plays with her fan.]
EPIKHODOV: Every day something unfortunate happens to me, and I, if I may so
           express myself, only smile, and even laugh.
270   [VARYA enters from the drawing-room.]

VARYA: Haven't you gone yet, Simeon? You really have no respect for anybody. [To DUNYASHA] You go away, Dunyasha. [To EPIKHODOV] You play billiards and break a cue, and walk about the drawing-room as if you were a visitor!

EPIKHODOV: You cannot, if I may say so, call me to order.

VARYA: I'm not calling you to order, I'm only telling you. You just walk about from place to place and never do your work. Goodness only knows why we keep a clerk.

EPIKHODOV: [Offended] Whether I work, or walk about, or eat, or play billiards, is
280   only a matter to be settled by people of understanding and my elders.

VARYA: You dare to talk to me like that! [Furious] You dare? You mean that I know nothing? Get out of here! This minute!

EPIKHODOV: [Nervous] I must ask you to express yourself more delicately.

VARYA: [Beside herself] Get out this minute. Get out! [He goes to the door, she
285   follows] Two-and-twenty troubles! I don't want any sign of you here! I don't want to see anything of you! [EPIKHODOV has gone out; his voice can be heard outside: "I'll make a complaint against you."] What, coming back? [Snatches up the stick left by FIERS by the door] Go . . . go . . . go, I'll show you. . . . Are you going? Are you going? Well,
290   then take that. [She hits out as LOPAKHIN enters.]

LOPAKHIN: Much obliged.

VARYA: [Angry but amused] I'm sorry.

LOPAKHIN: Never mind. I thank you for my pleasant reception.

VARYA: It isn't worth any thanks. [Walks away, then looks back and asks gently] I
295   didn't hurt you, did I?

LOPAKHIN: No, not at all. There'll be an enormous bump, that's all.

VOICES FROM DRAWING-ROOM: Lopakhin's returned! Ermolai Alexeyevitch!

PISCHIN: Now we'll see what there is to see and hear what there is to hear. . . [Kisses LOPAKHIN] You smell of cognac, my dear, my soul. And we're all
300   having a good time.
         [Enter LUBOV ANDREYEVNA.]

LUBOV: Is that you, Ermolai Alexeyevitch? Why were you so long? Where's Leonid?

LOPAKHIN: Leonid Andreyevitch came back with me, he's coming. . . .

LUBOV: [Excited] Well, what? Is it sold? Tell me?

LOPAKHIN: [Confused, afraid to show his pleasure] The sale ended up at four o'clock. . . . We missed the train, and had to wait till half-past nine. [Sighs heavily] Ooh! My head's going round a little.
         [Enter GAEV; in his right hand he carries things he has bought, with his
310   left he wipes away his tears.]

LUBOV: Leon, what's happened? Leon, well? [Impatiently, in tears] Quick, for the love of God. . . .

GAEV: [Says nothing to her, only waves his hand; to FIERS, weeping] Here, take this. . . . Here are anchovies, herrings from Kertch. . . . I've had no
315   food to-day. . . . I have had a time! [The door from the billiard-room is open; the clicking of the balls is heard, and YASHA'S voice, "Seven, eighteen!" GAEV'S expression changes, he cries no more] I'm awfully tired. Help me change my clothes, Fiers.
         [Goes out through the drawing-room; FIERS after him.]

PISCHIN: What happened? Come on, tell us!

LUBOV: Is the cherry orchard sold?

LOPAKHIN: It is sold.

LUBOV: Who bought it?

LOPAKHIN: I bought it.

325   [LUBOV ANDREYEVNA is overwhelmed; she would fall if she were not standing by an armchair and a table. VARYA takes her keys off her belt, throws them on the floor, into the middle of the room and goes out.]

LOPAKHIN: I bought it! Wait, ladies and gentlemen, please, my head's going round, I can't talk. . . . [Laughs] When we got to the sale, Deriganov was there
330   already. Leonid Andreyevitch had only fifteen thousand roubles, and Deriganov offered thirty thousand on top of the mortgage to begin with. I saw how matters were, so I grabbed hold of him and bid forty. He went up to forty-five, I offered fifty-five. That means he went up by fives and I went up by tens. . . . Well, it came to an end. I bid ninety more than
335   the mortgage; and it stayed with me. The cherry orchard is mine now, mine! [Roars with laughter] My God, my God, the cherry orchard's mine! Tell me I'm drunk, or mad, or dreaming. . . . [Stamps his feet] Don't laugh at me! If my father and grandfather rose from their graves and looked at the whole affair, and saw how their Ermolai, their beaten
340   and uneducated Ermolai, who used to run barefoot in the winter, how that very Ermolai has bought an estate, which is the most beautiful thing in the world! I've bought the estate where my grandfather and my father were slaves, where they weren't even allowed into the kitchen. I'm asleep, it's only a dream, an illusion. . . . It's the fruit of imagination,
345   wrapped in the fog of the unknown. . . . [Picks up the keys, nicely smiling] She threw down the keys, she wanted to show she was no longer mistress here. . . . [Jingles keys] Well, it's all one! [Hears the band tuning up] Eh, musicians, play, I want to hear you! Come and look at Ermolai Lopakhin laying his axe to the cherry orchard, come and look
350   at the trees falling! We'll build villas here, and our grandsons and great-grandsons will see a new life here. . . . Play on, music! [The band plays. LUBOV ANDREYEVNA sinks into a chair and weeps bitterly. LOPAKHIN continues reproachfully] Why then, why didn't you take my advice? My poor, dear woman, you can't go back now. [Weeps] Oh, if
355   only the whole thing was done with, if only our uneven, unhappy life were changed!

PISCHIN: [Takes his arm; in an undertone] She's crying. Let's go into the drawing-room and leave her by herself . . . come on. . . . [Takes his arm and leads him out.]

LOPAKHIN: What's that? Bandsmen, play nicely! Go on, do just as I want you to! [Ironically] The new owner, the owner of the cherry orchard is coming! [He accidentally knocks up against a little table and nearly upsets the candelabra] I can pay for everything! [Exit with PISCHIN]

[In the reception-room and the drawing-room nobody remains except
365   LUBOV ANDREYEVNA, who sits huddled up and weeping bitterly. The band plays softly. ANYA and TROFIMOV come in quickly. ANYA goes up to her mother and goes on her knees in front of her. TROFIMOV stands at the drawing-room entrance.]

ANYA: Mother! mother, are you crying? My dear, kind, good mother, my beautiful
370 mother, I love you! Bless you! The cherry orchard is sold, we've got it
no longer, it's true, true, but don't cry mother, you've still got your life
before you, you've still your beautiful pure soul . . . Come with me,
come, dear, away from here, come! We'll plant a new garden, finer than
this, and you'll see it, and you'll understand, and deep joy, gentle joy
375 will sink into your soul, like the evening sun, and you'll smile, mother!
Come, dear, let's go!

CURTAIN

ACT FOUR

[The stage is set as for Act I. There are no curtains on the windows, no pictures;
only a few pieces of furniture are left; they are piled up in a corner as if for sale. The
emptiness is felt. By the door that leads out of the house and at the back of the stage,
portmanteaux and travelling paraphernalia are piled up. The door on the left is open;
the voices of VARYA and ANYA can be heard through it. LOPAKHIN stands and
waits. YASHA holds a tray with little tumblers of champagne. Outside,
EPIKHODOV is tying up a box. Voices are heard behind the stage. The peasants have
come to say good-bye. The voice of GAEV is heard: "Thank you, brothers, thank
you."]

YASHA: The common people have come to say good-bye. I am of the opinion,
Ermolai Alexeyevitch, that they're good people, but they don't
understand very much.
[The voices die away. LUBOV ANDREYEVNA and GAEV enter. She
5 is not crying but is pale, and her face trembles; she can hardly speak.]
GAEV: You gave them your purse, Luba. You can't go on like that, you can't!
LUBOV: I couldn't help myself, I couldn't! [They go out.]
LOPAKHIN: [In the doorway, calling after them] Please, I ask you most humbly! Just a
little glass to say good-bye. I didn't remember to bring any from town
10 and I only found one bottle at the station. Please, do! [Pause] Won't you
really have any? [Goes away from the door] If I only knew—I wouldn't
have bought any. Well, I shan't drink any either. [YASHA carefully puts
the tray on a chair] You have a drink, Yasha, at any rate.
YASHA: To those departing! And good luck to those who stay behind! [Drinks] I can
15 assure you that this isn't real champagne.
LOPAKHIN: Eight roubles a bottle. [Pause] It's devilish cold here.
YASHA: There are no fires to-day, we're going away. [Laughs]
LOPAKHIN: What's the matter with you?
YASHA: I'm just pleased.
LOPAKHIN: It's October outside, but it's as sunny and as quiet as if it were summer.
Good for building. [Looking at his watch and speaking through the door]
Ladies and gentlemen, please remember that it's only forty-seven
minutes till the train goes! You must go off to the station in twenty
minutes. Hurry up.
25 [TROFIMOV, in an overcoat, comes in from the grounds.]

TROFIMOV: I think it's time we went. The carriages are waiting. Where the devil are my goloshes? They're lost. [Through the door] Anya, I can't find my goloshes! I can't!

LOPAKHIN: I've got to go to Kharkov. I'm going in the same train as you. I'm going
30 to spend the whole winter in Kharkov. I've been hanging about with you people, going rusty without work. I can't live without working. I must have something to do with my hands; they hang about as if they weren't mine at all.

TROFIMOV: We'll go away now and then you'll start again on your useful labours.

LOPAKHIN: Have a glass.

TROFIMOV: I won't.

LOPAKHIN: So you're off to Moscow now?

TROFIMOV: Yes. I'll see them into town and to-morrow I'm off to Moscow.

LOPAKHIN: Yes. . . . I expect the professors don't lecture nowadays; they're waiting
40 till you turn up!

TROFIMOV: That's not your business.

LOPAKHIN: How many years have you been going to the university?

TROFIMOV: Think of something fresh. This is old and flat. [Looking for his goloshes] You know, we may not meet each other again, so just let me give you a
45 word of advice on parting: "Don't wave your hands about! Get rid of that habit of waving them about. And then, building villas and reckoning on their residents becoming freeholders in time—that's the same thing; it's all a matter of waving your hands about. . . . Whether I want to or not, you know, I like you. You've thin, delicate fingers, like those of an artist,
50 and you've a thin, delicate soul. . . ."

LOPAKHIN: [Embraces him] Good-bye, dear fellow. Thanks for all you've said. If you want any, take some money from me for the journey.

TROFIMOV: Why should I? I don't want it.

LOPAKHIN: But you've nothing!

TROFIMOV: Yes, I have, thank you; I've got some for a translation. Here it is in my pocket. [Nervously] But I can't find my goloshes!

VARYA: [From the other room] Take your rubbish away! [Throws a pair of rubber goloshes on to the stage.]

TROFIMOV: Why are you angry, Varya? Hm! These aren't my goloshes!

LOPAKHIN: In the spring I sowed three thousand acres of poppies, and now I've made forty thousand roubles net profit. And when my poppies were in flower, what a picture it was! So I, as I was saying, made forty thousand roubles, and I mean I'd like to lend you some, because I can afford it. Why turn up your nose at it? I'm just a simple peasant. . . .

TROFIMOV: Your father was a peasant, mine was a chemist, and that means absolutely nothing. [LOPAKHIN takes out his pocket-book] No, no. . . . Even if you gave me twenty thousand I should refuse. I'm a free man. And everything that all you people, rich and poor, value so highly and so dearly hasn't the least influence over me; it's like a flock
70 of down in the wind. I can do without you, I can pass you by. I'm strong and proud. Mankind goes on to the highest truths and to the highest happiness such as is only possible on earth, and I go in the front ranks!

LOPAKHIN: Will you get there?

TROFIMOV: I will. [Pause] I'll get there and show others the way. [Axes cutting the
75   trees are heard in the distance.]
LOPAKHIN: Well, good-bye, old man. It's time to go. Here we stand pulling one
            another's noses, but life goes its own way all the time. When I work for a
            long time, and I don't get tired, then I think more easily, and I think I get
            to understand why I exist. And there are so many people in Russia,
80   brother, who live for nothing at all. Still, work goes on without that.
            Leonid Andreyevitch, they say, has accepted a post in a bank; he will get
            sixty thousand roubles a year. . . . But he won't stand it; he's very lazy.
ANYA: [At the door] Mother asks if you will stop them cutting down the orchard
            until she has gone away.
TROFIMOV: Yes, really, you ought to have enough tact not to do that. [Exit.]
LOPAKHIN: All right, all right . . . yes, he's right. [Exit.]
ANYA: Has Fiers been sent to the hospital?
YASHA: I gave the order this morning. I suppose they've sent him.
ANYA: [To EPIKHODOV, who crosses the room] Simeon Panteleyevitch, please
90   make inquiries if Fiers has been sent to the hospital.
YASHA: [Offended] I told Egor this morning. What's the use of asking ten times!
EPIKHODOV: The aged Fiers, in my conclusive opinion, isn't worth mending; his
            forefathers had better have him. I only envy him. [Puts a trunk on a hat-
            box and squashes it] Well, of course. I thought so! [Exit.]
YASHA: [Grinning] Two-and-twenty troubles.
VARYA: [Behind the door] Has Fiers been taken away to the hospital?
ANYA: Yes.
VARYA: Why didn't they take the letter to the doctor?
ANYA: It'll have to be sent after him. [Exit.]
VARYA: [In the next room] Where's Yasha? Tell him his mother's come and wants to
            say good-bye to him.
YASHA: [Waving his hand] She'll make me lose all patience!
            [DUNYASHA has meanwhile been bustling round the luggage; now that
            YASHA is left alone, she goes up to him.]
DUNYASHA: If you only looked at me once, Yasha. You're going away, leaving me
            behind.
            [Weeps and hugs him round the neck.]
YASHA: What's the use of crying? [Drinks champagne] In six days I'll be again in
            Paris. To-morrow we get into the express and off we go. I can hardly
110   believe it. Vive la France! It doesn't suit me here, I can't live here . . .
            it's no good. Well, I've seen the uncivilized world; I have had enough of
            it. [Drinks champagne] What do you want to cry for? You behave
            yourself properly, and then you won't cry.
DUNYASHA: [Looks in a small mirror and powders her face] Send me a letter from
115   Paris. You know I loved you, Yasha, so much! I'm a sensitive creature,
            Yasha.
YASHA: Somebody's coming.
            [He bustles around the luggage, singing softly. Enter LUBOV
            ANDREYEVNA, GAEV, ANYA, and CHARLOTTA IVANOVNA.]
GAEV: We'd better be off. There's no time left. [Looks at YASHA] Somebody
            smells of herring!

LUBOV: We needn't get into our carriages for ten minutes. . . . [Looks round the room] Good-bye, dear house, old grandfather. The winter will go, the spring will come, and then you'll exist no more, you'll be pulled down.
125   How much these walls have seen! [Passionately kisses her daughter] My treasure, you're radiant, your eyes flash like two jewels! Are you happy? Very?

ANYA: Very! A new life is beginning, mother!

GAEV: [Gaily] Yes, really, everything's all right now. Before the cherry orchard was
130   sold we all were excited and we suffered, and then, when the question was solved once and for all, we all calmed down, and even became cheerful. I'm a bank official now, and a financier . . . red in the middle; and you, Luba, for some reason or other, look better, there's no doubt about it.

LUBOV: Yes. My nerves are better, it's true. [She puts on her coat and hat] I sleep well. Take my luggage out, Yasha. It's time. [To ANYA] My little girl, we'll soon see each other again. . . . I'm off to Paris. I'll live there on the money your grandmother from Yaroslav sent along to buy the estate—bless her!—though it won't last long.

ANYA: You'll come back soon, soon, mother, won't you? I'll get ready, and pass the exam at the Higher School, and then I'll work and help you. We'll read all sorts of books to one another, won't we? [Kisses her mother's hands] We'll read in the autumn evenings; we'll read many books, and a beautiful new world will open up before us. . . . [Thoughtfully] You'll
145   come, mother. . . .

LUBOV: I'll come, my darling. [Embraces her.]
        [Enter LOPAKHIN. CHARLOTTA is singing to herself.]

GAEV: Charlotta is happy; she sings!

CHARLOTTA: [Takes a bundle, looking like a wrapped-up baby] My little baby, bye-
150   bye. [The baby seems to answer, "Oua! Oua!"] Hush, my nice little boy. ["Oua! Oua!"] I'm so sorry for you! [Throws the bundle back] So please find me a new place. I can't go on like this.

LOPAKHIN: We'll find one, Charlotta Ivanovna, don't you be afraid.

GAEV: Everybody's leaving us. Varya's going away . . . we've suddenly become
155   unnecessary.

CHARLOTTA: I've nowhere to live in town. I must go away. [Hums] Never mind.
        [Enter PISCHIN.]

LOPAKHIN: Nature's marvel!

PISCHIN: [Puffing] Oh, let me get my breath back. . . . I'm fagged out . . . My
160   most honoured, give me some water. . . .

GAEV: Come for money, what? I'm your humble servant, and I'm going out of the way of temptation. [Exit.]

PISCHIN: I haven't been here for ever so long . . . dear madam. [To LOPAKHIN] You here? Glad to see you . . . man of immense brain . . . take
165   this . . . take it. . . . [Gives LOPAKHIN money] Four hundred roubles. . . . That leaves 840. . . .

LOPAKHIN: [Shrugs his shoulders in surprise] As if I were dreaming. Where did you get this from?

PISCHIN: Stop . . . it's hot. . . . A most unexpected thing happened. Some
170   Englishmen came along and found some white clay on my land. . . .
           [To LUBOV ANDREYEVNA] And here's four hundred for you . . .
           beautiful lady. . . . [Gives her money] Give you the rest later. . . .
           [Drinks water] Just now a young man in the train was saying that some
           great philosopher advises us all to jump off roofs. "Jump!" he says, and
175   that's all. [Astonished] To think of that, now! More water!
LOPAKHIN: Who were these Englishmen?
PISCHIN: I've leased off the land with the clay to them for twenty-four years. . . .
           Now, excuse me, I've no time. . . . I must run off. . . . I must go to
           Znoikov and to Kardamonov . . . I owe them all money. . . . [Drinks]
180   Good-bye. I'll come in on Thursday.
LUBOV: We're just off to town, and to-morrow I go abroad.
PISCHIN: [Agitated] What? Why to town? I see furniture . . . trunks. . . . Well,
           never mind. [Crying] Never mind. These Englishmen are men of
           immense intellect. . . . Never mind. . . . Be happy. . . . God will help
185   you. . . . Never mind. . . . Everything in this world comes to an
           end. . . . [Kisses LUBOV ANDREYEVNA'S hand] And if you should
           happen to hear that my end has come, just remember this old . . . horse
           and say: "There was one such and such a Simeonov-Pischin, God bless
           his soul. . . ." Wonderful weather . . . yes. . . . [Exit deeply moved,
190   but returns at once and says in the door] Dashenka sent her love! [Exit.]
LUBOV: Now we can go. I've two anxieties, though. The first is poor Fiers [Looks at
           her watch] We've still five minutes. . . .
ANYA: Mother, Fiers has already been sent to the hospital. Yasha sent him off this
           morning.
LUBOV: The second is Varya. She's used to getting up early and to work, and now
           she's no work to do she's like a fish out of water. She's grown thin and
           pale, and she cries, poor thing. . . . [Pause] You know very well,
           Ermolai Alexeyevitch, that I used to hope to marry her to you, and I
           suppose you are going to marry somebody? [Whispers to ANYA, who
200   nods to CHARLOTTA, and they both go out] She loves you, she's your
           sort, and I don't understand, I really don't, why you seem to be keeping
           away from each other. I don't understand!
LOPAKHIN: To tell the truth, I don't understand it myself. It's all so strange. . . . If
           there's still time, I'll be ready at once . . . Let's get it over, once and for
205   all; I don't feel as if I could ever propose to her without you.
LUBOV: Excellent. It'll only take a minute. I'll call her.
LOPAKHIN: The champagne's very appropriate. [Looking at the tumblers] They're
           empty, somebody's already drunk them. [YASHA coughs] I call that
           licking it up. . . .
LUBOV: [Animated] Excellent. We'll go out. Yasha, allez. I'll call her in. . . . [At
           the door] Varya, leave that and come here. Come! [Exit with YASHA.]
LOPAKHIN: [Looks at his watch] Yes. . . . [Pause.]
           [There is a restrained laugh behind the door, a whisper, then VARYA
           comes in.]
VARYA: [Looking at the luggage in silence] I can't seem to find it. . . .
LOPAKHIN: What are you looking for?
VARYA: I packed it myself and I don't remember. [Pause.]

LOPAKHIN: Where are you going to now, Barbara Mihailovna?

VARYA: I? To the Ragulins. . . . I've got an agreement to go and look after their
220   house . . . as housekeeper or something.

LOPAKHIN: Is that at Yashnevo? It's about fifty miles. [Pause] So life in this house is
        finished now. . . .

VARYA: [Looking at the luggage] Where is it? . . . perhaps I've put it away in the
        trunk. . . . Yes, there'll be no more life in this house. . . .

LOPAKHIN: And I'm off to Kharkov at once . . . by this train. I've a lot of business
        on hand. I'm leaving Epikhodov here . . . I've taken him on.

VARYA: Well, well!

LOPAKHIN: Last year at this time the snow was already falling, if you remember, and
        now it's nice and sunny. Only it's rather cold. . . . There's three
230   degrees of frost.

VARYA: I didn't look. [Pause] And our thermometer's broken. . . . [Pause.]

VOICE AT THE DOOR: Ermolai Alexeyevitch!

LOPAKHIN: [As if he has long been waiting to be called] This minute. [Exit quickly.]
        [VARYA, sitting on the floor, puts her face on a bundle of clothes and
235   weeps gently. The door opens. LUBOV ANDREYEVNA enters
        carefully.]

LUBOV: Well? [Pause] We must go.

VARYA: [Not crying now, wipes her eyes] Yes, it's quite time, little mother. I'll get
        to the Ragulins to-day, if I don't miss the train. . . .

LUBOV: [At the door] Anya, put on your things. [Enter ANYA, then GAEV,
        CHARLOTTA IVANOVNA. GAEV wears a warm overcoat with a
        cape. A servant and drivers come in. EPIKHODOV bustles around the
        luggage] Now we can go away.

ANYA: [Joyfully] Away!

GAEV: My friends, my dear friends! Can I be silent, in leaving this house for
        evermore?—can I restrain myself, in saying farewell, from expressing
        those feelings which now fill my whole being . . .?

ANYA: [Imploringly] Uncle!

VARYA: Uncle, you shouldn't!

GAEV: [Stupidly] Double the red into the middle. . . . I'll be quiet.
        [Enter TROFIMOV, then LOPAKHIN.]

TROFIMOV: Well, it's time to be off.

LOPAKHIN: Epikhodov, my coat!

LUBOV: I'll sit here one more minute. It's as if I'd never really noticed what the walls
255   and ceilings of this house were like, and now I look at them greedily,
        with such tender love. . . .

GAEV: I remember, when I was six years old, on Trinity Sunday, I sat at this window
        and looked and saw my father going to church. . . .

LUBOV: Have all the things been taken away?

LOPAKHIN: Yes, all, I think. [To EPIKHODOV, putting on his coat] You see that
        everything's quite straight, Epikhodov.

EPIKHODOV: [Hoarsely] You may depend upon me, Ermolai Alexeyevitch!

LOPAKHIN: What's the matter with your voice?

EPIKHODOV: I swallowed something just now; I was having a drink of water.

YASHA: [Suspiciously] What manners. . . .

LUBOV: We go away, and not a soul remains behind.

LOPAKHIN: Till the spring.

VARYA: [Drags an umbrella out of a bundle, and seems to be waving it about. LOPAKHIN appears to be frightened] What are you doing? . . . I never
270 thought . . .

TROFIMOV: Come along, let's take our seats . . . it's time! The train will be in directly.

VARYA: Peter, here they are, your goloshes, by that trunk. [In tears] And how old and dirty they are. . . .

TROFIMOV: [Putting them on] Come on!

GAEV: [Deeply moved, nearly crying] The train . . . the station. . . . Cross in the middle, a white double in the corner. . . .

LUBOV: Let's go!

LOPAKHIN: Are you all here? There's nobody else? [Locks the side-door on the left]
280 There's a lot of things in there. I must lock them up. Come!

ANYA: Good-bye, home! Good-bye, old life!

TROFIMOV: Welcome, new life! [Exit with ANYA.]
[VARYA looks round the room and goes out slowly. YASHA and CHARLOTTA, with her little dog, go out.]

LOPAKHIN: Till the spring, then! Come on . . . till we meet again! [Exit.]
[LUBOV ANDREYEVNA and GAEV are left alone. They might almost have been waiting for that. They fall into each other's arms and sob restrainedly and quietly, fearing that somebody might hear them.]

GAEV: [In despair] My sister, my sister. . . .

LUBOV: My dear, my gentle, beautiful orchard! My life, my youth, my happiness, good-bye! Good-bye!

ANYA'S VOICE: [Gaily] Mother!

TROFIMOV'S VOICE: [Gaily, excited] Coo-ee!

LUBOV: To look at the walls and the windows for the last time. . . . My dead
295 mother used to like to walk about this room. . . .

GAEV: My sister, my sister!

ANYA'S VOICE: Mother!

TROFIMOV'S VOICE: Coo-ee!

LUBOV: We're coming! [They go out.]
300 [The stage is empty. The sound of keys being turned in the locks is heard, and then the noise of the carriages going away. It is quiet. Then the sound of an axe against the trees is heard in the silence sadly and by itself. Steps are heard. FIERS comes in from the door on the right. He is dressed as usual, in a short jacket and white waistcoat; slippers on his
305 feet. He is ill. He goes to the door and tries the handle.]

FIERS: It's locked. They've gone away. [Sits on a sofa] They've forgotten about me. . . . Never mind, I'll sit here. . . . And Leonid Andreyevitch will have gone in a light overcoat instead of putting on his fur coat. . . .
[Sighs anxiously] I didn't see. . . . Oh, these young people! [Mumbles
310 something that cannot be understood] Life's gone on as if I'd never lived. [Lying down] I'll lie down. . . . You've no strength left in you, nothing left at all. . . . Oh, you . . . bungler!

[He lies without moving. The distant sound is heard, as if from the sky, of a breaking string, dying away sadly. Silence follows it, and only the sound is heard, some way away in the orchard, of the axe falling on the trees.]

315

CURTAIN

William Butler Yeats
Leda and the Swan

A sudden blow: The great wings beating still
Above the staggering girl, her thighs caressed
By the dark webs, her nape caught in the bill,
He holds her helpless breast upon his breast.

5 How can those terrified vague fingers push
The feathered glory from her loosening thighs?
And how can body, laid in that white rush,
But feel the strange heart beating where it lies?

A shudder in the loins engenders there
10 The broken wall, the burning roof and tower
And Agamemnon dead.

Being so caught up,
So mastered by the brute blood of the air,
Did she put on his knowledge with his power
15 Before the indifferent beak could let her drop?

—William Butler Yeats

Sailing to Byzantium

That is no country for old men. The young
In one another's arms, birds in the trees—
Those dying generations—at their song,
The salmon-falls, the mackerel-crowded seas,
5   Fish, flesh, or fowl, commend all summer long
Whatever is begotten, born, and dies.
Caught in that sensual music all neglect
Monuments of unageing intellect.

An aged man is but a paltry thing,
10   A tattered coat upon a stick, unless
Soul clap its hands and sing, and louder sing
For every tatter in its mortal dress,
Nor is there singing school but studying
Monuments of its own magnificence;
15   And therefore I have sailed the seas and come
To the holy city of Byzantium.

O sages standing in God's holy fire
As in the gold mosaic of a wall,
Come from the holy fire, perne in a gyre,
20   And be the singing-masters of my soul.
Consume my heart away; sick with desire
And fastened to a dying animal
It knows not what it is; and gather me
Into the artifice of eternity.

25   Once out of nature I shall never take
My bodily form from any natural thing,
But such a form as Grecian goldsmiths make
Of hammered gold and gold enamelling
To keep a drowsy Emperor awake;
30   Or set upon a golden bough to sing
To lords and ladies of Byzantium
Of what is past, or passing, or to come.

—*William Butler Yeats*

T.S. Eliot
The Love Song of J. Alfred Prufrock

S'io credesse che mia risposta fosse
A persona che mai tornasse al mondo,
Questa fiamma staria senza piu scosse.
Ma perciocche giammai di questo fondo
5 *Non torno vivo alcun, s'i'odo il vero,*
Senza tema d'infamia ti rispondo.

Let us go then, you and I,
When the evening is spread out against the sky
Like a patient etherized upon a table;
10 Let us go, through certain half-deserted streets,
The muttering retreats
Of restless nights in one-night cheap hotels
And sawdust restaurants with oyster-shells
Streets that follow like a tedious argument
15 Of insidious intent
To lead you to an overwhelming question. . .
Oh, do not ask, "What is it?"
Let us go and make our visit.

In the room the women come and go
20 Talking of Michelangelo.

The yellow fog that rubs its back upon the window-panes
The yellow smoke that rubs its muzzle on the window-panes
Licked its tongue into the corners of the evening.
Lingered upon the pools that stand in drains.
25 Let fall upon its back the soot that falls from chimneys.
Slipped by the terrace, made a sudden leap,
And seeing that it was a soft October night,
Curled once about the house, and fell asleep.

And indeed there will be time
30 For the yellow smoke that slides along the street,
Rubbing its back upon the window-panes;
There will be time, there will be time
To prepare a face to meet the faces that you meet;
There will be time to murder and create,
35 And time for all the works and days of hands
That lift and drop a question on your plate;
Time for you and time for me.
And time yet for a hundred indecisions,

And for a hundred visions and revisions,
40   Before the taking of a toast and tea.

In the room the women come and go
Talking of Michelangelo.

And indeed there will be time
To wonder, "Do I dare?" and, "Do I dare?"
45   Time to turn back and descend the stair,
With a bald spot in the middle of my hair—
[They will say: "How his hair is growing thin!"]
My morning coat, my collar mounting firmly to the chin,
My necktie rich and modest, but asserted by a simple pin—
50   [They will say: "But how his arms and legs are thin!"]
Do I dare
Disturb the universe?
In a minute there is time
For decisions and revisions which a minute will reverse.

55   For I have known them all already, known them all:
Have known the evenings, mornings, afternoons,
I have measured out my life with coffee spoons;
I know the voices dying with a dying fall
Beneath the music from a farther room.
60   So how should I presume?

And I have known the eyes already, known them all—
The eyes that fix you in a formulated phrase,
And when I am formulated, sprawling on a pin,
When I am pinned and wriggling on the wall,
65   Then how should I begin
To spit out all the butt-ends of my days and ways?
        And how should I presume?

And I have known the arms already, known them all—
Arms that are braceleted and white and bare
70   [But in the lamplight, downed with light brown hair!]
Is it perfume from a dress
That makes me so digress?
Arms that lie along a table, or wrap about a shawl.
        And should I then presume?
75   And how should I begin?

                . . . . .

Shall I say, I have gone at dusk through narrow streets
And watched the smoke that rises from the pipes
Of lonely men in shirt-sleeves, leaning out of windows? . . .

I should have been a pair of ragged claws
80 Scuttling across the floors of silent seas.

        . . . . .

And the afternoon, the evening, sleeps so peacefully!
Smoothed by long fingers,
Asleep. . . tired . . . or it malingers,
Stretched on the floor, here beside you and me.
85 Should I, after tea and cakes and ices,
Have the strength to force the moment to its crisis?
But though I have wept and fasted, wept and prayed,
Though I have seen my head [grown slightly bald] brought in upon a platter,
I am no prophet—and here's no great matter;
90 I have seen the moment of my greatness flicker,
And I have seen the eternal Footman hold my coat, and snicker,
And in short, I was afraid.

And would it have been worth it, after all,
After the cups, the marmalade, the tea,
95 Among the porcelain, among some talk of you and me,
Would it have been worth while,
To have bitten off the matter with a smile,
To have squeezed the universe into a ball
To roll it toward some overwhelming question,
100 To say: "I am Lazarus, come from the dead,
Come back to tell you all, I shall tell you all"—
If one, settling a pillow by her head,
      Should say: "That is not what I meant at all.
      That is not it, at all."

105 And would it have been worth it, after all,
Would it have been worth while,
After the sunsets and the dooryards and the sprinkled streets,
After the novels, after the teacups, after the skirts that trail along the floor—
And this, and so much more?—
110 It is impossible to say just what I mean!
But as if a magic lantern threw the nerves in patterns on a screen:
Would it have been worth while
If one, settling a pillow, or throwing off a shawl,
And turning toward the window, should say:
115   "That is not it at all,
      That is not what I meant, at all."

        . . . . .

No! I am not Prince Hamlet, nor was meant to be;
Am an attendant lord, one that will do
To swell a progress, start a scene or two,
120 Advise the prince; no doubt, an easy tool,
Deferential, glad to be of use,
Politic, cautious, and meticulous;
Full of high sentence, but a bit obtuse;

At times, indeed, almost ridiculous—
125   Almost, at times, the Fool.

I grow old . . . I grow old . . .
I shall wear the bottoms of my trousers rolled.

Shall I part my hair behind? Do I dare to eat a peach?
I shall wear white flannel trousers, and walk upon the beach.
130   I have heard the mermaids singing, each to each.

I do not think that they will sing to me.

I have seen them riding seaward on the waves
Combing the white hair of the waves blown back
When the wind blows the water white and black.

135   We have lingered in the chambers of the sea
By sea-girls wreathed with seaweed red and brown
Till human voices wake us, and we drown.

—T.S. Elliot

The Waste Land

"Nam Sibyllam quidem Cumis ego ipse oculis meis
vidi in ampulla pendere, et cum illi pueri dicerent:
Sibylla ti theleis; respondebat illa: apothanein thelo."

I. THE BURIAL OF THE DEAD

April is the cruellest month, breeding
Lilacs out of the dead land, mixing
Memory and desire, stirring
Dull roots with spring rain.
5   Winter kept us warm, covering
Earth in forgetful snow, feeding
A little life with dried tubers.
Summer surprised us, coming over the Starnbergersee
With a shower of rain; we stopped in the colonnade,
10   And went on in sunlight, into the Hofgarten,
And drank coffee, and talked for an hour.
Bin gar keine Russin, stamm' aus Litauen, echt deutsch.
And when we were children, staying at the archduke's,
My cousin's, he took me out on a sled,
15   And I was frightened. He said, Marie,
Marie, hold on tight. And down we went.
In the mountains, there you feel free.
I read, much of the night, and go south in the winter.

What are the roots that clutch, what branches grow
20   Out of this stony rubbish? Son of man,
You cannot say, or guess, for you know only
A heap of broken images, where the sun beats,
And the dead tree gives no shelter, the cricket no relief,
And the dry stone no sound of water. Only
25   There is shadow under this red rock,
(Come in under the shadow of this red rock),
And I will show you something different from either
Your shadow at morning striding behind you
Or your shadow at evening rising to meet you;
30   I will show you fear in a handful of dust.
    Frisch weht der Wind
    Der Heimat zu
    Mein Irisch Kind,
    Wo weilest du?
35   "You gave me hyacinths first a year ago;
"They called me the hyacinth girl."

—Yet when we came back, late, from the Hyacinth garden,
Your arms full, and your hair wet, I could not
Speak, and my eyes failed, I was neither
40   Living nor dead, and I knew nothing,
Looking into the heart of light, the silence.
Od' und leer das Meer.

Madame Sosostris, famous clairvoyante,
Had a bad cold, nevertheless
45   Is known to be the wisest woman in Europe,
With a wicked pack of cards. Here, said she,
Is your card, the drowned Phoenician Sailor,
(Those are pearls that were his eyes. Look!)
Here is Belladonna, the Lady of the Rocks,
50   The lady of situations.
Here is the man with three staves, and here the Wheel,
And here is the one-eyed merchant, and this card,
Which is blank, is something he carries on his back,
Which I am forbidden to see. I do not find
55   The Hanged Man. Fear death by water.
I see crowds of people, walking round in a ring.
Thank you. If you see dear Mrs. Equitone,
Tell her I bring the horoscope myself:
One must be so careful these days.

60   Unreal City,
Under the brown fog of a winter dawn,
A crowd flowed over London Bridge, so many,
I had not thought death had undone so many.
Sighs, short and infrequent, were exhaled,
65   And each man fixed his eyes before his feet.
Flowed up the hill and down King William Street,
To where Saint Mary Woolnoth kept the hours
With a dead sound on the final stroke of nine.
There I saw one I knew, and stopped him, crying "Stetson!
70   "You who were with me in the ships at Mylae!
"That corpse you planted last year in your garden,
"Has it begun to sprout? Will it bloom this year?
"Or has the sudden frost disturbed its bed?
75   "Oh keep the Dog far hence, that's friend to men,
"Or with his nails he'll dig it up again!
"You! hypocrite lecteur!—mon semblable,—mon frere!"

II. A GAME OF CHESS

The Chair she sat in, like a burnished throne,
Glowed on the marble, where the glass
Held up by standards wrought with fruited vines
80   From which a golden Cupidon peeped out
(Another hid his eyes behind his wing)
Doubled the flames of sevenbranched candelabra
Reflecting light upon the table as
The glitter of her jewels rose to meet it,
85   From satin cases poured in rich profusion;
In vials of ivory and coloured glass
Unstoppered, lurked her strange synthetic perfumes,
Unguent, powdered, or liquid—troubled, confused
And drowned the sense in odours; stirred by the air
90   That freshened from the window, these ascended
In fattening the prolonged candle-flames,
Flung their smoke into the laquearia,
Stirring the pattern on the coffered ceiling.
Huge sea-wood fed with copper
95   Burned green and orange, framed by the coloured stone,
In which sad light a carved dolphin swam.
Above the antique mantel was displayed
As though a window gave upon the sylvan scene
The change of Philomel, by the barbarous king
100   So rudely forced; yet there the nightingale
Filled all the desert with inviolable voice
And still she cried, and still the world pursues,
"Jug Jug" to dirty ears.
And other withered stumps of time
105   Were told upon the walls; staring forms
Leaned out, leaning, hushing the room enclosed.
Footsteps shuffled on the stair.
Under the firelight, under the brush, her hair
Spread out in fiery points
110   Glowed into words, then would be savagely still.

"My nerves are bad to-night. Yes, bad. Stay with me.
"Speak to me. Why do you never speak. Speak.
"What are you thinking of? What thinking? What?
"I never know what you are thinking. Think."

115   I think we are in rats' alley
Where the dead men lost their bones.

"What is that noise?"
                    The wind under the door.
"What is that noise now? What is the wind doing?"
120   Nothing again nothing.

                                             "Do
"You know nothing? Do you see nothing? Do you remember
"Nothing?"

      I remember

125   Those are pearls that were his eyes.
"Are you alive, or not? Is there nothing in your head?"
                                                      But
O O O O that Shakespeherian Rag—
It's so elegant

130   So intelligent
"What shall I do now? What shall I do?"
I shall rush out as I am, and walk the street
"With my hair down, so. What shall we do to-morrow?
"What shall we ever do?"

135   The hot water at ten.
And if it rains, a closed car at four.
And we shall play a game of chess,
Pressing lidless eyes and waiting for a knock upon the door.

When Lil's husband got demobbed, I said—

140   I didn't mince my words, I said to her myself,
HURRY UP PLEASE ITS TIME
Now Albert's coming back, make yourself a bit smart.
He'll want to know what you done with that money he gave you
To get yourself some teeth. He did, I was there.

145   You have them all out, Lil, and get a nice set,
He said, I swear, I can't bear to look at you.
And no more can't I, I said, and think of poor Albert,
He's been in the army four years, he wants a good time,
And if you don't give it him, there's others will, I said.

150   Oh is there, she said. Something o' that, I said.
Then I'll know who to thank, she said, and give me a straight look.
HURRY UP PLEASE ITS TIME
If you don't like it you can get on with it, I said.
Others can pick and choose if you can't.

155   But if Albert makes off, it won't be for lack of telling.
You ought to be ashamed, I said, to look so antique.
(And her only thirty-one.)
I can't help it, she said, pulling a long face,
It's them pills I took, to bring it off, she said.

160   (She's had five already, and nearly died of young George.)
The chemist said it would be alright, but I've never been the same.
You are a proper fool, I said.
Well, if Albert won't leave you alone, there it is, I said,
What you get married for if you don't want children?

165   HURRY UP PLEASE ITS TIME

Well, that Sunday Albert was home, they had a hot gammon,
And they asked me in to dinner, to get the beauty of it hot -
HURRY UP PLEASE ITS TIME
HURRY UP PLEASE ITS TIME
170 Goonight Bill. Goonight Lou. Goonight May. Goonight.
Ta ta. Goonight. Goonight.
Good night, ladies, good night, sweet ladies, good night, good night.

III. THE FIRE SERMON

The river's tent is broken: the last fingers of leaf
Clutch and sink into the wet bank. The wind
175 Crosses the brown land, unheard. The nymphs are departed.
Sweet Thames, run softly, till I end my song.
The river bears no empty bottles, sandwich papers,
Silk handkerchiefs, cardboard boxes, cigarette ends
Or other testimony of summer nights. The nymphs are departed.
180 And their friends, the loitering heirs of city directors;
Departed, have left no addresses.
By the waters of Leman I sat down and wept . . .
Sweet Thames, run softly till I end my song,
Sweet Thames, run softly, for I speak not loud or long.
185 But at my back in a cold blast I hear
The rattle of the bones, and chuckle spread from ear to ear.
A rat crept softly through the vegetation
Dragging its slimy belly on the bank
While I was fishing in the dull canal
190 On a winter evening round behind the gashouse
Musing upon the king my brother's wreck
And on the king my father's death before him.
White bodies naked on the low damp ground
And bones cast in a little low dry garret,
195 Rattled by the rat's foot only, year to year.
But at my back from time to time I hear
The sound of horns and motors, which shall bring
Sweeney to Mrs. Porter in the spring.
O the moon shone bright on Mrs. Porter
200 And on her daughter
They wash their feet in soda water
Et O ces voix d'enfants, chantant dans la coupole!

Twit twit twit
Jug jug jug jug jug jug
205 So rudely forc'd.
Tereu

Unreal City
Under the brown fog of a winter noon
Mr. Eugenides, the Smyrna merchant
210   Unshaven, with a pocket full of currants
C.i.f. London: documents at sight,
Asked me in demotic French
To luncheon at the Cannon Street Hotel
Followed by a weekend at the Metropole.

205   At the violet hour, when the eyes and back
Turn upward from the desk, when the human engine waits
Like a taxi throbbing waiting,
I Tiresias, though blind, throbbing between two lives,
Old man with wrinkled female breasts, can see
220   At the violet hour, the evening hour that strives
Homeward, and brings the sailor home from sea,
The typist home at teatime, clears her breakfast, lights
Her stove, and lays out food in tins.
Out of the window perilously spread
225   Her drying combinations touched by the sun's last rays,
On the divan are piled (at night her bed)
Stockings, slippers, camisoles, and stays.
I Tiresias, old man with wrinkled dugs
Perceived the scene, and foretold the rest—
230   I too awaited the expected guest.
He, the young man carbuncular, arrives,
A small house agent's clerk, with one bold stare,
One of the low on whom assurance sits
As a silk hat on a Bradford millionaire.
235   The time is now propitious, as he guesses,
The meal is ended, she is bored and tired,
Endeavours to engage her in caresses
Which still are unreproved, if undesired.
Flushed and decided, he assaults at once;
240   Exploring hands encounter no defence;
His vanity requires no response,
And makes a welcome of indifference.
(And I Tiresias have foresuffered all
Enacted on this same divan or bed;
245   I who have sat by Thebes below the wall
And walked among the lowest of the dead.)
Bestows one final patronising kiss,
And gropes his way, finding the stairs unlit . . .

She turns and looks a moment in the glass,
250   Hardly aware of her departed lover;
Her brain allows one half-formed thought to pass:
"Well now that's done: and I'm glad it's over."
When lovely woman stoops to folly and

Paces about her room again, alone,
255 She smoothes her hair with automatic hand,
And puts a record on the gramophone.

"This music crept by me upon the waters"
And along the Strand, up Queen Victoria Street.
O City city, I can sometimes hear
260 Beside a public bar in Lower Thames Street,
The pleasant whining of a mandoline
And a clatter and a chatter from within
Where fishmen lounge at noon: where the walls
Of Magnus Martyr hold
265 Inexplicable splendour of Ionian white and gold.

The river sweats
Oil and tar
The barges drift
With the turning tide
270 Red sails
Wide
To leeward, swing on the heavy spar.
The barges wash
Drifting logs
275 Down Greenwich reach
Past the Isle of Dogs.
Weialala leia
Wallala leialala

Elizabeth and Leicester
280 Beating oars
The stern was formed
A gilded shell
Red and gold
The brisk swell
285 Rippled both shores
Southwest wind
Carried down stream
The peal of bells
White towers
290 Weialala leia
Wallala leialala

"Trams and dusty trees.
Highbury bore me. Richmond and Kew
Undid me. By Richmond I raised my knees
295 Supine on the floor of a narrow canoe."

"My feet are at Moorgate, and my heart
Under my feet. After the event

He wept. He promised 'a new start'.
I made no comment. What should I resent?"
300 "On Margate Sands.
I can connect
Nothing with nothing.
The broken fingernails of dirty hands.
My people humble people who expect
305 Nothing."
        la la

To Carthage then I came

Burning burning burning burning
O Lord Thou pluckest me out
310 O Lord Thou pluckest

burning

IV. DEATH BY WATER

Phlebas the Phoenician, a fortnight dead,
Forgot the cry of gulls, and the deep sea swell
And the profit and loss.
315   A current under sea
Picked his bones in whispers. As he rose and fell
He passed the stages of his age and youth
Entering the whirlpool.
                              Gentile or Jew
320 O you who turn the wheel and look to windward,
Consider Phlebas, who was once handsome and tall as you.

V. WHAT THE THUNDER SAID

After the torchlight red on sweaty faces
After the frosty silence in the gardens
After the agony in stony places
325 The shouting and the crying
Prison and palace and reverberation
Of thunder of spring over distant mountains
He who was living is now dead
We who were living are now dying
330 With a little patience

Here is no water but only rock
Rock and no water and the sandy road
The road winding above among the mountains
Which are mountains of rock without water
335 If there were water we should stop and drink
Amongst the rock one cannot stop or think
Sweat is dry and feet are in the sand

If there were only water amongst the rock
Dead mountain mouth of carious teeth that cannot spit
340 Here one can neither stand nor lie nor sit
There is not even silence in the mountains
But dry sterile thunder without rain
There is not even solitude in the mountains
But red sullen faces sneer and snarl
345 From doors of mudcracked houses
                              If there were water

And no rock
If there were rock
And also water
350 And water
A spring
A pool among the rock
If there were the sound of water only
Not the cicada
355 And dry grass singing
But sound of water over a rock
Where the hermit-thrush sings in the pine trees
Drip drop drip drop drop drop drop
But there is no water

360 Who is the third who walks always beside you?
When I count, there are only you and I together
But when I look ahead up the white road
There is always another one walking beside you
Gliding wrapt in a brown mantle, hooded
365 I do not know whether a man or a woman
—But who is that on the other side of you?

What is that sound high in the air
Murmur of maternal lamentation
Who are those hooded hordes swarming
370 Over endless plains, stumbling in cracked earth
Ringed by the flat horizon only
What is the city over the mountains
Cracks and reforms and bursts in the violet air
Falling towers
375 Jerusalem Athens Alexandria
Vienna London
Unreal

A woman drew her long black hair out tight
And fiddled whisper music on those strings
380 And bats with baby faces in the violet light
Whistled, and beat their wings
And crawled head downward down a blackened wall
And upside down in air were towers

Tolling reminiscent bells, that kept the hours
385   And voices singing out of empty cisterns and exhausted wells.

In this decayed hole among the mountains
In the faint moonlight, the grass is singing
Over the tumbled graves, about the chapel
There is the empty chapel, only the wind's home.
390   It has no windows, and the door swings,
Dry bones can harm no one.
Only a cock stood on the rooftree
Co co rico co co rico
In a flash of lightning. Then a damp gust
395   Bringing rain

Ganga was sunken, and the limp leaves
Waited for rain, while the black clouds
Gathered far distant, over Himavant.
The jungle crouched, humped in silence.
400   Then spoke the thunder
DA
Datta: what have we given?
My friend, blood shaking my heart
The awful daring of a moment's surrender
405   Which an age of prudence can never retract
By this, and this only, we have existed
Which is not to be found in our obituaries
Or in memories draped by the beneficent spider
Or under seals broken by the lean solicitor
410   In our empty rooms
DA
Dayadhvam: I have heard the key
Turn in the door once and turn once only
We think of the key, each in his prison
415   Thinking of the key, each confirms a prison
Only at nightfall, aetherial rumours
Revive for a moment a broken Coriolanus
DA
Damyata: The boat responded
420   Gaily, to the hand expert with sail and oar
The sea was calm, your heart would have responded
Gaily, when invited, beating obedient
To controlling hands

I sat upon the shore
425   Fishing, with the arid plain behind me
Shall I at least set my lands in order?
London Bridge is falling down falling down falling down
Poi s'ascose nel foco che gli affina
Quando fiam ceu chelidon—O swallow swallow

430   Le Prince d'Aquitaine a la tour abolie
        These fragments I have shored against my ruins
        Why then Ile fit you. Hieronymo's mad againe.
        Datta. Dayadhvam. Damyata.
                    Shantih   shantih   shantih

NOTES ON "THE WASTE LAND"

Not only the title, but the plan and a good deal of the
incidental symbolism of the poem were suggested
by Miss Jessie L. Weston's book on the Grail legend:
From Ritual to Romance. Indeed,
so deeply am I indebted, Miss Weston's book will elucidate
the difficulties of the poem much better than my notes can do;
and I recommend it (apart from the great interest of the book itself)
to any who think such elucidation of the poem worth the trouble.
To another work of anthropology I am indebted in general, one which has
influenced our generation profoundly; I mean The Golden Bough; I have
used especially the two volumes Adonis, Attis, Osiris. Anyone who is
acquainted with these works will immediately recognise in the poem
certain references to vegetation ceremonies.

I. THE BURIAL OF THE DEAD

Line 20. Cf. Ezekiel 2:1.
23. Cf. Ecclesiastes 12:5.
31. V. Tristan und Isolde, i, verses 5-8.
42. Id. iii, verse 24.
46. I am not familiar with the exact constitution of the Tarot pack
of cards, from which I have obviously departed to suit my own convenience.
The Hanged Man, a member of the traditional pack, fits my purpose
in two ways: because he is associated in my mind with the Hanged God
of Frazer, and because I associate him with the hooded figure in
the passage of the disciples to Emmaus in Part V. The Phoenician Sailor
and the Merchant appear later; also the "crowds of people," and
Death by Water is executed in Part IV. The Man with Three Staves
(an authentic member of the Tarot pack) I associate, quite arbitrarily,
with the Fisher King himself.
60. Cf. Baudelaire:

        "Fourmillante cite;, cite; pleine de reves,
        Ou le spectre en plein jour raccroche le passant."

63. Cf. Inferno, iii. 55-7.

> "si lunga tratta
di gente, ch'io non avrei mai creduto
che morte tanta n'avesse disfatta."

64. Cf. Inferno, iv. 25-7:

> "Quivi, secondo che per ascoltare,
"non avea pianto, ma' che di sospiri,
"che l'aura eterna facevan tremare."

68. A phenomenon which I have often noticed.

74. Cf. the Dirge in Webster's White Devil .

76. V. Baudelaire, Preface to Fleurs du Mal.

II. A GAME OF CHESS

77. Cf. Antony and Cleopatra, II. ii., l. 190.

92. Laquearia. V. Aeneid, I. 726:

> dependent lychni laquearibus aureis incensi, et noctem flammis
> funalia vincunt.

98. Sylvan scene. V. Milton, Paradise Lost, iv. 140.

99. V. Ovid, Metamorphoses, vi, Philomela.

100. Cf. Part III, l. 204.

115. Cf. Part III, l. 195.

118. Cf. Webster: "Is the wind in that door still?"

126. Cf. Part I, l. 37, 48.

138. Cf. the game of chess in Middleton's Women beware Women.

III. THE FIRE SERMON

176. V. Spenser, Prothalamion.

192. Cf. The Tempest, I. ii.

196. Cf. Marvell, To His Coy Mistress.

197. Cf. Day, Parliament of Bees:

> "When of the sudden, listening, you shall hear,
"A noise of horns and hunting, which shall bring
"Actaeon to Diana in the spring,
"Where all shall see her naked skin . . ."

199. I do not know the origin of the ballad from which these lines
are taken: it was reported to me from Sydney, Australia.

202. V. Verlaine, Parsifal.

210. The currants were quoted at a price "carriage and insurance
free to London"; and the Bill of Lading etc. were to be handed
to the buyer upon payment of the sight draft.

Notes 196 and 197 were transposed in this and the Hogarth Press edition,
but have been corrected here.

210. "Carriage and insurance free"] "cost, insurance and freight"-Editor.

218. Tiresias, although a mere spectator and not indeed a "character,"
is yet the most important personage in the poem, uniting all the rest.
Just as the one-eyed merchant, seller of currants, melts into
the Phoenician Sailor, and the latter is not wholly distinct

from Ferdinand Prince of Naples, so all the women are one woman,
and the two sexes meet in Tiresias. What Tiresias sees, in fact,
is the substance of the poem. The whole passage from Ovid is
of great anthropological interest:

'. . . Cum Iunone iocos et maior vestra profecto est
Quam, quae contingit maribus,' dixisse, 'voluptas.'
Illa negat; placuit quae sit sententia docti
Quaerere Tiresiae: venus huic erat utraque nota.
Nam duo magnorum viridi coeuntia silva
Corpora serpentum baculi violaverat ictu
Deque viro factus, mirabile, femina septem
Egerat autumnos; octavo rursus eosdem
Vidit et 'est vestrae si tanta potentia plagae,'
Dixit 'ut auctoris sortem in contraria mutet,
Nunc quoque vos feriam!' percussis anguibus isdem
Forma prior rediit genetivaque venit imago.
Arbiter hic igitur sumptus de lite iocosa
Dicta Iovis firmat; gravius Saturnia iusto
Nec pro materia fertur doluisse suique
Iudicis aeterna damnavit lumina nocte,
At pater omnipotens (neque enim licet inrita cuiquam
Facta dei fecisse deo) pro lumine adempto
Scire futura dedit poenamque levavit honore.

221. This may not appear as exact as Sappho's lines, but I had in mind
the "longshore" or "dory" fisherman, who returns at nightfall.
253. V. Goldsmith, the song in The Vicar of Wakefield.
257. V. The Tempest, as above.
264. The interior of St. Magnus Martyr is to my mind one of
the finest among Wren's interiors. See The Proposed Demolition
of Nineteen City Churches (P. S. King & Son, Ltd.).
266. The Song of the (three) Thames-daughters begins here. From line 292 to
306 inclusive they speak in turn. V. Gutterdsammerung, III. i: the Rhine-daughters.
279. V. Froude, Elizabeth, Vol. I, ch. iv, letter of De Quadra
to Philip of Spain:
"In the afternoon we were in a barge, watching the games on the river.
(The queen) was alone with Lord Robert and myself on the poop,
when they began to talk nonsense, and went so far that Lord Robert
at last said, as I was on the spot there was no reason why they
should not be married if the queen pleased."
293. Cf. Purgatorio, v. 133:
"Ricorditi di me, che son la Pia;
Siena mi fe', disfecemi Maremma."
307. V. St. Augustine's Confessions: "to Carthage then I came,
where a cauldron of unholy loves sang all about mine ears."
308. The complete text of the Buddha's Fire Sermon (which corresponds
in importance to the Sermon on the Mount) from which these words are taken,
will be found translated in the late Henry Clarke Warren's Buddhism
in Translation (Harvard Oriental Series). Mr. Warren was one

of the great pioneers of Buddhist studies in the Occident.

309. From St. Augustine's Confessions again. The collocation
of these two representatives of eastern and western asceticism,
as the culmination of this part of the poem, is not an accident.

V. WHAT THE THUNDER SAID

In the first part of Part V three themes are employed:
the journey to Emmaus, the approach to the Chapel Perilous
(see Miss Weston's book) and the present decay of eastern Europe.
357. This is Turdus aonalaschkae pallasii, the hermit-thrush
which I have heard in Quebec County. Chapman says (Handbook of
Birds of Eastern North America) "it is most at home in secluded
woodland and thickety retreats. . . . Its notes are not remarkable
for variety or volume, but in purity and sweetness of tone and
exquisite modulation they are unequalled." Its "water-dripping song"
is justly celebrated.
360. The following lines were stimulated by the account of one
of the Antarctic expeditions (I forget which, but I think one
of Shackleton's): it was related that the party of explorers,
at the extremity of their strength, had the constant delusion
that there was one more member than could actually be counted.
367-77. Cf. Hermann Hesse, Blick ins Chaos:
"Schon ist halb Europa, schon ist zumindest der halbe Osten Europas auf dem
Wege zum Chaos, fährt betrunken im heiligem Wahn am Abgrund entlang
und singt dazu, singt betrunken und hymnisch wie Dmitri Karamasoff sang.
Ueber diese Lieder lacht der B͵rger beleidigt, der Heilige
und Seher hˆrt sie mit Tränen."

402. "Datta, dayadhvam, damyata" (Give, sympathize,
control). The fable of the meaning of the Thunder is found
in the Brihadaranyaka-Upanishad, 5, 1. A translation is found
in Deussen's Sechzig Upanishads des Veda, p. 489.
408. Cf. Webster, The White Devil, v. vi:
                              ". . . they'll remarry
  Ere the worm pierce your winding-sheet, ere the spider
  Make a thin curtain for your epitaphs."
412. Cf. Inferno, xxxiii. 46:
      "ed io sentii chiavar l'uscio di sotto
      all'orribile torre."
Also F. H. Bradley, Appearance and Reality, p. 346:
"My external sensations are no less private to myself than are my
thoughts or my feelings. In either case my experience falls within
my own circle, a circle closed on the outside; and, with all its
elements alike, every sphere is opaque to the others which surround
it. . . . In brief, regarded as an existence which appears in a soul,
the whole world for each is peculiar and private to that soul."
425. V. Weston, From Ritual to Romance; chapter on the Fisher King.

428. V. Purgatorio, xxvi. 148.

>"'Ara vos prec per aquella valor
>'que vos guida al som de l'escalina,
>'sovegna vos a temps de ma dolor.'
> Poi s'ascose nel foco che gli affina."

429. V. Pervigilium Veneris. Cf. Philomela in Parts II and III.
430. V. Gerard de Nerval, Sonnet El Desdichado.
432. V. Kyd's Spanish Tragedy.
434. Shantih. Repeated as here, a formal ending to an Upanishad.
'The Peace which passeth understanding' is a feeble translation
of the content of this word.

Albert Camus
The Guest

Translated by Justin O'Brien

The schoolmaster was watching the two men climb toward him. One was on horseback, the other on foot. They had not yet tackled the abrupt rise leading to the schoolhouse built on the hillside. They were toiling onward, making slow progress in the snow, among the stones, on the vast expanse of the high deserted plateau. From time to time the horse stumbled. Without hearing anything yet, he could see the breath issuing from the horse's nostrils. One of the men, at least, knew the region. They were following the trail although it had disappeared days ago under a layer of dirty white snow. The schoolmaster calculated that it would take them half an hour to get onto the hill. It was cold; he went back into the school to get a sweater.

He crossed the empty, frigid classroom. On the blackboard the four rivers of France, drawn with four different colored chalks, had been flowing toward their estuaries for the past three days. Snow had suddenly fallen in mid-October after eight months of drought without the transition of rain, and the twenty pupils, more or less, who lived in the villages scattered over the plateau had stopped coming. With fair weather they would return. Daru now heated only the single room that was his lodging, adjoining the classroom and giving also onto the plateau to the east. Like the class windows, his window looked to the south. On that side the school was a few kilometers from the point where the plateau began to slope toward the south. In clear weather could be seen the purple mass of the mountain range where the gap opened onto the desert.

Somewhat warmed, Daru returned to the window from which he had first seen the two men. They were no longer visible. Hence they must have tackled the rise. The sky was not so dark, for the snow had stopped falling during the night. The morning had opened with a dirty light which had scarcely become brighter as the ceiling of clouds lifted. At two in the afternoon it seemed as if the day were merely beginning. But still this was better than those three days when the thick snow was falling amidst unbroken darkness with little gusts of wind that rattled the double door of the classroom. Then Daru had spent long hours in his room, leaving it only to go to the shed and feed the chickens or get some coal. Fortunately the delivery truck from Tadjid, the nearest village to the north, had brought his supplies two days before the blizzard. It would return in forty-eight hours.

Besides, he had enough to resist a siege, for the little room was cluttered with bags of wheat that the administration left as a stock to distribute to those of his pupils whose families had suffered from the drought. Actually they had all been victims because they were all poor. Every day Daru would distribute a ration to the children. They had missed it, he knew, during these bad days. Possibly one of the fathers or big brothers would come this afternoon and he could supply them with grain. It was just a matter of carrying them over to the next harvest. Now shiploads of wheat were arriving from France and the worst was over. But it would be hard to forget that poverty, that army of ragged ghosts wandering in the sunlight, the plateaus burned to a cinder month after month, the earth shriveled up little by little, literally scorched, every stone bursting into dust under one's foot. The sheep had died then by thousands and even a few men, here and there, sometimes without anyone's knowing.

In contrast with such poverty, he who lived almost like a monk in his remote schoolhouse, nonetheless satisfied with the little he had and with the rough life, had felt like a lord with his whitewashed walls, his narrow couch, his unpainted shelves, his well, and his weekly provision of water and food.

And suddenly this snow, without warning, without the foretaste of rain. This is the way the region was, cruel to live in, even without men—who didn't help matters either. But Daru had been born here. Everywhere else, he felt exiled.

He stepped out onto the terrace in front of the schoolhouse. The two men were now halfway up the slope. He recognized the horseman as Balducci, the old gendarme he had known for a long time. Balducci was holding on the end of a rope an Arab who was walking behind him with hands bound and head lowered. The gendarme waved a greeting to which Daru did not reply, lost as he was in contemplation of the Arab dressed in a faded blue jellaba, his feet in sandals but covered with socks of heavy raw wool, his head surmounted by a narrow, short *chèche*. They were approaching. Balducci was holding back his horse in order not to hurt the Arab, and the group was advancing slowly.

Within earshot, Balducci shouted: "One hour to do the three kilometers from El Ameur!" Daru did not answer. Short and square in his thick sweater, he watched them climb. Not once had the Arab raised his head. "Hello," said Daru when they got up onto the terrace. "Come and warm up." Balducci painfully got down from his horse without letting go of the rope. From under his bristling mustache he smiled at the schoolmaster. His little dark eyes, deepset under a tanned forehead, and his mouth surrounded with wrinkles made him look attentive and studious. Daru took the bridle, led the horse to the shed, and came back to the two men, who were now waiting for him in the school. He led them into his room. "I am going to heat up the classroom," he said. "We'll be more comfortable there." When he entered the room again Balducci was on the couch. He had undone the rope tying him to the Arab, who had squatted near the stove. His hands still bound, the *chèche* pushed back on his head, he was looking toward the window. At first Daru noticed only his huge lips, fat, smooth, almost Negroid; yet his nose was straight, his eyes were dark and full of fever. The *chèche* revealed an obstinate forehead and, under the weathered skin now rather discolored by the cold, the whole face had a restless and rebellious look that struck Daru when the Arab, turning his face toward him, looked him straight in the eyes. "Go into the other room," said the schoolmaster, "and I'll make you some mint tea." "Thanks," Balducci said. "What a chore! How I long for retirement." And addressing his prisoner in Arabic: "Come on, you." The Arab got up and, slowly, holding his bound wrists in front of him, went into the classroom.

With the tea, Daru brought a chair. But Balducci was already enthroned on the nearest pupil's desk and the Arab had squatted against the teacher's platform facing the stove, which stood between the desk and the window. When he held out the glass of tea to the prisoner, Daru hesitated at the sight of his bound hands. "He might perhaps be untied." "Sure," said Balducci. "That was for the trip." He started to get to his feet. But Daru, setting the glass on the floor, had knelt beside the Arab. Without saying anything, the Arab watched him with his feverish eyes. Once his hands were free, he rubbed his swollen wrists against each other, took the glass of tea, and sucked up the burning liquid in swift little sips.

"Good," said Daru. "And where are you headed?"

Balducci withdrew his mustache from the tea. "Here, son."

"Odd pupils! And you're spending the night?"

"No. I'm going back to El Ameur. And you will deliver this fellow to Tinguit. He is expected at police headquarters."

Balducci was looking at Daru with a friendly little smile.

"What's this story?" asked the schoolmaster. "Are you pulling my leg?"

"No, son. Those are the orders."

"The orders? I'm not . . ." Daru hesitated, not wanting to hurt the old Corsican. "I mean, that's not my job."

"What! What's the meaning of that? In wartime people do all kinds of jobs."

"Then I'll wait for the declaration of war!"

Balducci nodded.

"O.K. But the orders exist and they concern you too. Things are brewing, it appears. There is talk of a forthcoming revolt. We are mobilized, in a way."

Daru still had his obstinate look.

"Listen, son," Balducci said. "I like you and you must understand. There's only a dozen of us at El Ameur to patrol throughout the whole territory of a small department and I must get back in a hurry. I was told to hand this guy over to you and return without delay. He couldn't be kept there. His village was beginning to stir; they wanted to take him back. You must take him to Tinguit tomorrow before the day is over. Twenty kilometers shouldn't faze a husky fellow like you. After that, all will be over. You'll come back to your pupils and your comfortable life."

Behind the wall the horse could be heard snorting and pawing the earth. Daru was looking out the window. Decidedly, the weather was clearing and the light was increasing over the snowy plateau. When all the snow was melted, the sun would take over again and once more would burn the fields of stone. For days, still, the unchanging sky would shed its dry light on the solitary expanse where nothing had any connection with man.

"After all," he said, turning around toward Balducci, "what did he do?" And, before the gendarme had opened his mouth, he asked: "Does he speak French?"

"No, not a word. We had been looking for him for a month, but they were hiding him. He killed his cousin."

"Is he against us?"

"I don't think so. But you can never be sure."

"Why did he kill?"

"A family squabble, I think. One owed the other grain, it seems. It's not at all clear. In short, he killed his cousin with a billhook. You know, like a sheep, *kreezk!*"

Balducci made the gesture of drawing a blade across his throat and the Arab, his attention attracted, watched him with a sort of anxiety. Daru felt a sudden wrath against the man, against all men with their rotten spite, their tireless hates, their blood lust.

But the kettle was singing on the stove. He served Balducci more tea, hesitated, then served the Arab again, who, a second time, drank avidly. His raised arms made the jellaba fall open and the schoolmaster saw his thin, muscular chest.

"Thanks, kid," Balducci said. "And now, I'm off."

He got up and went toward the Arab, taking a small rope from his pocket.

"What are you doing?" Daru asked dryly.

Balducci, disconcerted, showed him the rope.

"Don't bother."

The old gendarme hesitated. "It's up to you. Of course, you are armed?"

"I have my shotgun."

"Where?"

"In the trunk."

"You ought to have it near your bed."

"Why? I have nothing to fear."

"You're crazy, son. If there's an uprising, no one is safe, we're all in the same boat."

"I'll defend myself. I'll have time to see them coming."

Balducci began to laugh, then suddenly the mustache covered the white teeth. "You'll have time? O.K. That's just what I was saying. You have always been a little cracked. That's why I like you, my son was like that."

At the same time he took out his revolver and put it on the desk.

"Keep it; I don't need two weapons from here to El Ameur."

The revolver shone against the black paint of the table. When the gendarme turned toward him, the schoolmaster caught the smell of leather and horseflesh.

"Listen, Balducci," Daru said suddenly, "every bit of this disgusts me, and first of all your fellow here. But I won't hand him over. Fight, yes, if I have to. But not that."

The old gendarme stood in front of him and looked at him severely.

"You're being a fool," he said slowly. "I don't like it either. You don't get used to putting a rope on a man even after years of it, and you're even ashamed—yes, ashamed. But you can't let them have their way."

"I won't hand him over," Daru said again.

"It's an order, son, and I repeat it."

"That's right. Repeat to them what I've said to you: I won't hand him over."

Balducci made a visible effort to reflect. He looked at the Arab and at Daru. At last he decided.

"No, I won't tell them anything. If you want to drop us, go ahead; I'll not denounce you. I have an order to deliver the prisoner and I'm doing so. And now you'll just sign this paper for me."

"There's no need. I'll not deny that you left him with me."

"Don't be mean with me. I know you'll tell the truth. You're from hereabouts and you are a man. But you must sign, that's the rule."

Daru opened his drawer, took out a little square bottle of purple ink, the red wooden penholder with the "sergeant-major" pen he used for making models of penmanship, and signed. The gendarme carefully folded the paper and put it into his wallet. Then he moved toward the door.

"I'll see you off," Daru said.

"No," said Balducci. "There's no use being polite. You insulted me."

He looked at the Arab, motionless in the same spot, sniffed peevishly, and turned away toward the door. "Good-by, son," he said. The door shut behind him. Balducci appeared suddenly outside the window and then disappeared. His footsteps were muffled by the snow. The horse stirred on the other side of the wall and several chickens fluttered in fright. A moment later Balducci reappeared outside the window leading the horse by the bridle. He walked toward the little rise without turning around and disappeared from sight with the horse following him. A big stone could be heard bouncing down. Daru walked back toward the prisoner, who, without stirring, never took his eyes off him. "Wait," the schoolmaster said in Arabic and went toward the bedroom. As he was going through the door, he had a second thought, went to the desk, took the revolver, and stuck it in his pocket. Then, without looking back, he went into his room.

For some time he lay on his couch watching the sky gradually close over, listening to the silence. It was this silence that had seemed painful to him during the first days here, after the war. He had requested a post in the little town at the base of the foothills separating the upper plateaus from the desert. There, rocky walls, green and black to the north, pink and lavender to the south, marked the frontier of eternal summer. He had been named to a post farther north, on the plateau itself. In the beginning, the solitude and the silence had been hard for him on these wastelands peopled only by stones. Occasionally, furrows suggested cultivation, but they had been dug to uncover a certain kind of stone good for building. The only plowing here was to harvest rocks. Elsewhere a thin layer of soil accumulated in the hollows would be scraped out to enrich paltry village gardens. This is the way it was: bare rock covered three quarters of the region. Towns sprang up, flourished, then disappeared; men came by, loved one another or fought bitterly, then died. No one in this desert, neither he nor his guest, mattered. And yet, outside this desert neither of them, Daru knew, could have really lived.

When he got up, no noise came from the classroom. He was amazed at the unmixed joy he derived from the mere thought that the Arab might have fled and that he would be alone with no decision to make. But the prisoner was there. He had merely stretched out between the stove and the desk. With eyes open, he was staring at the ceiling. In that position, his thick lips were particularly noticeable, giving him a pouting look. "Come," said Daru. The Arab got up and followed him. In the bedroom, the schoolmaster pointed to a chair near the table under the window. The Arab sat down without taking his eyes off Daru.

"Are you hungry?"

"Yes," the prisoner said.

Daru set the table for two. He took flour and oil, shaped a cake in a frying-pan, and lighted the little stove that functioned on bottled gas. While the cake was cooking, he went out to the shed to get cheese, eggs, dates, and condensed milk. When the cake was done he set it on the window sill to cool, heated some condensed milk diluted with water, and beat up the eggs into an omelette. In one of his motions he knocked against the revolver stuck in his right pocket. He set the bowl down, went into the classroom, and put the revolver in his desk drawer. When he came back to the room, night was falling. He put on the light and served the Arab. "Eat," he said. The Arab took a piece of the cake, lifted it eagerly to his mouth, and stopped short.

"And you?" he asked.

"After you. I'll eat too."

The thick lips opened slightly. The Arab hesitated, then bit into the cake determinedly.

The meal over, the Arab looked at the schoolmaster. "Are you the judge?"

"No, I'm simply keeping you until tomorrow."

"Why do you eat with me?"

"I'm hungry."

The Arab fell silent. Daru got up and went out. He brought back a folding bed from the shed, set it up between the table and the stove, perpendicular to his own bed.

From a large suitcase which, upright in a corner, served as a shelf for papers, he took two blankets and arranged them on the camp bed. Then he stopped, felt useless, and sat down on his bed. There was nothing more to do or to get ready. He had to look at this man. He looked at him, therefore, trying to imagine his face bursting with rage. He couldn't do so. He could see nothing but the dark yet shining eyes and the animal mouth.

"Why did you kill him?" he asked in a voice whose hostile tone surprised him. The Arab looked away. "He ran away. I ran after him."

He raised his eyes to Daru and they were full of a sort of woeful interrogation. "Now what will they do to me?"

"Are you afraid?"

He stiffened, turning his eyes away."Are you sorry?"

The Arab stared at him openmouthed. Obviously he did not understand. Daru's annoyance was growing. At the same time he felt awkward and self-conscious with his big body wedged between the two beds.

"Lie down there," he said impatiently. "That's your bed."

The Arab didn't move. He called to Daru: "Tell me!"

The schoolmaster looked at him.

"Is the gendarme coming back tomorrow?"

"I don't know."

"Are you coming with us?"

"I don't know. Why?"

The prisoner got up and stretched out on top of the blankets, his feet toward the window. The light from the electric bulb shone straight into his eyes and he closed them at once.

"Why?" Daru repeated, standing beside the bed.

The Arab opened his eyes under the blinding light and looked at him, trying not to blink.

"Come with us," he said.

In the middle of the night, Daru was still not asleep. He had gone to bed after undressing completely; he generally slept naked. But when he suddenly realized that he had nothing on he hesitated. He felt vulnerable and the temptation came to him to put his clothes back on. Then he shrugged his shoulders; after all, he wasn't a child and, if need be, he could break his adversary in two. From his bed he could observe him, lying on his back, still motionless with his eyes closed under the harsh light. When Daru turned out the light, the darkness seemed to coagulate all of a sudden. Little by little, the night came back to life in the window where the starless sky was stirring gently. The schoolmaster soon made out the body lying at his feet. The Arab still did not move, but his eyes seemed open. A faint wind was prowling around the schoolhouse. Perhaps it would drive away the clouds and the sun would reappear.

During the night the wind increased. The hens fluttered a little and then were silent. The Arab turned over on his side with his back to Daru, who thought he heard him moan. Then he listened for his guest's breathing, become heavier and more regular. He listened to that breath so close to him and mused without being able to go to sleep. In this room where he had been sleeping alone for a year, this presence bothered him. But it bothered him also by imposing on him a sort of brotherhood he knew well but refused to accept in the present circumstances. Men who share the same rooms, soldiers or prisoners, develop a strange alliance as if, having cast off their armor with their clothing, they fraternized every evening, over and above their differences, in the ancient community of dream and fatigue. But Daru shook himself; he didn't like such musings, and it was essential to sleep.

A little later, however, when the Arab stirred slightly, the schoolmaster was still not asleep. When the prisoner made a second move, he stiffened, on the alert. The Arab was lifting himself slowly on his arms with almost the motion of a sleepwalker. Seated upright in bed, he waited motionless without turning his head toward Daru, as if he were listening attentively. Daru did not stir; it had just occurred to him that the revolver was still in the drawer of his desk. It was better to act at once. Yet he continued to observe the prisoner, who, with the same slithery motion, put his feet on the ground, waited again, then began to stand up slowly. Daru was about to call out to him when the Arab began to walk, in a quite natural but extraordinary silent way. He was heading toward the door at the end of the room that opened into the shed. He lifted the latch with precaution and went out, pushing the door behind him but without shutting it. Daru had not stirred. "He is running away," he merely thought. "Good riddance!" Yet he listened attentively. The hens were not fluttering; the guest must be on the plateau. A faint sound of water reached him, and he didn't know what it was until the Arab again stood framed in the doorway, closed the door carefully, and came back to bed without a sound. Then Daru turned his back on him and fell asleep. Still later he seemed, from the depths of his sleep, to hear furtive steps around the schoolhouse. "I'm dreaming! I'm dreaming!" he repeated to himself. And he went on sleeping.

When he awoke, the sky was clear; the loose window let in a cold, pure air. The Arab was asleep, hunched up under the blankets now, his mouth open, utterly relaxed. But when Daru shook him, he started dreadfully, staring at Daru with wild eyes as if he had never seen him and such a frightened expression that the schoolmaster stepped back. "Don't be afraid. It's me. You must eat." The Arab nodded and said yes. Calm had returned to his face, but his expression was vacant and listless.

The coffee was ready. They drank it seated together on the folding bed as they munched their pieces of the cake. Then Daru led the Arab under the shed and showed him the faucet where he washed. He went back into the room, folded the blankets and the bed, made his own bed and put the room in order. Then he went through the classroom and out onto the terrace. The sun was already rising in the blue sky; a soft bright light was bathing the deserted plateau. On the ridge the snow was melting in spots. The stones were about to reappear. Crouched on the edge of the plateau, the schoolmaster looked at the deserted expanse. He thought of Balducci. He had hurt him, for he had sent him off in a way as if he didn't want to be associated with him. He could hear the gendarme's farewell and, without knowing why, he felt strangely empty and vulnerable. At that moment, from the other side of the schoolhouse, the prisoner coughed. Daru listened to him almost despite himself and then, furious, threw a pebble that whistled through the air before sinking into the snow. That man's stupid crime revolted him, but to hand him over was contrary to honor. Merely thinking of it made him smart with humiliation. And he cursed at one and the same time his own people who had sent him this Arab and the Arab too who had dared to kill and not managed to get away. Daru got up, walked in a circle on the terrace, waited motionless, and then went back into the schoolhouse.

The Arab, leaning over the cement floor of the shed, was washing his teeth with two fingers. Daru looked at him and said: "Come." He went back into the room ahead of the prisoner. He slipped a hunting-jacket on over his sweater and put on walking-shoes. Standing, he waited until the Arab had put on his *chèche* and sandals. They went into the classroom and the schoolmaster pointed to the exit, saying: "Go ahead." The fellow didn't budge. "I'm coming," said Daru. The Arab went out. Daru went back into the room and made a package of pieces of rusk, dates, and sugar. In the classroom, before going out, he hesitated a second in front of his desk, then crossed the threshold and locked the door. "That's the way," he said. He started toward the east, followed by the prisoner. But, a short distance from the schoolhouse, he thought he heard a slight sound behind them. He retraced his steps and examined the surroundings of the house; there was no one there. The Arab watched him without seeming to understand. "Come on," said Daru.

They walked for an hour and rested beside a sharp peak of limestone. The snow was melting faster and faster and the sun was drinking up the puddles at once, rapidly cleaning the plateau, which gradually dried and vibrated like the air itself. When they resumed walking, the ground rang under their feet. From time to time a bird rent the space in front of them with a joyful cry. Daru breathed in deeply the fresh morning light. He felt a sort of rapture before the vast familiar expanse, now almost entirely yellow under its dome of blue sky. They walked an hour or more, descending toward the south. They reached a level height made up of crumbly rocks. From there on, the plateau sloped down, eastward toward a low plain where there were a few spindly trees and, to the south, toward outcroppings of rock that gave the landscape a chaotic look.

Daru surveyed the two directions. There was nothing but the sky on the horizon. Not a man could be seen. He turned toward the Arab, who was looking at him blankly. Daru held out the package to him. "Take it," he said. "There are dates, bread, and sugar. You can hold out for two days. Here are a thousand francs too." The Arab took the package and the money but kept his full hands at chest level as if he didn't know what to do with what was being given him. "Now look," the schoolmaster said as he pointed in the direction of the east, "there's the way to Tinguit. You have a two-hour walk. At Tinguit you'll find the administration and the police. They are expecting you." The Arab looked toward the east, still holding the package and the money against his chest. Daru took his elbow and turned him rather roughly toward the south. At the foot of the height on which they stood could be seen a faint path. "That's the trail across the plateau. In a day's walk from here you'll find pasturelands and the first nomads. They'll take you in and shelter you according to their law." The Arab had now turned toward Daru and a sort of panic was visible in his expression. "Listen," he said. Daru shook his head: "No, be quiet. Now I'm leaving you." He turned his back on him, took two long steps in the direction of the school, looked hesitantly at the motionless Arab, and started off again. For a few minutes he heard nothing but his own step resounding on the cold ground and did not turn his head. A moment later, however, he turned around. The Arab was still there on the edge of the hill, his arms hanging now, and he was looking at the schoolmaster. Daru felt something rise in his throat. But he swore with impatience, waved vaguely, and started off again. He had already gone some distance when he again stopped and looked. There was no longer anyone on the hill.

Daru hesitated. The sun was now rather high in the sky and was beginning to beat down on his head. The schoolmaster retraced his steps, at first somewhat uncertainly, then with decision. When he reached the little hill, he was bathed in sweat. He climbed it as fast as he could and stopped, out of breath, at the top. The rock-fields to the south stood out sharply against the blue sky, but on the plain to the east a steamy heat was already rising. And in that slight haze, Daru, with heavy heart, made out the Arab walking slowly on the road to prison.

A little later, standing before the window of the classroom, the schoolmaster was watching the clear light bathing the whole surface of the plateau, but he hardly saw it. Behind him on the blackboard, among the winding French rivers, sprawled the clumsily chalked-up words he had just read: "You handed over our brother. You will pay for this." Daru looked at the sky, the plateau, and, beyond, the invisible lands stretching all the way to the sea. In the vast landscape he had loved so much, he was alone.